Writing for Video Game Genres

Writing for Video Game Genres

From FPS to RPG

edited by

Wendy Despain

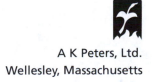

A K Peters, Ltd.
Wellesley, Massachusetts

Editorial, Sales, and Customer Service Office

A K Peters, Ltd.
888 Worcester Street, Suite 230
Wellesley, MA 02482
www.akpeters.com

Library of Congress Cataloging-in-Publication Data

Writing for video game genres : from FPS to RPG / edited by Wendy Despain.
    p. cm.
  ISBN 978-1-56881-417-9 (alk. paper)
  1. Video games–Authorship. 2. Video games–Design. 3. Video genres. I. Despain, Wendy.
  GV1469.34.A97W75 2009
  794.8–dc22

        2009001763

Printed in the United States of America
13 12 11 10 09   10 9 8 7 6 5 4 3 2 1

To RRB and ARB. You don't know who you are, but I do.

And special thanks to Kim Sparks, Ben Serviss,
Ahmad Saad, and Beth Dillon, who helped edit this book.
No one could ask for better minions.

Contents

4 Writing for Action-Adventure Games
(John Feil) **29**

5 Writing for Platform Games
(Andrew S. Walsh) **37**

6 Writing for First-Person Shooters
(Lucien Soulban and Haris Orkin) **51**

Preface

Anytime game writers get together and start debating the minutiae of the craft, someone invariably throws up their hands saying, "But writing for an FPS is completely different from writing for an MMO." And that kills the conversation just as surely as if they had mentioned Hitler. Everyone morosely wanders off in their minds for a moment, thinking of what a lonely and strange job this is. How even when we've found kindred spirits who know how to dig deep into the ugly underbelly of branching dialogue trees, we still have these irreconcilable differences. Predictably enough, the inevitable next step in this oft-repeated conversation is to head to a bar, if not already in one.

This book offers an alternative to drowning our sorrows and crying in our beer. I approached writers who have non-trivial experience in each video game genre, and I've asked them to go there. Sit down and put on paper exactly what it is that makes writing for an FPS so different from writing for an MMO. Instead of moping about how alone we are, I've asked these writers to talk about what makes these genres unique from a writing perspective.

Because we're not alone. It's not like there's only one writer who ever gets hired for every RPG being made this year. More than one person has written a story for a platformer. I guarantee game writers out there get asked to cross genres all the time. And speaking selfishly, I would love to have someone with experience in this genre download their brain for me.

So here it is. Info-dumps from 21 different experts, looking into the nitty-gritty of what makes writing for one genre different from writing for another. I enjoyed reading every one of them, and here's what surprised me—there are elements from every chapter I can use in the game I'm writing for today. Sure, they need adapting to the circumstances, but good flow charts are good flow charts. It doesn't matter that I learned it from a writer of sandbox games and I'm working on an RPG.

How to Use This Book

Let's face it, when it comes to writing for video games, we're all working in uncharted territory. The medium is still inventing itself, and the horizon just keeps getting foggier. It's hard to look ahead and know what's coming. Changes in technology, tools, market preferences, and development strategies force course corrections all the time. But what we can do is look around at where we are and tell you about where we've been.

That's what this book is for. It's written by a group of experts who have been down the dark, twisty passages and have brought back a map. Now they're sharing it with you. You'll see the landscape of video game genres is quite varied. Some paths look pretty familiar, whether you're in the craggy mountains of MMORPGs or the stuffy corridors of a FPS, but each region has its own pitfalls and dead ends. The experts who wrote the chapters in this book are sharing their own tips for navigating the terrain they've traveled. Think of it as a travel guide book, not a definitive scientific treatise. We're not saying this is the only way to do things, we're just saying this is how we've done them, and we hope our experience helps you enjoy your trip through your own game writing tasks.

Start with the first page, or skip around to the sections that interest you most. The chapters were written to stand on their own, but you might be surprised what you can learn from a genre you've never worked in before. Nuggets of wisdom are tucked in all over the place. I mostly work in alternate reality games and RPG/adventure games, but I learned a lot from every chapter. I tell ya, there's gold in them thar hills.

What You Need to Know to Make the Most of It

This is not a book about the basics of how to write. The basics are still important—grammar, spelling, narrative fundamentals—all these things matter, but they're not covered in this book. We're examining the nuts and bolts of how to get the work done: how to get to the end of the 635th piece of quest dialogue, how to make your sports commentators sound believable, how to write help text that makes sense. Other books talk about the hero's journey and how to format a script. We've even written some of them.

Our first book, *Game Writing: Narrative Skills for Video Games*, is an excellent introduction to the art and craft of game writing. We build on that foundation and expand on it in *Professional Techniques for Video Game Writing*. These are excellent resources for building up a solid understanding of the basic mechanics.

This book is intended as a starting point from which we can work together to improve the state of the art. Writing for television, murder mystery novels and podcasts all require more than just a passing grade in English 101. It's the same for video game writing. There are specific genres within the medium, and each one has its own quirks and requirements. Experienced, working game writers share their methods in each chapter so everyone doesn't have to reinvent the wheel every time they sit down to a new project. If we could all start out knowing what the experts know, we could build on that standard and lift the art of video games to new heights.

Online Resources

The experts contributing to this book were all drawn from the International Game Developers Association Game Writing Special Interest Group (IGDA Writing SIG). We have built a community of people interested in the craft of interactive narrative, and we welcome new members. Our website and mailing list subscription information can be found at http://www.igda.org/writing.

Also on that website, at http://www.igda.org/writing/library, you'll find our online script library. Longer versions of the script samples included in this book can be found there, along with additional scripts and sample documents. We hope you'll find it useful and maybe even contribute samples of your own work. We're all in this together.

And that's the attitude we've taken in every chapter of this book. They're written as personal essays with the individual style of each author intact. And we want to make this a conversation, so please enjoy the book and join us on the Internet to tell us what you think about it.

Wendy Despain

1

Writing for Massively Multiplayer Online Games

Steve Danuser and Tracy A. Seamster

1.1 Introduction

Writing for massively multiplayer online games (commonly referred to as MMOs or MMOGs, or as MMORPGs when the term "role-playing" gets thrown in the mix) requires most of the same talents and disciplines as writing for any other type of game. Since we are, when all is said and done, talking about making a game, the goal of your writing should be to bring fun and enjoyment to the player regardless of whether the tone is joyous, scary, or anywhere in between. There are, however, some aspects of MMOs that require unique approaches to story planning and dialogue writing that are worth consideration.

Before we delve too deeply into the particulars, it's worth noting that calling a game an MMO refers more to its player interaction model than to its genre or style. You can have a fantasy adventure like *World of Warcraft*, a sci-fi setting like *Tabula Rasa*, a shooter like *PlanetSide*, or even a freeform social space like *Second Life*. The common element is a persistent world in which thousands of players interact together. Since this book is focused on writing, this chapter will assume that we're discussing an MMO with at least some degree of directed storytelling and character dialogue.

Various companies use writers in different ways. Some MMOs may hire freelance writers; others have full-time writers on staff. Still other companies do not have a separate job title for writers, lumping them under the catch-all umbrella of "game designer." Titles are not that important, of course, as long as the writer's talents are recognized and utilized effectively. When in the course of this chapter we refer to "the writer," we mean anyone who is tasked with writing copy for an MMO as part or the sum of their contribution to the project.

1

1.2   The Play's the Thing

As writers, we instinctively want to tell the richest story possible. This is especially true in MMOs, a style of game with a generally slower pace than platformers or shooters, which therefore allows for more emphasis on plot development. But we must never forget that we're making a game, a medium based around player-driven action. We mustn't fall into the trap of confusing the goal of inspiring play with leading players by the nose through a story we stubbornly insist on telling.

Play is instinctive. Like animals, we begin to play soon after we are born, using play to practice fundamental behaviors that we will employ later in life. From peek-a-boo we graduate to other forms of play, moving from the simple and childlike games to team sports, as well as games of logic and chance.

Personal computers and consoles have helped sophisticated gameplay flourish, because they allow an intellectual expression of many of the same primal behaviors present in simpler types of games. But at the same time, these gaming platforms have pulled us back from gaming as a shared experience to games that we engage in individually, or at least on a smaller scale.

MMOs are compelling because they break that mold, taking the personal computer or console and connecting it to thousands of others. The intellectual and personal game becomes social, making it a team experience once again. In fact, one of the core tenets of MMOs is team building, whether it's a group that comes together to fight in a dungeon or a guild that comes together to take on raid challenges.

1.3   Story and Play in Harmony

In contrast to play, storytelling is learned behavior unique to humans. Animals communicate, but as far as we know, they don't share stories with one another. Storytelling is a skill we develop, used to convey lessons, histories, and shared experiences.

As much as we want to tell a good story, we must never lose sight of the fact that this medium is about playing. Therefore, the storytelling must serve the game, since there won't be an opportunity to tell the story unless the person playing your MMO finds the gameplay satisfying.

We must not see ourselves as writing a story onto which someone else will tack a game. Such an approach will fail, because computers and consoles are inherently inefficient mediums for expressing the subtlety of good stories. What we are doing is building a game, all the parts of which are carefully crafted to fit together and inherently convey a story without it needing to be explicitly spelled out.

Fortunately for us, computers and consoles give us lots of tools to work with beyond written words. For starters, we have colors, movement, and sound—extremely powerful tools with which to create mood and convey story. We can use them to all sorts of effects upon the people playing our game, from scaring them to thrilling them to making them sad. It's our job to craft play that elicits the emotional reactions that dialogue and written words do in other mediums.

Does that mean we should avoid using the written word in MMOs? Absolutely not. The beauty of MMOs is that they are so massive in scope that they aren't about playing all the time. Though few people want to sit on a football field and build a campfire around which to tell stories, most MMO players want to be able to take their characters into social situations where the focus shifts from play to other forms of interaction. This is an excellent place to make more traditional forms of storytelling available to people outside of play mode through books they can buy, scrolls they can read, and non-player characters (NPCs) they can interact with. *Warhammer Online: Age of Reckoning* has a feature called the Tome of Knowledge, which allows players to unlock pieces of game lore that can be read at the player's leisure for a deeper look into the story of the game.

1.4   Unique Challenges of MMO Writing

So what makes writing for MMOs different from writing for other games? There are several special considerations that the writer must consider, four of which we will examine here:

1. Since the world is intended to be persistent for years to come, the story of the world does not end.

2. The game's story can't focus on a single character, because every player is his or her own protagonist.

3. Unlike most storytelling mediums, the writer has little control over pacing.

4. The stories you tell are going to be far less memorable and entertaining than the ones that evolve through the interactions of your player base.

Please don't look upon the preceding points as problems that need to be solved, necessarily; rather, they are properties of the medium itself and are intrinsically tied to the very things that make MMOs popular in the first place. The clever writer will see them as opportunities rather than roadblocks.

The Never-Ending Story

As of this writing, every commercial MMO released to the public has been marketed with the intent of continuing indefinitely (not all of them have, of course, but the intent was there). To support this business model, most MMOs are designed to tell stories that never end—a fact which separates this medium from pretty much every other type of narrative computer or console game. Sure, a lot of story-driven titles leave room for a sequel, but most of the time they set out to give the player a satisfying ending that provides some sense of closure to the events that just took place.

The ongoing nature of MMOs, however, means that, in many cases, their stories are told in a format similar to the old movie serials of the 1930s. The hero is put in jeopardy by a dastardly villain; said villain is overcome in a harrowing battle; next week another even more dastardly foe surfaces to repeat the process. The quest format established by games like *EverQuest II* and *World of Warcraft* moves the player through a series of small vignettes that often conclude in the defeat of one foe and lead into a conflict with the next. Expansions to these games throw even bigger bad guys into ever grander settings, hopefully building upon what has gone before so that the story arc builds consistency.

While this has proven to be an economically successful model, it isn't necessarily the most satisfying. Even fans of half-hour sitcoms like to see the stories wrap up neatly, and MMOs tend to leave a lot of dangling threads. As writers, we can do better. While older MMOs had a lot of limitations on technology, newer titles can apply some of the newer features developed to enhance the methodology of storytelling.

For example, games like *Pirates of the Burning Sea* and *Lord of the Rings Online* use instancing (a method of making unique copies of a given area for each group of players) to enhance storytelling. Players can journey through a story-driven instance and achieve their objective (defeat the bad guy, obtain the treasure, etc.). Next time they enter the instance, the population and setting has changed to reflect their actions last time through without affecting the experience for players who will be enjoying that content for the first time.

Though the challenge of telling dynamic stories while maintaining a persistent shared world remains, techniques like those noted above can be used to tell a good story without ignoring the desire to keep the game running for many years to come.

Wherefore Art Thou, Romeo371?

The movie *Star Wars* may have featured multiple characters, but there was only one Luke Skywalker who went from being a farm boy on Tatooine to becoming a great Jedi Knight. His was the classic heroic story arc, a journey countless fans would love to take.

A massively multiplayer game allows thousands or millions of players to undertake a similar heroic journey. The problem is, they all undertake pretty much the same journey, and they may be doing it at pretty much the same time. Besides those minor details, the writer won't know the character's name or what sorts of motivations lurk within the player behind the keyboard. Do the players even really care about saving the world, or are they only in it for the loot?

While an MMO can strictly guide players along a single path, it is more in tune with the dynamic and varied richness of the genre to offer players multiple ways to enjoy the game in the way they want to experience it. This can be accomplished in a variety of ways, some of which are easy and some of which can be very costly in terms of time and resources.

One of the easier means of letting the player feel like he has a unique voice is to offer multiple dialogue options when interacting with an NPC. Give the player varying options to be polite, rude, helpful, intimidating, neutral, or disinterested. This will make the players who care about such choices feel like they are taking a direct hand in their characters' development, which is much harder to convey with a simple "yes/no" or "accept/decline" dialogue box.

Say an NPC named Orrin the Wise offers a quest, ending with the line, "Will you bring me the sacred chalice?" Give the player responses that can allow for different role-playing choices.

Here is an example:

Response 1: What's in it for me?

Response 2: Of course I'll help you.

Response 3: And if I don't?

Response 4: I don't want to get involved.

Note that the response choices are fairly neutral, yet they allow players to infer certain motivations for themselves. Response 1 is motivated by greed; it's not necessarily an evil response, yet it could certainly be taken that way. Response 2 could be seen as the good or helpful response. Then again, the player may intend to retrieve the sacred chalice and use it in some other way (provided you give the player that option). Response 3 could be evil or good. This response indicates a desire to know more about the consequences and allows you to give more backstory. Response 4 gives the player a way to decline a quest she doesn't want.

Does every quest need four different player responses? Definitely not. Two might be all you need to make sense in the context of the quest offering. The variety of response options can give your quest more depth. In the end, the only choice the player makes is whether or not to accept the quest. To that end, even when you are offering a variety of responses, you must always move the player toward a decision. Hopefully, the player will be swayed by your masterful way with words and accept the mission or quest that is offered. Either that or the player is quickly clicking through the dialogue tree and has no idea what to do or why she wants to do it.

Another way to make players feel heroic and important is to give NPCs the ability to recognize and respond to things they have achieved or done. Perhaps after returning the chalice to Orrin the Wise, this NPC will evermore call out to the player character when he walks by. Or perhaps when the character achieves a certain level of reputation with the city guards, they will salute when the character comes into town. Little details like this immerse players in the game by making them feel that their actions have meaning, and they can make them forget for a little while that many other players have achieved a lot of the same things they have.

Setting the Pace

In a book, the writer has absolute freedom to take a character from Point A to Point B in whichever manner she chooses. In a film, the director and editor decide how much to show the viewer in order to tell the story. Peter Jackson didn't feel the need to show you every step of Frodo's journey to Mordor—just the interesting bits.

Unfortunately, MMO writers don't always have the luxury of controlling pacing. You can have an NPC offer a quest, but you can't be sure whether the player is going to jump right to the first step, take on another quest instead, go back to town and buy food, duel with a friend, or any other of a number of potential activities.

In this respect, the quest log of the modern MMO is both a blessing and a curse. It gives the player character a constant stream of things to do, yet it can pull the player in so many different directions that the narrative can be lost. Quests become a shopping list of objectives rather than a means to tell a deep and memorable story.

Consider offering fewer quests to the player at any particular point in time, and instead make each of them more immersive and meaningful. But don't become so enthralled with the idea of offering depth that you make it easy for the player to get lost within complexity. Remember that MMOs are not an ideal canvas for storytelling, so you should try to be as clear and direct as you can. Making your story points too subtle will cause them to be lost; go for clear and accessible instead.

It also helps to keep the objective of the quest very near to the quest giver so that the player is more likely to try to complete the quest right away. It's far more likely that the player will retrieve the sacred chalice for Orrin the Wise if the person who stole it is in a hideout just down the street. If the thief is hiding halfway across the world, the player is likely to look for a more accessible objective that offers immediate gratification.

Players will excuse exceptions to the above rule of thumb if the quest is clearly important or rewarding enough to merit immediate action. If returning the sacred chalice will cause Orrin to reward him with the Mighty Sword of Endless Victories, the player may be so enthused he'll spend hours working his way to confront the thief. If the quest reward is only a handful of copper, though, expect your sweeping storyline to be ignored.

Since pacing is so much out of the writer's control and so much within the player's, it becomes very important to take every opportunity to keep progress regular and meaningful. Players will like it, and you'll find that your story is much more likely to be recognized and enjoyed.

Players Are the Real Storytellers

Take a look at early MMOs like *Ultima Online* and *EverQuest*. Compared to modern games, there was much less NPC dialogue to read and far fewer blocks of prose to digest. You'd find named NPCs inside dungeons and begin to piece together the framework of a story, leaving most of the details to your own imagination.

Modern MMOs, largely through their emphasis on questing, provide players a lot more to read and thus lay the context out in a much more black-and-white fashion. This takes away one aspect of player storytelling but can't touch its fundamental core: the stories that result purely from what happens when a bunch of people share a gaming experience.

Ask veterans of MMOs for their favorite stories from early games and few of them will focus on something written by a content designer. Almost all the stories will be about how their grouped wiped while fighting in Lower Guk, or how they were jumped by PKs in the bottom of Destard and later took revenge. Just as football fanatics remember great touchdowns or baseball fans remember a grand slam that clinches a game, MMO players remember those moments of exhilarating success and brilliant failure that result from someone in their guild doing something profoundly smart or extraordinarily dumb. There's a reason that Leeroy Jenkins became an answer on *Jeopardy!*

Our job, then, is to provide a framework for players to tell their own stories. Sure, we will continue to provide them with engaging quest text to read and dialogue to listen to, but we've got to get our writer egos out of the equation. Our stories, no matter how lovingly crafted, usually aren't going to be as memorable as the stories that come about through play.

1.5   Telling Stories: More than Words

If you're a writer who has been considering working on an MMO, perhaps you're feeling a bit uneasy after reading to this point. If so, take heart; you're a storyteller, and you have a whole toolbox of talents to draw from. That's a good thing, because it allows you to frame the play (and thereby the story) using both words and the visceral experience.

The trick is to tie the two together as seamlessly as possible. A dungeon called Sleeper's Tomb in the *Scars of Velious* expansion of *EverQuest* is a good example of tying gameplay together with storytelling.

For the most part, Sleeper's Tomb was a dungeon like any other. There were nasty mobs to kill and treasures to acquire, though the difficulty was considerable, and it took a long time to crawl through the place. What set it apart was what you encountered at the very bottom.

Beyond a final gate in a massive square room lay an enormous prismatic dragon named Kerafyrm, asleep on a pedestal. Around the perimeter of the room, walkways connected four corners. At each corner stood one of the four warders, huge dragons in their own right. By their placement in the room, it was clear they had a relationship to the slumbering beast in the middle.

Assuming you paid attention to the quest you went through to gain the key to enter Sleeper's Tomb, you know that Kerafyrm was the unlawful offspring of two dragons that were not supposed to mate. Their union resulted in the birth of an ultra-powerful prismatic dragon, tranquilized and locked away under the care of four warders charged with making sure junior stayed asleep.

So why am I holding this up as a good example of MMO storytelling? Because even if you didn't read any of the lore leading up to the Sleeper's chamber, the things you see with your own eyes allow you to start piecing together a story. Sleeping dragon. Four other dragons standing nearby. Yeah, pretty sure they're standing guard. And when you kill all four of them and Kerafyrm wakes up, the fact that he starts killing everything in sight is a pretty good indicator that you just did a bad thing.

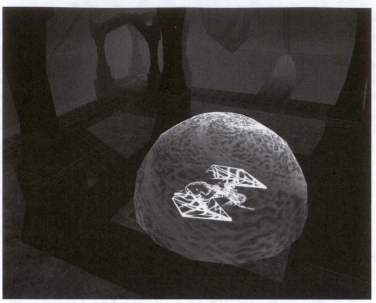

Figure 1.1. The sleeping prismatic dragon Kerafyrm in the Sleeper's Tomb dungeon in *EverQuest*.

The beauty of all this is that the story got across to the players whether they paid attention to the writing along the way or not.

1.6   Pitfalls: When the Story Doesn't Get Through

Sometimes you visualize a story so clearly in your mind that it doesn't occur to you that every player won't be seeing the game through the same camera you have in your head. The free-flowing nature of MMOs means that players aren't on rails, giving them the freedom to veer away from your best-laid plans.

An example of this can be found in *The Fallen Dynasty* adventure pack for *EverQuest II*. I implemented a quest called "The Pirate's Bride," in which the player is trying to find out how pirates found the location of a remote island. When investigating suspicious behavior among the local villagers, the player observes that a young lady strolls down to the shore every night and throws a bottle into the sea.

Sounds great, right? On paper that's a reasonable way to visually demonstrate to the player that something fishy is going on. The trouble is, I couldn't control what the player's camera saw, nor could I control at what in-game time of day the player took the quest to observe the NPC. Because of this loss of control, I couldn't be sure the storyline was being conveyed in the way I had intended.

I tuned the quest to have the guilty villager make her trip more frequently, which addressed the gameplay fault of forcing the player to wait for a certain time of day to see the quest through (hint: players won't wait around in MMOs; if you bore them, they move on to another quest). However, the mistake of hanging the story on a small action that was easy for the wandering eye of the player to miss still hindered the storytelling of the quest.

Another tempting trap you can fall into as an MMO writer is that you try so hard to make your NPC characters interesting that you overshadow player characters. Sometimes this is done in subtle ways, such as dressing town guards in fancier armor than the player can ever hope to obtain. Other times it is more blatant, such as putting nigh-invulnerable NPCs into situations so that you can erase any doubt of the player attacking them and interfering with your carefully scripted story.

Challenging your players is one thing, but making them feel consistently less than heroic is another. At the launch of *EverQuest II*, we decided that one way we would demonstrate the evil city of Freeport's nature was by having its residents berate the players on a regular basis. Bad idea. It wouldn't have been so bad if we had things start out that way and have the city NPCs recognize early on that the players were heroes in the process of saving Freeport, but we never gave them that opportunity. Instead, it just made players feel unappreciated. When we later released a revamped newbie experience, one of the major changes we made was changing the tone and recognizing the players as heroes.

1.7   Planning is the Key to Consistency

The world of any MMO is a massive place, populated by thousands of NPCs, quests, places, and stories. Because these games are so monstrous in scope, it takes a whole team of writers and designers to make them come to life. Yet, like episodes of a television show written by a staff of people working on different scripts, all aspects of your game world need to share a single, recognizable voice.

Beyond your own work, players who stay with your game for years should be able to feel as though the world they've invented within your game is consistent with the game's overall storyline. Not every player takes role-playing to heart, but you need to keep a consistent story throughout the multitudes of levels, especially when expansions or other additions to the world are being considered.

It is vitally important that the game team have a go-to person tasked with maintaining the vision of the project's overall story. This individual will be consulted throughout the process of building the world to ensure that all the threads tie together. Indispensable to this person's job are two crucial documents: the story bible and the style guide. The story bible includes all the basic information a writer will need to know about the world to make it come alive in a way that is consistent with what everyone else on the team will be doing. The style guide ensures a consistent voice and quality to the writing that helps make it feel like it comes from a single source.

And though it should go without saying (yet, sadly, it often isn't said at all), there is no substitute for getting the writing team together into a room regularly to share story ideas and identify conflicts. For example, during the planning and implementation of expansions for *EverQuest II*, the designers would meet regularly to discuss the various storylines that the expansions would reveal. They had to be consistent with each other as well as with lore previously released. As the team's designers all wrote their own quests, it was an important facet that everyone else knew where the stories intersected.

EverQuest II's *Echoes of Faydwer* expansion brought the primary lore writers together to discuss details of the War of the Fay, an event that took place hundreds of years before the current game's setting. We actually placed a map of the area on a tabletop and marched armies (of office supplies, as we were short of *D&D* figurines) across it like World War II generals, to see which units would be where, how they'd get there, and when. It's that level of designer immersion that allowed us to prepare intersecting viewpoints that are revealed to the players via dozens of seemingly unrelated quests scattered throughout the game world.

While some stories eventually receded into the background as others become more important, having those discussions allowed the team glimpses of the stories to be told and quest lines to be written. As the details are revealed, they give players a sense of world order and history, which again allows them to feel part of the bigger picture, regardless of their own level of role-playing within the game.

Without documentation and communication, an MMO is likely to feel like a misshapen collection of random ideas instead of a cohesive whole. The time invested early on pays countless dividends down the road, because your team won't have to waste resources creating content that is rejected because it doesn't fit with the established fiction of the game world.

1.8   Got All That? Now Go Forth and Write!

Games are largely a visual medium, yet writers still have a vital role to play. Writing for MMOs takes many forms and is integral to the process of designing complex game worlds. Whether conveying stories through words, through visuals in the game, or somewhere in between, great stories enhance great gameplay. Forge solid connections between both, and your players will be the ones who benefit.

2

Writing for Role-Playing Games

Daniel Erickson

2.1   The RPG Challenge: Writing without a Protagonist

Of all video game genres, it is the western role-playing game (RPG) that most takes advantage of the unique aspects of the interactive medium. It is also arguably the most challenging to write for, as many of a writer's tools are removed from the toolbox and set aside—traded, if you will—for the chance to give the player agency[1] and participation in not just the results of the narrative but in its tone, progress, and character development.

The most marked example of this trade is the tradition of not having a set protagonist to drive the plot. By allowing the player to create a protagonist from scratch (often of either gender, and choosing from multiple backgrounds, classes, and even occasionally ages) we throw away thousands of years of storytelling tradition. We're writing *Death of a Salesman* with no Willy Loman, *Braveheart* without William Wallace, *Detective Comics* sans Batman. In short, we're on our own here. With an understanding of interactive storytelling, however, and a few key tools—most importantly how to make choices matter, how to keep players in the moment, and how to reinforce a player's personal fiction—we'll do just fine.

2.2   Understanding Interactive Storytelling

For years now, there has been a growing trend of people standing up at various conferences and debating whether or not storytelling can be done in games at the same level as in movies or books. In general, the firebrands like to take the negative position as it assures some controversy and a chance to stand up and make ridiculous speeches the next year as well, but the fact is, they keep missing the point that the fundamental question is flawed. True, you couldn't do *Citizen Kane* as a game and

---

[1] For more on player agency, see Chapter 3 of the book *Game Writing: Narrative Skills for Videogames*, edited by Chris Bateman.

have the same impact. Neither could you do it as a ballet. So what? Games are further from movies than early movies were from plays, and there is no chance of understanding interactive storytelling without understanding we're exploring a new art form that is still in its infancy. Many of the old rules of storytelling do not apply. Let's start understanding then, with a quick definition and the smallest bit of history.

A Controversial Definition

The term RPG has been tossed around and twisted for all sorts of perverse uses in the years since *Dungeons & Dragons* appeared in the United States. These days, it is often slapped onto any game that is either fantasy or—more commonly—has stats and a level-based progression system. For this chapter, we're going to be a bit stricter and define an RPG in the classic sense: a story-based game wherein the player creates and takes on a role that he has chosen, making decisions and actions that affect the game's outcome. So *Fallout*, *Baldur's Gate*, and *Oblivion* qualify. Interestingly, so do *Deus Ex* and several non-traditional RPGs. Not qualifying would be *World of Warcraft* (no game-mandated role-playing, actions don't affect game story) or the *Final Fantasy* series (pre-made protagonist who's going to act the fool no matter what the player does.)

The Protagonist as Early Explorer

In the 1970s, the introduction of both *Dungeons & Dragons* and the immensely popular *Choose Your Own Adventure* books took the idea of audience-driven storytelling and made it something understandable to people of all ages. What was once a tradition of bedtime stories made up on the spot ("But I want to be a princess!" "Okay, then, you're a princess.") and playing make-believe with friends ("I blew you up!" "Nope, I had laser-proof shorts on!") all of a sudden had rules and structure, and the seeds of what would one day be computer RPGs (CRPGs) were planted.

The Virtual Dungeon Master Analogy

It comes as little surprise that many of the great writers and designers of CRPGs were either enthusiasts or previously employed in the pen-and-paper RPG world. Many of the principles of what makes good pacing, storytelling, and wish-fulfillment fantasy are best learned with a group of real people and a set of dice. A successful dungeon master, or DM, quickly learns not to run roughshod over the players or attempt to force a plot twist that requires the players' characters to act against their core concepts. The DM cannot decide that the paladin who leads the party will fall in love, will sacrifice his life for a noble cause, or will be fooled by the villain who is masquerading as a friend.

The DM, like the successful CRPG writer, learns that player agency is the essential appeal of the art form and that there is no story twist brilliant enough to convince players to sacrifice more than the smallest part of that agency. Thus the CRPG writer must become a master of giving as much agency as possible to players, allowing them to be the protagonist they wish to be and giving them the choices and obstacles that will make their impact on the game world undeniable.

2.3   Making Choices and Making them Matter

The entire RPG genre is about choice. Choice in character creation. Choice in dialogue. Choice in story. Without important, frequent choices that impact either the player's story or the state of the game world, the player may as well go watch a movie. Below are some rules to live by when adding choices to an RPG.

Only Present a Choice When it Matters

At first glance, this may seem counter to the idea of the RPG story being choice-centric, but players will quickly tire of pointless false choices and button pushing as busy work. In story, choices should come at critical moments where the player really has the option to change the course of the narrative. In dialogue, choices should come after complete, interesting ideas have been presented by an NPC or when the player is being asked a direct, meaningful question.

Make All Responses Specific

This rule primarily applies to dialogue and is broken constantly in the genre. The sloppiest way to approximate interactive dialogue without actually having to go through the trouble of writing for all the possibilities the player may want to choose is simply to make all of the responses by the NPCs vague. Hand-craft the great majority of the responses to reflect the subtleties of a player's choice, and you'll complete the illusion of living, breathing characters involved in conversation.

Every Choice Should Be a Valid Choice

Related to, but distinct from, the notion of only presenting choices when there is something important happening, it is also vital that when choices are presented, those choices are valid possibilities. Letting a player attempt to sneak past a dragon is worthless if the game mechanics make it impossible. The same goes for asking a player what he wants to do next when there is no choice, or which reward he would like to choose when only one is available. False choice is often worse than no choice. The same goes for bait and switch. Nothing good comes from allowing a player to believe he's accomplished or earned the alternative choice when you're just going to push him back to the rejected choice at the last minute.

Let Players Be Self-Destructive

Allowing players to do stupid things is perhaps the single most empowering decision you can make during the design and writing of a story. It is also one of the most dangerous. Players love to test limits and to act against any restrictions placed upon them. It is this urge that makes the ability to be self-destructive in the relatively safe confines of the game world so appealing. The most simple way to enable such a feature is to just allow random slaughter and put the onus on the player to accept the consequences if the plot breaks as a result. This is exactly what the *Baldur's Gate* series did, as did many of the games in the *Elder Scrolls* series. The decision to just let the players run amok and suffer the consequences slides uncomfortably toward a "let the buyer beware" school of story design, however, and breaks one of the core tenants of game and story design listed above: every choice should be a valid choice. Actions that bring the plot to a screeching halt are not valid choices.

There are three great ways to allow self-destructive behavior without letting players simply turn the game into a slaughterhouse: alternate paths, punishment, and penance. In the alternate paths model, there is simply a separate—and usually more difficult, supporting the thematic consequences of having gone "bad"—path that can be used to accomplish the goals that can no longer be accomplished because of the deviant behavior. The alternate path could even be the "good" path in a game focusing more clearly on the battle against a player's internal evil, making players work for their moral high ground. In the punishment model, there are consequences that stop forward progress but do not break the plot. Examples of this would include being thrown in prison, hated by a particular group, or having certain stores or resources closed to the player. Each of these could be further enhanced by the third choice of penance. In heroic myth, a misdeed can often be expunged by some great bravery. Allowing players to experience this cycle can be extremely compelling, whatever the magnitude of the misdeed. A farmer's wife that you tried to bully now won't help you, until you help with her concerns. A kingdom whose prince you killed forces you to defeat the dragon he trained his whole life to slay. At the end of the day, the player has freedom to push against the edges of the story but still stays in the world, and the story stays intact.

2.4   Keeping Players in the Moment

You can give a player all of the brilliant choices in the world, make him master of his own destiny, and litter his path with great accomplishments, but if he doesn't escape himself, if he doesn't lose himself in the story, then nothing else matters. That is why it is vitally important to, at all times, pay attention to the little details that make the world seem solid, predictable in its rules (though never its outcomes) and even in its delivery of information. Techniques to keep players in the moment must be practiced and perfected as they require a precise touch that only constant use can achieve.

Ground the Player

When the player encounters a new situation, take a moment to ease the transition. Remember that RPGs are comprised of several different player states—combat, exploration, dialogue, mercantile—and that state changes are jarring. Unlike a book or movie where the inactive audience is fully tuned to the story unfolding before them, an RPG player is just as likely to have been thinking of combat strategies, experience points, or how to upgrade his armor in the moment before he transitions back to story. So when that first line of dialogue starts, remind the player where he left the story and what the situation is. Draw out the first idea of the new story moment a bit longer than seems necessary or even repeat the notion—not the actual dialogue— to make sure the player has grasped the new situation. If states change too fast, if dialogue begins and the player can't immediately follow it, the player will stop and separate himself from the experience, which is the moment we never want to allow.

Don't Ask Players to Track the Plot Alone

For the same reasons it is important to ground the player, it is equally important to give the player some ability to track the plot besides memory. RPGs tend to be longer and more complicated than games from other genres, and the constant state changes make keeping track of plot harder than in even the longest book. A comprehensive journal system, on-demand playback of key story moments, lines for traveling companions that remind the player of past events—all of these can be used to great affect to make certain the player never has to wonder where he is and what he was supposed to be doing.

The Infantilizing of Linearity and the Tyranny of Choice

We've already touched upon the need for choice to enable player agency, but it is the balance between too few and too many options that preserves the momentum of the story. Remove all options from a particular scene, dialogue, or plot and it will quickly become apparent to the player. The player feels infantilized by the sudden shift to linearity, not trusted to make decisions, and therefore disconnects from the experience.

On the flip side, giving a player too many choices creates a sense of paralysis that can just as easily cause a disconnect. Having to stop, either in dialogue or otherwise, and consider more than three to four routes or possibilities at one time means the player can neither decide quickly nor keep all of the various choices in mind at once. The result is a sense of pressure and confusion that quickly becomes oppressive.

Don't Write Game Instructions as Dialogue

Easily one of the worst offenses for world consistency, the writing of gameplay instructions (as opposed to in-story directions on where to go next) as in-game dialogue negates any ability for the player to suspend disbelief and live within the game world. On-screen pop-ups, interactive tutorials, or even instructions accessible through the options menu are all preferable to putting instructions in the mouths of characters who are supposed to be living, breathing people grounded in the world.

Let the Player Do More Listening than Talking

This is a fairly straightforward rule and obviously applies to dialogue writing. Don't confuse player control and agency with shoving a ton of words in the player's mouth. The player should lead, choose, react, and interpret. The player should not narrate.

Remember that you do not have a classical protagonist, and if you insist on treating the player as one, then you will very quickly run into the trap of having the player say or do something that he would not have chosen to do.

Anticipate Smart Players

It is always a mistake to talk down to your audience, doubly so when writing an RPG. Due to the very nature of the complexity of an RPG, the audience tends to be savvy when it comes to storylines, twists, and plot holes. Much as you wouldn't expect a simple flanking maneuver to surprise a modern strategy game enthusiast, don't for a moment think the large plot hole you've exposed to your players will not be seen and either exploited or mocked. Don't force players into obvious ambushes, make them the agents of their own destruction, or ask them to believe their in-game avatar is at any point less able than the players themselves.

2.5   Reinforcing a Player's Personal Fiction

Making sure that the world the player moves through stays consistent and provides a space for the player to make decisions is only the first part of the puzzle. To complete the experience, we must make sure to continually reinforce the decisions and self-expression that come naturally to players who have been asked to create a protagonist from scratch. There are a few simple techniques that can help achieve this goal, all fairly easy to use if planned for ahead of time.

Don't Imply Character History for the Player

While it is fine at the beginning of a game to fill in a bit of character background for the player—as long as it still allows for some interpretation and self-expression—it is absolutely not okay to spring new details or character background on the player while in mid-story. An NPC commenting out of the blue about the PC's sister when the player assumed no family connections or an NPC making a declaration of some wondrous or heinous deed the player's character is supposed to have done can shatter the player's entire image for the character. The single exception to this would be if the plot were actually about the fact that the player's character didn't know this information, but in general, this is something to be stringently avoided.

Feedback on the Self-Expression Choices a Player Makes

When a player makes a decision about what class or race to play, what gender to be, even what color hair to have, that player has given you a great opportunity to bring his unique world to life. Having NPCs comment on these decisions, especially on the unusual ones, will validate the player's choices and make the entire experience more immersive. If the player has chosen a strangely fat elf, say something. If the player is a dwarf without facial hair and that isn't the norm, say something. If the player is a stereotype, comment on that as well. It's easy to do with a few variables and pays huge dividends.

Make Sure All Requests to the PC are Valid

This is one of the most often violated rules for RPG writing and one that's the most easily fixed. Simply put, you shouldn't ever ask a noble paladin to take a break from saving the world to kill a bunny rabbit. The RPG genre is strewn with terrible, pointless quests that not only make little sense dramatically (who is this random peasant and why is he approaching an armed warrior about some missing apples?), but they also fly in the face of the fiction surrounding the player character, usually a great hero. In the world of video games, it's just as easy to model a dire rat as a sewer rat, a dragon as a lizard, a great wizard as a peasant. So don't sell the player and your story short out of pure lazy writing. Think of something dramatic, action packed, and worthy of the player's attention. Then ask the player character to go do that.

If Writing Dialogue Trees, Keep Player Character Dialogue Broad

When writing for the main character, it is vital to remember that this is the on-screen representation of a thousand different fantasies. One player sees himself as a smooth rogue, with a ready wit and a charming smile. Another player sees herself as educated and well-heeled, ready for any delicate situation. Therefore the player character's dialogue must be carefully written to avoid too many particular parts of speech that denote class or temper. A simple line of modest vocabulary can be read in many different ways, with many different inflections. The exception to this rule comes in the increasingly likely event that there is full voiceover for the PC. In such a case, lines must still be kept broad where it's possible, but an interpretation of the lines must be made.

2.6   Conclusion

The only way to create vibrant, immersive, high-quality RPG stories and dialogue is to first take both the subject matter and the art form seriously. If you approach interactive storytelling the same way you would approach traditional fiction, it will show. This is a new art we have on our hands, less than two decades old and ripe for revolution and experiment. In this new space, the place of a protagonist has been removed, and player agency and world consistency must be the primary narrative concerns. The tools of the interactive storyteller must therefore necessarily be different. Creating choices that matter, keeping players in the moment, and reinforcing a player's personal fiction are the first steps. After that, it's practice, patience, and belief that giving a player control of a story can create a different and fantastic form of storytelling.

3
Writing for Adventure Games

Lee Sheldon

IF you would like to start with some history, GOTO "*Plus ça change, plus c'est la même chose*"

IF you would like to jump to the theme of this chapter, GOTO "Writer as Designer"

IF you would like to jump to the red meat, GOTO "Player Character"

IF you reached this chapter by mistake, GOTO "END"

3.1   *Plus ça change, plus c'est la même chose*

In 1996, the then dominant video game magazine *Computer Gaming World* published a book called *Graphic Adventure Companion*. As co-designer of one of its featured games, *The Riddle of Master Lu*, I wrote a sidebar that included the following:

> Adventure games these days at least pretend to story and character. Puzzles should therefore be designed in the context of the story and characters. It should be one of the "Poetics" of adventure game design.

Speaking to the players, I added:

> Unless the game designer is unconcerned with-or unfamiliar with-story and character logic, the "learn context" method can be a shortcut to correct actions, encourage your suspension of disbelief, draw you further into the story, and provide a far more satisfying overall experience than the "how do I get by the next puzzle roadblock" mindset.

Writing in context—that is, making sure adventure game puzzles directly contribute to your story and help reveal your characters—has remained my mantra ever since.

3.2   Writer as Designer

All video games have unique requirements. Hence this book. However, an adventure game, more than any other type of video game, demands that writing and design be inexorably intertwined. In context, puzzles become dramatic obstacles, whether they take the form of physical impediments or of non-player characters with agendas of their own. Only in my recent work in alternate reality games have I found the same necessary symbiosis. So let's keep this in mind as we explore some of the challenges of adventure game writing.

3.3   Player Character

Before we can have story, we must have character. Character exposes our theme, produces the drama and comedy, and creates the conflict that drives the story. Choosing the character the player gets to play in an adventure determines the structure of the story and the design.

If you are adapting from another medium, some choices become simpler, others more difficult. In *The Riddle of Master Lu*, the player character was a real person, Robert Ripley, supposedly one of the main inspirations for Indiana Jones. Here was a man who in his heyday was known as an adventurer who sought out bizarre relics from the far corners of the planet. Yet he also had a widely publicized, unconventional private life involving relationships with numerous women. Since the game was intended to be an adventure game and not *Ripley's Playboy Mansion*, his spirit, his boyish enthusiasm, his fascination with the fantastic, and his love of adventure were the traits to focus on.

Figure 3.1. *Ripley's Believe It or Not!: The Riddle of Master Lu*, Sanctuary Woods, Inc., 1995.

Recently I was given the task of adapting some of Agatha Christie's books as point-and-click adventure games. The first two were *And Then There Were None* and *Murder on the Orient Express*. The second of these presented a daunting challenge. The detective, Hercule Poirot, is one of the most famous fictional detectives ever, probably surpassed only by Sherlock Holmes. Everyone who is not a writer often jumps to the conclusion that players would have the most fun playing Poirot. But is that truly the best answer?

We've seen him in almost every imaginable medium. We know him. It was my belief that the fun of Poirot's character, as is the fun of Sherlock Holmes, derives from watching him do his thing, being surprised by his deductions and conclusions, and being amused by his eccentric behavior. To put the player inside the mind of such a character spoiled the surprise and the humor.

So instead, I enlarged the role of a peripheral character, combined him with another character from the book, and changed his sex to female. That person became the player character. She could be far more active than the sedentary Poirot, she could be more adventurous, she allowed the player to make deductions and to make mistakes (something Poirot rarely did), and she allowed the player to experience Poirot in all his brilliant, eccentric glory.

The most important rule for characters adapted from another medium? Make sure you remain true to them. Don't force them into situations or choices they didn't make before. James Bond does not gun down innocent civilians.

If you are creating a brand-new story, you have much more freedom. Here are a few suggestions to think about as you create your player character.

- Create a character who makes sense in the world he'll inhabit. He doesn't have to be at home in that world, but his place there should not strain the player's credulity. A fish out of water is fine: for example, a middle-class character whom players can identify with thrust into the world of politics or high society. This gives you lots of opportunities for puzzles, surprises and comedy.

- Create a character who makes sense in an adventure game. Somebody who thinks with his fists, or who is at home firing automatic weapons, may not be the best choice for the more cerebral pleasures of the adventure game.

- Create a character who doesn't know everything. It's much more interesting for players if their avatars don't have all the skills necessary to complete the story but must learn some along the way. Consider hindering the skills they do have at some point. Feel free to break a leg or temporarily blind them.

- Just as in a TV series, make sure the character is someone with shoes we'd want to slip into. The character may have faults but should be someone who is interesting, someone with whom you would want to spend a considerable amount of time.

- Think about the other characters your avatar will meet and the arena in which you set your story. Both should be chosen for the potential of conflict and obstacles as in any good drama.

- Keep the details of the avatar interesting but sketchy. Allow room for the player to fill out the corners of the character.

- Avoid stereotypes. Nobody wants to play a character who is utterly predictable and devoid of life.

- Resist cliché. Avoid amnesia. Try not to kill off or maim innocent members of the avatar's family just to give the player a reason to ride out for revenge.

IF you would like to read more about character, GOTO "Non-Player Characters" THEN GOTO "Major Characters" THEN GOTO "Minor Characters" THEN GOTO "Death"

IF you would like to jump to the next main topic, GOTO "Dialogue"

ELSE GOTO "END"

3.4   Non-Player Characters

Non-player characters (NPCs) can be divided into two camps: major characters (villains, mentors, sidekicks) and minor characters (servants, pets, extras, cannon fodder). We don't have time to go into detail about each subgroup and how it is written, but here are some general points to keep in mind. First, *any* live character can expose story in a more interesting and unobtrusive way than artifacts like books, journals, scrolls, audio recordings, video recordings, historic markers, or signage.

Major Characters

- They deserve our attention and respect. Treating them simply as obstacles or Central Exposition or hint systems is to ignore the fact that they are one of the most seamless ways of telling story. Properly developed, they are far more engaging than endless pages of text or canned speeches. Create full-blooded 3D characters with lives of their own. The three dimensions of character? Physical, sociological, and psychological. If you don't know these, look them up.

- Once you know who these people are, their usefulness in puzzle creation goes beyond mere roadblocks.

- They can also be tools to solve puzzles.

- They help us to develop the player character. He can react to them and the news or crises they bring. He can interact with them, hearing good counsel or opposing views. Drama results. Or comedy. Or both.

- They not only help us move the plot forward, they help us to generate emotion.

- Remember that the most interesting of villains have valid reasons for the havoc they create. They aren't just evil. In fact, they are often of the opinion that what they do is right and just. The difference between heroes and villains on the battlefield is determined by who wins.

- Give your major characters more than one purpose to bring them alive. A single character can be mentor, sidekick, *and* villain. Save some money in an already miniscule adventure game budget: combine character roles!

- Avoid stereotypes.

Minor Characters

- They do not need to be as fully fleshed out as major characters. Instead, they can be sketched in vibrant, memorable colors. Have a look at how Charles Dickens can bring a character alive by focusing on only a few distinctive traits, entertainingly revealed.

- Minor characters can—and should—fill more than one role.

- They bring the setting of the game to life.

- They can also be either obstacles or the solution to a puzzle.

- Avoid stereotypes.

In *Evil Under the Sun*, a cat and a dog become the obstacle and solution to a puzzle, as well as a literal running gag throughout the remainder of the game.

3.5 Death

The player's avatar dies repeatedly in many types of games. It is a convention. The player's avatar used to die repeatedly in adventure games as well. These days we're seeing less of it, and for good reason. Adventure games are more cerebral than visceral. In chess, the king dies once and the game is over. Avatar death adds nothing to the gameplay.

In fact, in a game where a player's effort to solve a puzzle ends in his avatar's death, the game falls into the trap of "learning by dying" that has plagued video games since the beginning. It made sense in *Dragon's Lair* to force the player to find each step in a sequence to escape death. Every step cost another quarter. But the branching trees of death in certain full motion video (FMV) games like *Silent Steel* helped kill FMVs.

To use player character death to raise the stakes, or create suspense, is fruitless. We've already trivialized it with "Save and save often!" and easy resets. (Remember when avatar death meant restarting an entire game?) It may be a standard practice

Figure 3.2. *Agatha Christie: Evil Under the Sun*, The Adventure Company, 2007.

elsewhere, but sacrificing suspense for shock doesn't help out storytelling much. Too bad Alfred Hitchcock isn't designing games. He knew the difference.

IF you would like to read about dialogue, GOTO "Dialogue" THEN GOTO "Exposition"

IF you would like to jump to the next main topic, GOTO "Puzzles"

ELSE GOTO "END"

3.6   Dialogue

Dialogue is often an important element in adventure games, *Myst* being a notable exception. It can be handled in a number of different ways. We have the standard dialogue trees of *Hotel Dusk* and their several variations like "draining the bucket" where all menu choices remain until selected, or "race to the finish" where every choice leads to more choices until the conversation completes.

We can suggest types of choices rather than actual dialogue such as "Be Masterful" or "Insinuate You Know More Than You Really Do," or the easier than it sounds "Say Something Witty." Text can be replaced with icons or dialogue choices selected on a mood meter that ranges from "Bully" to "Sycophant."

However your dialogue is delivered, here are some general rules:

- Know your characters: where they're from, their education level, and their profession. All will help determine how they sound.

- If writing an accent or dialect, avoid trying to spell everything phonetically. No one will be able to read it. Instead rely on rhythm, cadence, and sentence structure with the occasional regionalism or foreign word added for flavor.

- Colloquial dialogue is not enough. Find an edge, something that will catch the ear of the player because it is not what they usually hear in the real world.

- Vary paragraph, sentence, word, and syllable length for variety. Too many of the same size of any of these in a row can be soporific.

- Do not write huge speeches unless a huge speech is specifically called for. Keep lines short and to the point.

- Use every line to reveal character and advance the story.

- Avoid anachronisms and cheap humor untethered from character or time or place.

One other point about dialogue: consider return visits. Allow NPCs to have memories of the avatar. Then provide variations for an NPC to re-greet the avatar when you go back to her based on time or distance, e.g., (a) if the player exits the NPC's room, then turns around and goes back in: "Was there something else?" or (b) if the player travels to Thailand and returns to the NPC's room in Chicago: "Hi! Long time no see!"

3.7 Exposition

Keep exposition simple and clear. Break it into bits and pieces and scatter it throughout the game. Don't stop the game for exposition. Give it to the player as she plays.

IF you would like to read about puzzles, GOTO "Puzzles"

IF you would like to read about story and structure, GOTO "Story and Structure"

IF you would like to jump to the conclusion, GOTO "Conclusion"

ELSE GOTO "END"

3.8 Puzzles

Puzzles are the heart and soul of adventure games. Because writing and design are so closely linked, your writing chores may often include puzzle design. Puzzles can involve creation (build an impromptu ladder to reach the roof), destruction (break open the strongbox), questing ("Find me the sacred pickle, and I'll reveal what I know"), and many other jobs large or small that the player is asked to accomplish.

All puzzles are composed of an obstacle that must be overcome (a literal or metaphorical lock) and a means of overcoming it (a literal or metaphorical key). Puzzles can be mechanical or character-based or mental, or a combination of these. Mechanical puzzles can be inventory-based (combine the poison with the coffee and the cup) or require only manipulation of objects in the world (push lever to the right and down to put the car in gear). Character puzzles may require dialogue (threat, cajole, outsmart), subterfuge (create a diversion), or violence (time for that mace you picked up earlier) to name just a few. Mental puzzles can be riddles, math problems, or social, scientific, or psychological conundrums (solve global warming).

Puzzles can be combined in puzzle suites (many thematically linked pieces of a larger obstacle), or chained together in series to create elaborate puzzle structures.

Some puzzling considerations for writers:

- Puzzles can pose moral dilemmas. To combat evil, must I become evil? Does the end justify the means?

- Consequences of certain puzzle solutions may not be readily apparent. I opened the water valve so I could swim across the ravine, but the flood drowned poor Toto.

- Puzzles can provide exposition: reassembling this bomb, I can match it against the techniques of known bomb makers and maybe identify who made this one.

- Every good puzzle has a crisis, a climax, and a resolution, just like a good story.

- Keep in mind that your task is not to create puzzles so hard that the player cannot solve them, and that you can easily modify a puzzle's level of difficulty with skillful writing.

- Play fair! All the information needed to solve a puzzle should be available somewhere within the game.

Remember above all that if you want to integrate all the elements of your adventure game, your puzzles must be in context. In the recent series of Agatha Christie adventure games I wrote and designed, I tried to make every puzzle, every obstacle, every action the player takes relate directly to the story and the characters, make them logical within the fiction of the game world, and keep them thematically consistent.

3.9   Story and Structure

The structure of an adventure game is not a sandbox. The player cannot invent the story and make it her own as other types of games try to do. The adventure game is a progression from point to point. This does not mean it has to be linear! Don't make that mistake! But even if it isn't linear, it forces players to assemble the story in concrete pieces that do not allow for much emergent gameplay as we typically define it.

Even if the puzzles can be solved in any order, they must be solved, or the game is not a true adventure game. This is one of several reasons adventure games have fallen out of fashion in recent years in the face of wide-open worlds that promise a unique experience for every player.

However, by giving the player choices that grant players agency, alter the gameplay, relationships with characters, the difficulty of challenges, etc., adventure games can be much more than a linear progression from puzzle A to puzzle B to puzzle C.

Here are some things to think about when constructing an adventure game story:

- Make the puzzles as integral a part of the story as any other element of a story.

- Use the setting, geography, and weather to create obstacles that need solving.

- Begin with simple challenges as a tutorial and as the player settles into the story.

- Adventure games are notoriously tricky when it comes to pace. As you near the endgame, consider not just continually ratcheting up the difficulty level but actually decreasing the difficulty level to increase pace.

- Another way to increase pace is to narrow the world: cut off physical locations as part of a story (landslides, loss of a boat), reduce the number of characters (a plague or simply a switch to a more isolated location), or reduce the player's inventory. (I love this one. Very late in *The Riddle of Master Lu*, I had a bad guy knock Robert Ripley out and go through his pockets, removing all those incredibly useful inventory items adventure gamers are so fond of, so that players had to start from scratch in the endgame.)

- Use time. An adventure game by its very nature is turn-based. (I hate real-time puzzles added simply to change up the gameplay!) Use what I call "event time" to increase suspense. In one design, the player avatar was locked in a trunk and dumped into a lake. There were four or five steps the player had to take to escape the trunk that was filling with water. I designed the puzzle so the water rose in the trunk only after the correct completion of a step, guaranteeing by the end the avatar would be up to his neck. It increased the suspense, felt as if the water was simple rising on its own, but... the avatar couldn't die.

3.10   Conclusion

Writing for adventure games presents a number of the same challenges writing for all games presents. But as we've briefly discussed, there are quite a few that are peculiarly our own. And there are certainly many not faced in other media. But don't fall into the trap of thinking that because we're a relatively new medium (not all that new anymore) that we can throw out methods of good character development and storytelling that have worked for thousands of years. Differentiate between elements from other media that work and elements that don't and directly apply the useful ones, adapt others to our unique needs, and embrace the new ones we can call our own.

Remember to write and design in tandem, and in context, to create an adventure game experience that is an integrated whole—and all the more richer for it.

END

4

Writing for Action-Adventure Games

John Feil

4.1 Introduction: "Hey, You Put Some Adventure in My Action!"

The action genre of games is very wide. Basically, any game that focuses on simulating physical movement can be placed in it. One genre that can't be placed in the action bucket is the adventure game. Adventure games, focusing on puzzles and story, rarely use action to entertain their audiences.

Action-adventure games thus combine elements of both genres into one. While generally focusing on physical movement, they steal gameplay from the adventure genre to serve the needs of the story of the game. For instance, though a Spider-Man game is generally about web-swinging through the streets of Manhattan, there are also adventure game elements in that Spidey gets to stop and talk to people, parts of the game only open themselves up after certain conversations, and there is usually a heavy story element involved in driving the player from the beginning of the game to the end.

Generally, action-adventure games tend to identify themselves by their story-driven nature. Most games based on a license, like comic books or movies, fall into this genre, as do most games that have a very strong narrative element. Games focusing on characters such as Indiana Jones, Spider-Man, and Shrek are generally lumped into the action-adventure pile. Games that aren't action-adventure but share a lot of the gameplay of the genre can include role-playing games like *Fallout 3*, MMORPGs like *World of Warcraft*, survival horror games like *Resident Evil*, and first-person shooter games like *Half-Life*. These games also focus on story to drive their action, but they tend to be identified with a specific, smaller niche.

4.2   Story and Action, Not the Best of Friends

You may have noticed this before: story does not belong in games. Sure, I know this must be shocking, written in a book about how to write stories in games, but it's true. Games require a certain level of heightened focus and reaction time to defeat, especially action games, where you are running, dodging, attacking, defending, and jumping to get to the end. There's not a lot of time to pay attention to what the characters say, much less what the written text on the screen says.

To give a real-life statistic, people who try to talk on cell phones while they drive suffer a 40% loss of attention from driving. If you're fighting the boss at the end of a level, listening to your character's mentor trying to tell him something is likely to get filtered out as a distraction.

However, people crave stories, as stories give them a framework, a motivation, for all that running and jumping and slaying. Furthermore, game developers also tend to want to make their games about something more than just running around.

So here we are, stuck trying to mash story into an activity that isn't very friendly to the idea.

So, if we want players to pay attention to and enjoy our story, we're going to have to tell it in the spaces in between the action.

4.3   The Cracks

Where are the cracks in the gameplay when players have enough attention span to learn about your carefully crafted plot and dialogue? Here's a list:

- **Cutscenes**. Also called cinematics, these are the little movies where control is removed from the player and we show him what the game is doing now that he's reached level 4. Cutscenes are the default standard in action-adventure games to tell story. The good thing is that when you remove the player from having to concentrate on gameplay, you can get his full attention on what's happening. The bad thing is that players don't want to be interrupted if they are having fun, so they'll skip the cinematic as fast as their thumbs can hit "X." Furthermore, cutscenes are expensive and time consuming. They require tons of unique animations that are never used anywhere else in the game, and they can cost hundreds of thousands of dollars to create. They are also hard to change if the story suddenly needs to be altered, so they can either tie you down to the story you contrived at 2:00 a.m. right before the script deadline, or they have to be dropped totally, wasting the work of several artists, animators, and sound guys as well as the money you paid them.

- **Between the beats.** Humans are multitasking machines. We can handle some story shoved at us when we're in action, but not much. If you want to tell the player something while he's out defeating the hordes of enemies he's facing, you have to keep it short and audible. Text messages go largely ignored, so you're stuck with dialogue. Called "shout-outs," these snippets of dialogue should only contain one idea like "go left" or "kill the red guy." Keep these shout-outs as short as you can, generally less than 10 seconds. To complicate your job, these snippets also have to be said in such a way as to relate important details about your non-player character's personality. To do this, always push for the best voice talent you can get, as tone and delivery will transmit volumes of information even behind lines like "Watch out!"

- **On the ground.** A popular way to tell stories in games is to place bits and pieces of it in journals and books and newspapers that the player can find and read throughout the game. You can also have non-player characters stand around and wait for the player to talk with them. This is a good way to tell story, but it relies totally on the player's desire to learn about the game's world and his ability to find these bits and pieces of story in the first place. This almost forces you to make your story somewhat non-linear. You have to allow for the player to find story bit A and C, but not B and D.

- **Quests.** Quests are a good way of relating story. As you know, quests are missions or tasks you ask the player to complete. From the nature and content of the quests you give the player, you can detail your important plot points. "Go fight the zombie horde attacking the town to the west" tells the player that the land is being overrun by the undead and from which direction they are coming. Players, once again, have little patience for the specifics, so keep things as quick and as simple as you can.

- **Semiotics.** Semiotics is the study of signs and symbols. While not totally within the realm of the writer, adding signs and symbols to the game's environment can help you tell your story. The problem with symbols and signs are that most of them are highly culture-specific. A red octagon usually says "stop sign" in the United States but can mean something totally different to a player in Korea. One type of sign that tends to reach beyond culture is facial expressions. Smiles, frowns, etc. can communicate a lot of information to the player. Fortunately, today's technology allows games to do a decent job of facial animation, allowing us to use these powerful symbols. Another way to use semiotics in your game is to establish your own set of symbols specific to the world of your game. A good example of this is the way *World of Warcraft* uses exclamation marks to indicate that a quest is available from the character it is floating over.

4.4   Characters

Your characters are going to be your primary method of delivering what you write to your audience. By what they say and do, you'll expose the beats of the story, reveal the personalities of the characters, and unveil your plot.

The Player Character: Putting Words into the Player's Mouth

One of the most difficult things about making games is managing expectations. If the player expects one thing and gets another, you run the risk of creating a disconnect, a point where the player breaks his suspension of disbelief and loses his immersion in your game. One of the easiest ways to create a disconnect is to have the player character say something that the player doesn't feel is appropriate to that character. For instance, one of the biggest complaints about the original *Thief* game was that the main character would sometimes make wry remarks at unexpected times. These remarks would kick the player's immersion right out of the game.

To avoid disconnects like this, you have to establish the personality and dialogue style of the main character from the very beginning of the game and stick to it throughout the entire experience. Further, pay attention to the action in the game: if the player is trying to be stealthy, don't have his player character talk while he's in a sneaky section. Work with designers and programmers to make sure you know when gameplay like this will happen.

Another facet of modern games is that almost all of them are about power fantasies. As such, one of your jobs as a writer is to make the player character say things that make the player feel smarter, funnier, or tougher than the universe he's walking around in. The main character doesn't have to know everything, but, in any verbal joust, he needs to come out on top.

Non-Player Characters: Your Most Important Characters

Non-player characters (NPCs) should be the primary vehicle for exposition in your game. They can tell the player where to go, where the plot currently stands, and information that the player needs to overcome the various puzzles he will face. Most importantly, the dialogue of your NPCs helps reinforce the personality of the game world. This makes it important to make sure your NPCs' voices don't betray things like anachronisms or cultural references that your audience will feel are inappropriate to the setting. For example, don't have the NPC say "Dude!" if the game takes place in a medieval world.

One of the best ways to tell story through dialogue is by having two non-player characters talk with one another. In this way, you are not putting words or unwanted emotions into the player's mouth. However, just like any time the player must choose between words and action, you must always assume the player will choose action. The player may not want to stick around to hear the NPCs talk; thus you are back to those cracks we talked about above.

An interesting way to keep the player around is to have his companions do a lot of talking. The companions stick to the player like glue, so the player can't get away from the conversation. However, the state of companion AI being what it is, this can make things very hard on the game's programmers.

One of the best uses of this is in the *Jak and Daxter* series of platformers. Jak is silent, but Daxter is a motor-mouth who comments on anything and everything the player sees. Companion AI is cleverly avoided by making Daxter into what amounts to a second head for Jak, as the funny critter spends the entire game riding on Jak's shoulder.

The Villain: The Most Important Character in the Game

The most important NPCs you will write for are the villains. Villains should be interesting and believable and give the player a good reason to want to defeat them. Action-adventure games, being very story-oriented, require that the villains be the primary drivers of the action. Generally, the main character is reactive, rather than proactive. The villain's plans are driving the main character from place to place, sending him to fight fires more than requiring him to prevent the fires in the first place.

The villains of the game should have their presence felt at all times. Even if the main character doesn't know the identity of the villain, all the events that the player is reacting to should have some element that reflects the villain's hand behind them. While the old Batman villains seem campy now, they are an excellent (if overly blatant) example of how a villain's style and methodology can be just as central to their character as their dialogue.

4.5   Locations

Action-adventure games are generally divided into distinctive locations, or levels. The player journeys from location to location, sometimes returning over the same terrain, sometimes not. These locations are the setting for your story and, as in any storytelling vehicle, should reinforce your narrative and characters.

A Location Is Worth a Thousand Words

No part of the game promotes and reinforces immersion more than the locations that the player travels through. As the writer, you use that setting to reinforce your narrative to make the game even more immersive.

Game environments tend to rely heavily on cliché. Western fantasy settings usually root themselves in a *Dungeons & Dragons*–like mishmash of western medieval culture and mythologies. Science fiction settings have advanced weaponry, cars, and are generally either very shiny or very rusty. Modern action games take their settings straight from Bond, Bourne, or whatever recent action film has captured the development team's imagination.

As a writer, it will be your job to leverage that cliché in modest ways but still find some new angle that comes at that cliché in a way that seems totally original and unique. Yeah, it's not easy at all.

Luckily, as mentioned, action-adventure games tend to use a familiar intellectual property (IP) as their basis, so some of that responsibility will be removed from your shoulders. However, working within someone else's world can be very frustrating.

4.6   Writing for Licensed Games

Writing for games based on a license can be one of the most frustrating experiences imaginable. Here's why.

Let's say that you are working at an independent developer hired by a publisher to develop on a game based on a movie. The publisher will have definite ideas of what they want from the game, and your designers will respond to that, trying to make sure they make the game their team will have fun making while also making sure the publisher is happy.

Once the publisher is happy with the direction of the game, they'll send it on to the people who actually own the license, as there will probably be some sort of agreement in their contract with these people that lets the license holder have some say over the product the publisher is trying to get your developer to create. In this case, the people who control the license are not only the people who are making the film but also the people responsible for publishing the books the film is based on, plus the agents of the author who wrote that book, plus the author herself.

Let's list this out. People in charge of the direction of your game include the following:

1. Developer's team management (lead designer, lead producer, etc.).

2. Developer's upper management (studio head, creative directors, etc.).

3. Publisher's primary liaison to the developer (i.e. their producer).

4. Publisher's upper management.

5. Film license holder (this may be split up amongst several distinct companies).

6. Book publisher.

7. Author's agents.

8. Author.

So, basically, you can have more people telling you what to do with your writing than there are people on your development team. In the case above, there may be infighting between factions that can cause you to wonder who has the ultimate authority.

In any case, what I'm getting at here is that you'll be pulled in a lot of directions and may have to chart a course for your story and dialogue that you do not like one little bit.

To survive this, here are some tips:

- **Research the IP.** Get to know the characters inside and out, as well as their setting. Constantly ask for research material so you can know exactly how your characters will act and react in any circumstance. The better you can hit this mark, the more the people who read your writing will trust you and leave you alone to do your work. One note, however: not only will you need to know the characters of the license inside and out, but you'll have to figure out how these characters are interpreted by the people who give you your orders.

  For instance, for your lead designer, the plucky boy wizard is primarily focused on making trouble for his arch-nemesis. The author might feel that the key to the character is his relationship with his friends. The publisher's producer may feel that the character's real appeal is the powers he wields and how that appeals to his preteen fans' need for empowerment. All these people may be right, but you'll need to spend a lot of time listening so you can walk that line that keeps your every word from being edited 16 times.

- **Build consensus amongst your own team and your studio.** As the writer, you probably won't be invited to high-level meetings reviewing the work you do. You need to make friends and get buy-in with the people who will be there. Your producer, the studio head, etc. will be the ones defending your writing to the publisher, so they need to believe in your talent and resist changes being handed down from above. They also need to be familiar enough with your efforts to be able to understand why you are writing the story the way you are.

  Once again, listening is key here. Make sure your benefactors know you are there to make the game they want to make. To do that, you need to really understand what they want, which takes a lot of being quiet and listening and not expounding on your own take of the characters you are writing for.

- **Be flexible.** Most writers are highly defensive about their work and will fight to keep it unchanged even if they know it's not quality. Don't be one of those guys: keep communication open and make sure you aren't making everyone else's day worse by clinging to your precious prose. Try very hard to stay energetic and involved in making sure that you and the people trying to modify your writing are working together to make the game everybody feels they want to make.

  Don't do an end-run around process: generally, it won't be your job to contact and talk to the publishers or the license holders. It is a hard thing to not want to shorten communication lines and try to understand why these people don't seem to agree with any of the directions you have taken. However, doing an end-run around your bosses, even if it improves things, will put your career in jeopardy.

4.7   Conclusion

Writing for action-adventure games isn't that different from writing for most story-based console games. Your characters need to be strong, your villains engaging, your dialogue short, entertaining, and dense with information. You'll find that your prose will always be challenged by various forces, and you'll need to spend more of your time in meetings listening, suggesting, and agreeing than you will actually writing. It's not the easiest job on your ego, for certain.

However, there is no industry on Earth that lets you write in so many styles and formats, all in one product. From long journal entries to pithy one-liners, from movie scripting for cutscenes to in-game help text, you get to stretch those literary muscles and strut your stuff before audiences (especially if you consider piracy) that most novelists can only dream of.

5

Writing for Platform Games

Andrew S. Walsh

5.1   Jump, Die, Repeat

> The sewers stretched before him broken, potholed, decayed. It was a vast net-
> work, at times towering five stories above a brick-lined floor that oozed with
> New York's fetid effluent and seethed with giant, snapping crabs that awaited
> his slightest mistake. With a twirl of his moustache, he turned to his brother.
> They shared an unspoken bond, jump, die, repeat—they will make it to the
> other side.

So could read the opening of *Mario Bros.*, one of the earliest, and certainly one
of the most famous, platform games (or platformer). First appearing in *Donkey Kong*
in 1981, the Mario brand has gone on to sell more than 200 million units world-
wide, with most of these sales being platformers. Such financial accomplishments
contributed to the platform genre representing around a third of the games market
in the 1980s. This success rested, in part, on the fact that platform games produced
some of the industry's most iconic characters—Mario, Sonic the Hedgehog, Lara
Croft, and the Prince of Persia to name but a few. Yet, despite being dominated by
world-renowned, franchise-building characters, most people do not associate platformers with narrative, or with writers.

The failure to connect narrative with the platform genre seems yet stranger considering the fact that narrative appeared in the very first platform game, *Donkey
Kong*. Despite limited technology, this early game boasted a clear hero, impos-
ing villain, cutscenes, a beginning, middle, and end, and an objective. Things
didn't stop there, either. The genre continued to be a source of new narrative
models and technology from then until now. So forget perception. The uneven,
dangerous worlds of the platformer do contain great opportunities for story and
character.

Death by Gravity: A Brief Definition of Platform Games

To tame the beast, it is always best to first understand it, so what is a platform game? At their core, platformers are games that require players to make their way through environments composed of broken ground by leaping from one safe area (a platform) to another. The in-game challenges can include other obstacles, but the player must always defeat the game via acrobatic gameplay. Early 2D games could only offer dangerous falls and the occasional elevator as obstacles, but game technology and design has gone on to evolve additional elements from physical impediments such as jumping enemies, armed opponents, and booby traps to more cerebral physics and puzzle problems. As this technology has advanced, the traditional platformer market share has declined, though while the pure platformer is a rarer beast than it once was, the genre continues, and its staple ingredients have been incorporated into a wide variety of other games. Titles such as *Splinter Cell* and *Assassin's Creed* are not straightforward platformers, but they contain gameplay sequences and design principles that owe their heritage to the pure platformer. It is worth bearing in mind that the advice in this chapter can be translated to cover platform sections of gameplay in many games, even if the game as a whole is not a platformer.

5.2   Learning to Run: Story and Game Objectives

In every story, the protagonist has to have a motive, every plot a denouement. Equally, every game has to have a gameplay objective, be it stacking blocks (*Tetris*) or surviving gun battles by killing everything in sight (*Doom*). For gaming stories to work well, the protagonist's motive and the game's gameplay objective should match. If you are writing a game that involves shooting guns, then the story must involve conflict so the player can frame his gun-toting actions. In the case of platformers, the objective is simple—the main character must travel to somewhere. Platform gameplay is all about movement, with the game character being required to go from one geographical point to another. The story goal for reaching the next geographical point can be anything you decide, but the story must involve travel, because that is what the game is about.

Early platformers often involved the main character needing to reach a villain to put right a wrong. In *Kirby's Dream Land*, Kirby is trying to retrieve the food that King Dedede has stolen from the land's inhabitants. In *Super Mario Bros.*, *Super Mario Bros. 2*, *Super Mario Land*, *Super Mario World*, *New Super Mario Bros.*, and *Super Mario Galaxy*, Mario must rescue a kidnapped princess. Such basic settings serve as story frames; they outline an objective so the player is given a motive for his gameplay actions. The game character is not just traveling; he is traveling to something. Mario is not just out for a morning jog; he is rescuing a princess. Providing an objective is the most basic purpose of any game story.

The Mario games, the Kirby series, and *Sonic the Hedgehog* do not have deep, twelve-act structures loaded with Freudian conflict or Jungian angst, and even though as a writer you might yearn to pen such stuff, they don't need this depth. There are games that are happy with basic story frames, and there always will be. This does not mean that there cannot be deep stories in platform games, but it should demonstrate that there is nothing wrong with game stories this elementary. The decision to implement a complex narrative rather than a simple story frame comes down to the game's intended audience. Audience is a factor that exerts a keen influence in the platform genre.

Story Genre and Audience

Game writing is based firmly on the genre of game in which it is set. Otherwise, you wouldn't be reading this book, right? So, game genre comes first, narrative genre second. This does not make the narrative genre a poor cousin, but the game genre sets the boundaries within which the narrative genre must exist. Once the game genre has been determined, the next predominant factor in deciding story genre is the age range of the game's intended audience. From their original release to today, *Crash Bandicoot* and *Sonic the Hedgehog* have been aimed at the "family" market as games intended to be accessible to all ages. As a general rule, the industry seems to assume that family titles must employ simple stories, often cartoons, as this is all a family audience can handle (despite both television and film regularly proving that family audiences are open to satire and other more complex forms). Since the release of the original *Sonic*, the game market has fractured and diversified. Gamers have grown older, and there has been an increase in demand for a more mature gaming experience. This in turn has left family games being aimed even more squarely at a younger audience and simpler stories. There are titles, however, that have taken the expected, a cartoon setting, running and jumping challenges, and then subverted it. Psychonauts is one example of this. *Psychonauts* is a cartoon platformer with a teen rating[1] that maintains the family elements people have come to expect from many platformers but then laces it with satire and social commentary.

While the plethora of Mario titles, new Sonic incarnations, and the focus on younger and younger audiences might suggest it, platform games do not have to be set in cartoon worlds. There are a number of more "realistic" games aimed at an older audience. Naughty Dog's *Uncharted: Drake's Fortune* boasts an age rating of teen[2], while Ubisoft's *Prince of Persia* series has regularly wandered into the mature rating. It should be noted that *Uncharted* and *Prince of Persia* don't aim to attract an older audience simply by containing swearing or violence. Both have more complex gameplay sequences and deeper story worlds than their cartoon contemporaries. The plot of *Uncharted: Drake's Fortune* follows its hard-bitten hero on a quest to discover

---

[1] ESRB Teen; PEGI and USK 12+.
[2] ESRB Teen; PEGI 16+; USK 16.

an "ancestral" treasure, uncovering a twisting plot of mercenaries, great evil, and the undead along the way. The most recent *Prince of Persia* tells the tale of a hero who must save the world from a corrupting evil while on a journey to discover himself. In each case, story is an integral part of the game package, and both titles seek to make their central characters much more than a simple avatar; they seek to create characters as deep as those found in other genres.

5.3   Holes in the Ground: The Pitfalls of Platformers

If audience need not hold back the platform game writer, then what are the limitations and challenges to the writer? There are three that stand out above others:

1. Perception.

2. Resources and technology.

3. Level design.

Perception

As stated earlier, despite the narrative history of the platformer, this genre is not as strongly associated with narrative as is the case with action, role-playing, or even shooting games. This is partly because the genre was at its strongest at a point when game writing was at its most peripheral (limited mainly to adventure games[3]). As we have seen, the genre is also often, unfairly, associated with being a children's market. While they are false, these assumptions can often be a barrier to a writer hoping to create a narrative in the platform genre because such perceptions stop companies from investing the time and money needed to provide the narrative resources a writer needs.

Thankfully, some designers and developers do realize that platformers can have strong stories and that, historically, platform games such as *Metroid*[4] have sold partly because of their approach to story.

Resources and Technology

Whatever the writer's vision, it requires the game developer to invest resources. Every word in a game has a cost associated with it, thus each game development team will decide how much should be spent on it. Will the game get a speech engine? What scripting tools will be developed? How much programmer time, artificial intelligence (AI) development, and animation work will be given to the story? Will the team invest in the hiring of voice actors, or time in a motion-capture studio? Without animation time, the scripted events will have to be cut, or toned down, and a lack

---

[3] Despite the early narrative contributions made by titles such as *Donkey Kong* and *Metroid*.

[4] *Metroid* introduced non-linear gameplay and variable story endings—opened by completing the game in different times—so giving the player a reward and incentive to try the game again in different ways.

of scripting tools means that dialogue and events will only be able to be played in a small number of set conditions. As such, the presence, abundance, or absence of each of these determines how a story is told.

Level Design

Making sense of the gameplay world. Framing a believable plot in a realistic *Grand Theft Auto IV* style game is a world away from making sense of the environment platformers take place in. To create the acrobatic gameplay found in a platform game, the action must occur in a broken world vastly different from anything the player will have encountered in real life or in fictional settings—a topography constructed from plunging abysses (*Mario Bros.*), endless rolling barrels (*Donkey Kong*), whirling sawblades (*Prince of Persia: Two Thrones*), and marauding chickens (*Chuckie Egg*). This environment is another reason many platform games choose a cartoon setting. Such a choice means the platform world makes sense without explanation. However, some effort needs to be spent explaining the world to the player when the decision is to go for more "realistic" human characters inhabiting a "real" world—not every nuance of it, but enough to establish the setting so it makes sense.

The credibility or believability gap that broken worlds present can be tackled by pushing the player into a world that seems familiar from other genres—*Uncharted: Drake's Fortune* takes the player into crumbled ancient ruins the player will have seen in adventure stories such as the *Indiana Jones* films—or by forcing the player into real-world settings such as scaffolding platforms hanging off a skyscraper (*Tomb Raider: Legend*).

Oddworld: Abe's Exoddus takes the simple approach (in a very elegantly constructed game) of setting the action in a giant, high-security food factory. This industrial setting allows the use of machinery as obstacles while making total sense to the player. The choice goes beyond this, and the setting proves (spoiler alert) to be the core of the story. Abe's journey is to discover what has happened to his people. It appears at first that they have been enslaved to operate the factory's machinery, but ultimately Abe learns that the machines through which he has journeyed are actually turning his people into food. This choice of environment not only explains the game's setting but is integral to the narrative journey bringing the character's motive and the gameplay objectives together.

Prince of Persia (2008) also uses the environment to tell the story. Throughout the game, the Prince's companion, Elika, informs the Prince of the history of the world through which they are passing. This history and the way the characters interact with it are not just key to the game's functions (the need to travel), but they reflect back onto the characters and make the game world a character in its own right.

A broken world = a broken narrative. Beyond the challenge of explaining the world, the broken nature of platforming worlds offers further challenges to the writer that, without careful thought, can send the narrative plunging down an abyss.

Figure 5.1. *Prince of Persia* (2008). © 2008 Ubisoft Entertainment. All Rights Reserved. Based on Prince of Persia® created by Jordan Mechner.

The need of the player to keep moving, the vertically stacked levels, and the constant danger limit the number of places that the story can be told because telling a section of story in a place where the main character can die opens up a large can of worms. Should the lines that played before the character died play again? If so, what happens if the lines are broken a second, third, fourth, twenty-fifth time? How can the player expect to both watch a scene from the story and concentrate on navigating a complex, acrobatic gameplay path? Are the sections of the map chosen for the story to be shown visible to the average player? And visible long enough for a story segment to play out before the player has run past it?

Such considerations have a huge effect on how the player experiences the story. There is a constant risk that narrative information might be lost, rendering the narrative unintelligible. Conversely, choosing to reiterate information by replaying lines or scenes can lead to irritating repetition. Similarly, a writer's choice to place a stationary, non-interactive cinematic in the middle of a fast-moving gameplay section can lead to frustration for designer and gamer alike. Such challenges demand that the writer knows the level design inside out if he is to ensure that the gameplay does not break the story, nor the story disrupt the gameplay flow. Correctly placing scenes is essential to telling stories in platform games.

5.4 Writing Techniques and Technology: Countering the Challenges in Platform Games

Cutscenes

The problems of broken ground can be solved by telling the story in cutscenes on safe ground. Non-interactive sections allow the writer to control what happens, guaranteeing that the scene can't be broken and so avoiding the need for repetition. The decision to use cutscenes can also help counter any problems of resources the writer is facing as cutscenes do not require huge arrays of scripting tools or AI support. Planning a set number and length of cutscenes also means it is easier to calculate and manage the amount of investment needed to make the game's story work. This is the reason that even games such as the *Oddworld* series or *Uncharted*, which contain a wide range of storytelling techniques, also rely on beautifully crafted cinematic cutscenes to tell the most complex parts of the story.

Where a writer is tackling new games on less sophisticated platforms (such as handheld devices), or where budget is a big factor (such as in low-budget, downloadable projects), cutscenes are often the only storytelling tool available. This does not have to be a curse. *SolaRola* is a physics-based platformer for mobile phones. It tells its cartoon story—two blobs trying to survive in a universe threatened by Ping the Unmerciless—through cutscenes and very small amounts of in-game text. These comic inserts serve to frame the gameplay and provide level objectives (from refueling the blobs' spaceship to releasing imprisoned characters) and an extra ingredient: entertainment. The use of cutscenes here is not a backward movement but simply a reflection of the storytelling technology made available by handheld device technology developed on a handheld device budget.

The use of cutscenes does not absolve the writer from thinking about level design. Cutscenes are, by their very nature, non-interactive. This means that they live most happily at the start and end of levels or gameplay sequences. Placing static cinematics in the middle of an acrobatic sequence can break the gameplay flow. Careful thought

Figure 5.2. *SolaRola.* © 2007 Eidos Interactive Ltd.

must, therefore, be given to how the cutscene can introduce or pay off interactive elements without getting in their way.

The decision to use cutscenes does not eradicate the danger of repetition. *Prince of Persia: The Two Thrones* employed numerous in-game cutscenes. However, the game frequently positioned these cutscenes within save points, meaning that a player who failed a gameplay sequence was forced to watch these events again and again. While this meant that the player was certain to see these scenes, it was also highly likely that he would become frustrated with them. Such problems underline the fact that a close working relationship between narrative and design is vital to get the best from both.

Scripted Events: Telling a Story on the Move

Telling the story does not mean that the player must lose control. Scripted events are cinematic elements that show story but allow the player to keep playing. Integrating the story into the game can help to create a deeper sense of immersion and reduce the risk of breaking gameplay flow. That said, using scripted events in platform games is not always straightforward.

The main problem in using scripted events is their placement. For scripted events to be seen, the camera must point at them long enough for the information in the scene to register. *Prince of Persia* (2008) introduces one of its main characters, the Mourning King, in just such a way. He is heard shouting before he becomes visible, then as the player rounds a corner, the gameplay path points the player toward the King, meaning the player can keep control but also has time to see the character in the distance. After this point, a cinematic plays out, keeping the character alive but not containing any vital information that the player needs to know. Such a brief event works well to bring life to the world and to communicate basic information (Elika's name, the fact that this mysterious character is pursuing her, and even making it clear that he commands other characters the player has seen). The level design, however, does mean that if the player continues to run (fast movement being key to most platform design), then the scene is quickly out of sight. The amount of information in each scene and how it is delivered must, therefore, be carefully crafted to fit the window of opportunity where the scene is visible without distracting the player from the gameplay challenge.

Writers and designers should note that even if scripted events are planned as short and snappy, should the level design, art, and narrative not be closely coordinated, then the speed the character is moving, the difficulty of communicating the gameplay path, or simple camera angles can lead to interactive scripted events being missed, needing to become non-interactive, or even to these scenes being cut. Writers must think carefully, then, for while such moments can build immersion, it is often wise to avoid trying to communicate deep or essential story information in such scenes for fear that they might be missed.

When the planning works, the results can be very rewarding. *Uncharted: Drake's Fortune* is a game that uses scripted events well. In one level, the game's protagonist,

Nathan Drake, is confronted with an impossible jump. To make things worse, armed guards pull up in a truck and start to shoot at him. To progress, the player must return fire. Shooting at the guards results in the barrels on the rear of the truck exploding, catapulting the truck into the air for it to then land in exactly the right place so the player can cross the previously impassable section of the map. While this is an example of a design-led scripted event, such moments provide opportunity for story and character, create a memorable moment in the game, and tie the narrative into the gameplay path.

In a game about movement, the writer need not always use characters to tell the story; using the environment can be a good trick. *Mirror's Edge*, for instance, uses advertisements placed to be visible on the gameplay path to help establish the game's oppressive world. *Abe's Oddysee* utilizes rolling text signs built into the levels to communicate both gameplay and narrative information. Such environmental tricks are generally both cheap and immersive and so can help writers to establish their story without heavy investment of vital resources.

Speech Design in Platformers

Set animated events such as cutscenes and scripted events form only part of the writer's storytelling arsenal. Another tool available to writers is dialogue.

On-demand dialogue. On-demand dialogue is triggered by a button press meaning that it is available "on demand" when the player wants it. *Oddworld: Abe's Oddysee* and *Oddworld: Abe's Exoddus* placed such an on-demand speech engine (GameSpeak) at the heart of the game. To progress through the levels, the player was required to talk to and interact with other characters. By using a series of basic commands such as "Wait" and "Follow Me," the games' hero, Abe, was able to guide his fellow Mudokons[5] through the levels of RuptureFarms and use them to solve the gameplay puzzles presented to him. This design element helped to bring the characters to life, added greatly to the atmosphere, and showed the huge extra dimension that can be added to games when the characters communicate.

The most recent installment of *Prince of Persia* features a complex on-demand dialogue system that allows the player to learn more about the world, characters, and story events as well as to taunt enemies and even gain hints when solving the game's puzzles. As the player progresses through the game, new dialogue opens and old dialogue closes, keeping the dialogue fresh and relevant. This on-demand system allows the player to choose where to experience the story. Players who want to run and jump and keep moving need not learn many of the details found in the on-demand system, but those who crave a deeper story world can gain it at the press of a button.

In both *Oddworld* and *Prince of Persia*, the on-demand element requires (in most cases) a loss of control for the duration of the dialogue. This loss of control is miti-

---

[5]The enslaved race Abe comes from.

gated by the fact that the player has chosen to play the dialogue, and the loss of player control helps to prevent the dialogue from being broken.

Scripted dialogue. Scripted dialogue is triggered automatically by a game event, or when the player passes a set point in a level rather than being triggered by player choice.

Just as with cutscenes and scripted events, the writer must think about where the dialogue is placed. If it is somewhere the character can die, will the dialogue tail off or cut off? Will the dialogue repeat when the player restarts, and what is the effect of repetition on the player? All such factors must be discussed with the design and the story team. When writing such scripted dialogue, it is often useful for the writer to include his thoughts on how the dialogue should be timed, e.g., should all the lines be played one after the other, a series of single lines broken by short pauses, or sporadic with larger gaps of time between them? That way, the scripter who implements the dialogue into the game can do so in a way that matches the writer's thoughts.

Prince of Persia: Sands of Time uses scripted dialogue to good effect in a level where the player is required to find his route through a series of doors. As the Prince searches, he hears the girl he is searching for calling out to him. This disembodied voice adds a sense of mystery and enfolds the player in the story with little cost and to great effect while leaving the player fully in control of the game character.

AI dialogue. AI dialogue (sometimes called barks or emotes) is triggered when something happens to the player or the non-player characters. Such dialogue can be triggered by events from pain to the protagonist jumping or falling, and with a little thought, such dialogue can add to the storytelling if new banks of AI dialogue open through the game, refreshing to reflect the characters' development. This adds a further immersive storytelling tool that does not interfere with the gameplay. AI dialogue does not have to be, as it often is, limited to basic, rote writing.

Voice Recording: Thinking Beyond the Page

As far back as games such as *Impossible Mission* in 1984, platform games have contained spoken dialogue. Recording voices for platformers offers its own unique challenges. Try reading the lines aloud and then read them again while jumping up and down. Voice alters with movement. This can mean that lines written to be delivered while on the move can break, not because of the line, but because they do not sound real. Such considerations might appear to be the preserve of the voice director and the audio team, but the writer needs to think about these things ahead of time. Bad voice acting creates a break in immersion that the writer can help to prevent.

5.5   Character Creation for Platformers

Character Types

The design of game characters often stems from a combination of the game genre and the narrative genre. The prevalence of platform titles aimed at younger audiences and set in cartoon worlds has led to an abundance of cartoon characters within the genre. From *Earthworm Jim* to *Rayman*, cartoon characters make sense in a cartoon world. In games with more realistic human characters, the protagonists' background often casts them as adventurers to match their adventure film feel. In *Tomb Raider*, it is not just Lara Croft's bosom that defies gravity as she bounds from one ledge to another, and such acrobatic feats need to be explained. Both *Tomb Raider* and *Uncharted* sketch their protagonist as "an adventurer" to frame their characters' abilities. Not all games follow the convention of explaining how the protagonists can do what they do. After all, Mario is a portly plumber rather than a lithe circus performer. *Oddworld's* first hero Abe is supposed to be fit but not special. His movements and landings have weight to them that make him feel more like a real "person" trapped in special circumstances. For such characterization to work, the animation, art, and narrative character design must tie together neatly. Though it is not essential to explain everything, writers should try to match their characters to their gameworld.

Companions

Historically, many platformers have featured a single protagonist with supporting characters who only appeared in cutscenes. The reason for this is the large amount of work needed to get non-player characters (NPCs) to function believably in dangerous environments without them becoming an annoying liability to the player. The investment in design time and in the programming resources needed to create high-level AI have often proved prohibitive to the inclusion of NPCs beyond the cutscene. Adding characters to the platforming sections of the game is fraught with danger. *Lego Indiana Jones* runs into this problem with many of the secondary characters getting in the way of the player with the result that the player falls off ledges and fails gameplay sections through no fault of his own. This is because creating the artificial intelligence needed for NPCs to navigate platform sections is notoriously difficult.

Some games get around the AI constraints by having the NPC shadow the main character, repeating everything he does. In *Sonic the Hedgehog 2*, Sonic is joined by a companion, Knuckles. This companion follows Sonic, but there is no real communication between them. All the character does is repeat Sonic's moves.

In *Uncharted: Drake's Fortune*, the protagonist is joined by a number of NPCs who are capable of interacting with their environment (operating switches ahead of the player and independently moving to the next point of interest). The *Oddworld* series sees both *Abe's Oddysee* and *Abe's Exoddus* utilize NPCs as part of the game design. It should be noted that *Uncharted* limits these NPCs to the flat safe areas of the game, while the *Oddworld* games make leading the NPCs through the world and the limitations of these characters part of the gameplay challenge.

The limited abilities of secondary characters are a factor in determining where and how the story can be told. If secondary characters break the game, then the protagonist will need to be alone for much of the game. This in turn may prompt

Figure 5.3. *Prince of Persia* (2008). © 2008 Ubisoft Entertainment. All Rights Reserved. Based on Prince of Persia® created by Jordan Mechner.

the writer to use narration or monologue to compensate for the loss of dialogue opportunities. If secondary characters are present, then the writer might need to delay story points until the protagonist reaches safe ground where the characters can join the protagonist. If the aim is to put dialogue into interactive sections but characters can't travel with the player character, then the writer and designer can look to create sections where NPCs call out to the player from safe ground while the player character performs a gameplay sequence.

Prince of Persia (2008), however, features a companion who is not only capable of doing everything the player character does but who is also able to react to her surroundings and perform in a way that keeps her feeling alive and out of the player's way. This allows the story to be told throughout the game as the protagonist always has another character to play off.

5.6   Linear Gameplay Equals Linear Narrative

As platform games involve traveling from A to B and are often contained in single linear worlds, this can lead to the narratives and story designs presented in platform games to also simply go from A to B. This does not need to be the case.

One Road, Many Endings: Multiple Story Outcomes

If further proof were needed that platform games aren't the limited story vehicles some perceive them to be, then the fact that some claim the platform game *Metroid* to be the first game with a multiple narrative ending should demonstrate this. Each of the different story endings, including the reveal that Metroid's main character is female, are reached by completing the game in faster and faster times. *Abe's Exoddus* also uses multiple story endings triggered by completing the gameplay in different ways. Here the two different endings open depending on how many Mudokons the player manages to rescue through the course of the game.

Evolving the Platform Game: Open Worlds in Platformers

While *Metroid* introduced multiple endings to a linear game, other more recent designs have presented free-roaming worlds incorporating multiple gameplay paths. Such non- linear games are often controlled through hubs. Such hubs seen in games such as *Psychonauts* and *Earthworm Jim 3D* use these central locations as a place to tell the central story and as a way of linking the levels together. The new *Prince of Persia* gives the player a wide choice of how to navigate through the gameworld but requires the player to return to a central temple to gain the magical powers that open the world up. Where the gameplay is open, central hubs such as these allow the writer areas of safe ground within which to tell the story and also allow the writer to maintain an element of linear control. In all such cases, the writer should find ways to extend the story out beyond the hub so that it continues into the rest of the gameworld, the writer but should also note that this design gives him an element of control in the midst of a dangerous, broken world.

5.7   Safe Landings

Despite the perception of platform games as a genre that doesn't employ narrative, its rich history disproves this. Knowledge of this history not only helps a writer to see how other games have mastered the challenges of a broken world he is about to tackle but also to put forward a case to gain the resources he needs to tell his story. Knowing the challenges that exist in the design enables not only the development of appropriate technology, such as companion AI or the triggers needed to start scripted events, but helps the writer to position the story at appropriate places in the gameworld. What is evident in platform games is that early decisions can solve a lot of narrative problems before they occur. So go forth. Fear not as you peer into the abyss and hear the whirr of a sawblade, for the uneven, dangerous worlds of the platformer do contain great opportunities for story and character, and platform games continue to provide narrative firsts that other genres can benefit from.

6

Writing for First-Person Shooters

Lucien Soulban and Haris Orkin

6.1   Introduction: FPS and the Nature of the Beast

Welcome to first-person shooters (or FPS), a style of game that parks you behind the main character's eyes. All games let you control and manipulate your environment to varying degrees, but almost no other genre of video game drops you closer to the action than an FPS. Conversely, you also share the limitations of your character. You can't see down the next corridor, can't see what's coming up behind you unless you turn your character around.

FPS is more than putting the player into the head of the protagonist; it's all about the direct corollaries. Your adrenaline is the character's adrenaline, your racing heart is the character's racing heart. And sometimes, even the reverse is true. You get startled, the character misses his shot, thank you very much *F.E.A.R.* You see ally soldiers in distress, you run to save them, thank you *Halo* and *Medal of Honor* series. The motivations are primal, the goals visceral. We are, after all, inside the character's head in a cinematic experience that plays in surround sight and sound.

The first-person shooter is a schizophrenic medium that makes narrative all the more challenging. For certain, it is the most cinematic of the genres, all the gory details played out before our eyes, the technology stretched closer and closer to the boundaries of realism. Perhaps for this reason, story can often get lost in the stampede to push the technology or gameplay, what Marshall McLuhan once pinpointed as, "The medium is the message." In other words, for most FPSs, the story is often the advancement of technology or the realization of interesting gameplay.

But that's changing, and with it, the importance of the first-person narrative. While companies will always push the technology or gameplay of the FPS first, there is a greater drive for improving its narrative structure as well. So, welcome to the front lines of writing for FPSs—a first-person experience of a different kind.

6.2   A Primer on First-Person Narrative

Drop the "shooter" in FPS, and video games are hardly the first medium to use the first-person perspective. It is, however, the only medium that has done it so spectacularly or made the experience so interactive.

First Person in Literature

From a literary standpoint, first person is a technique whereby the story is told in the voice of the main character. He relates his experiences and describes the events that unfold directly for you. There is rarely any duplicity in first-person narrative, though there is that edge of personal interpretation skewing perception. Take Chuck Palahniuk's brilliantly written *Fight Club* to understand not only first-person literature but how the protagonist's perceptions are limited. The advantage of this narrative style is that it opens the character's mind to the reader. You can grasp the protagonist's motivations and fears in his own words. You become invested in his plight. You are also limited by the breadth of his perceptions, never seeing beyond his five senses, discovering the same mysteries at exactly the same time he does.

First Person in Movies

You're probably wondering when, if ever, you've seen first person used in films. Actually, that's because there are two ways of going about it. The first is the physical first-person shift where the audience sees through the character's eyes. Snippets of this style exist in the opening combat of *Saving Private Ryan* and in horror movies when the camera briefly shows a quick sequence through the character's or monster's eyes. Of course, there's the first-person sequence in the movie *Doom*, but that's more an homage to the game than anything else.

Then there's the other use of first person, where the camera remains distinctly third-person but the film is narrated or explored through the main character. Take *Memento*, where the movie focuses on the trials of Leonard Shelby and his inability to remember anything past a few minutes. Few movies ever plant you that deeply into someone's perceptions without diving in behind their eyes.

Movies like *Cloverfield*, however, offer a cheat by using the documentary style of cinéma vérité or "cinema of truth." The camera itself is both witness and proxy for the first-person perspective of the main characters.

6.3   The Caveats

These are some of the hurdles facing writers for this genre.

- **1001 terrorists.** Gameplay relies on a high action quotient (this is the shooter chapter, after all), and that often means populating the story with a reason why there are dozens, if not hundreds, of enemies populating any given map. That means, more than most genres, enemy motivation throughout the game and throughout each level is paramount. There has to be a reason why the bad guys are at said location in such vast numbers.

- **The genre is the story.** Genres have certain rules that they follow, and the success of the story is not only how well you understand those rules but how well you can play with them. *F.E.A.R.*-style horror shooters, for example, rely on suspense, on handicapping the character somehow, and on using the unknown. Military shooters are all about warfare, technology, and geopolitics.

- **The slow play.** Some players are likely to take days, weeks, or even months between play sessions, and that means they may not remember the fine details of the plot. Therefore, it's important to seed stories with hints and reminders of past events.

6.4 A Very Short History of the FPS

The early history of the first-person shooter is somewhat shrouded in mystery. Some believe the first shooter was *Maze Wars*. However, Jim Bowery, the creator of *Spasim*, claims that his game was the first real FPS. *Spasim* was a multiplayer 3D space sim, where players flew in virtual space, piloting wire-framed space vehicles. Both were created in the early 1970s.

The next big stride forward in FPS technology came from arcade games. In the 1980s, Atari's *Battlezone*, a tank sim, allowed players to move through a virtual world and battle AI enemies.

Other games continued to push the genre forward, but the breakthrough was probably id Software's *Wolfenstein 3-D*, which was purportedly created by thirteen people in only two months (one of them being the legendary John Carmack). And so began the modern era of the single-player FPS. The main character is an American soldier named B.J. Blazkowicz. There are countless Nazi thugs, guard dogs, and rooms with hidden treasure and food, guns and ammo, and the ubiquitous med kits, a convention in FPS games to this day.

The following year, id Software released the game that both defined and kicked the genre into high-gear: *Doom*. The story was simple, yet resonant, and fit the run-and-gun gameplay perfectly. The player is a space marine sent to Mars for assaulting a senior officer after disobeying an order to kill innocent civilians. The rebellious soldier who bucks authority has been a mainstay of shooters ever since, from *Doom* straight through to *Gears of War*. On Mars, the space marine works for the Union Aerospace Corporation, a faceless conglomerate doing secret experiments with teleportation. Well, of course, something goes wrong. Suddenly creatures from Hell come out of the deportation gateways, and everyone is either brutally killed or turned into a zombie. Only one human is left alive. The player. The story was retold for *Doom 3* and made into a widely panned movie in 2005. Many FPS games since have used this as a template for their own narratives.

Wolfenstein and *Doom* were not only the dawn of a new kind of gameplay; they were the dawn of the FPS story.

6.5 Proven Methods for Telling FPS Stories: A Quick Primer

- **Text.** Used in everything from subtitles to mission briefings to loading screens to in-game documents, books, and e-mails, text is the cheapest and most direct way of communicating information and narrative.

- **Static images.** Artists' renditions. Photographs. Max Payne used frames from a graphic novel very effectively to help tell the story.

- **Cutscenes (in-engine).** A short animated movie presented to the player to help further the plot. In this case, the animation is created using the game's own engine, so once the cutscene is over, the world looks exactly the same, which can help keep the player immersed.

- **Cutscenes (pre-rendered).** A cutscene using more expensive CGI to create something the game engine isn't capable of producing. Blizzard games are famous for these high-quality mini-movies.

- **FMVs (full motion videos).** Live-action footage used for cutscenes. Most famously used in the *Command & Conquer* RTS games.

- **Scripted events.** Animations within the game that don't take away player control. First used in *Half-Life*. Careful level design is necessary to make sure the player doesn't miss or ignore the event if it's essential to the story.

- **The diary/answering machine/e-mail method.** As used in *Doom 3*, *F.E.A.R.*, and *Bioshock*. An inexpensive way to communicate story information, it can be used as an adjunct to other methods as a way to deepen the story.

- **Radio/video/psychic contact.** Very cost effective. Voiceover that helps direct the player, delivers story, deepens characters, and aids in building the atmosphere.

- **NPC (non-player character) dialogue.** Used in cutscenes and scripted events, but also in-game, in the midst of action so play isn't halted. Taunts from enemies. Orders from commanders. Shouts for help. *Far Cry*'s guards often would offer subtle hints in their seemingly random conversations.

- **Artifacts and inventory.** Text about in-game artifacts and inventory, like weapons or armor or even books and documents, that can help further the story as in *The Elder Scrolls IV: Oblivion*.

- **Environment.** Televisions, billboards, video kiosks, paintings, or just prop and environmental details. *Bioshock* told much of its story through the use of brilliant art direction and design elements.

- **Loading screens.** A good use of time otherwise wasted as the player waits for the game to begin. Often only text is used, but some games use music as well. *Call of Juarez* used voiceovers from the major characters to help tell the story while the levels loaded.

- **Mission briefings.** Often used in military games like *Medal of Honor* and the Clancy games (*Ghost Recon*, *Rainbow Six*, *Splinter Cell*).

6.6 Early Classics and How They Told Their Stories

Anyone who wants to become a novelist must read all the great novels. If someone wants to be a screenwriter, they need to read screenplays and watch the classic movies. Before pursuing any artistic endeavor, it's essential to study the masters. At least that's what I tell my wife when she wakes up to find me in the living room, playing a video game at 3:00 a.m.

- **Outlaws (LucasArts, 1997).** Written by Stephen R. Shaw and Matthew Jacobs. An iconic western tale about retired town marshal James Anderson, whose wife is murdered and daughter is kidnapped by a ruthless railroad baron who wants his land. The storyline is linear, and the story is told through text, cell-animated cutscenes, and NPC dialogue. The emotional resonance and complexity of *Outlaws* raised FPS stories to a whole new level.

- **Half-Life (Valve, 1998).** Written by Marc Laidlaw, Randall Pitchford, and Brian Hess. A teleportation experiment has gone disastrously wrong, allowing the invasion of aliens from another world. Physicist Gordon Freeman is caught between the alien invaders, Marine Special Forces, and a mysterious character known as the G-Man. *Half-Life* tells its story entirely in-game in real time with triggered scripted sequences and no cutscenes. A major FPS storytelling breakthrough. Though the voice acting is well done, the player's character has no voice at all. The idea was to make the player the protagonist.

- **Deus Ex (Ion Storm, 2000).** Written by Austin Grossman, Sheldon Pacotti, and Chris Todd. Set in a grim cyberpunk future, the story follows United Nations Anti-Terrorist Coalition agent JC Denton as he uncovers an ancient conspiracy. The story is told with scripted events, cutscenes, and NPC interaction where, in RPG fashion, the player can converse by choosing from a list of dialogue options. Part of the story is told through a text-reading system, where players can access terminals and notes, excerpts from newspapers, and even real-world books. A giant step forward in the evolution of FPS storytelling.

- **No One Lives Forever (Monolith, 2000).** Written by Craig Hubbard. A wonderfully funny and atmospheric spy spoof set in the 1960s. Cate Archer, a rare female protagonist, is an agent of U.N.I.T.Y. The story is told with great voice acting, cinematic cutscenes, hilarious NPC conversations, and entertaining mission briefings. There is also constant radio communication from headquarters, to help direct the player to the next objective. The first FPS with a comedic point of view.

- **Max Payne (Remedy, 2001).** Written by Sam Lake. A sophisticated film noir–style thriller with elements of a John Woo action movie. Even though it's a third-person shooter, Max Payne was influential in many future FPS stories. It used cinematic techniques like flashbacks and dream sequences. Each episode was preceded by panels of a graphic novel narrated by the titular character. There were scripted sequences and cutscenes, phone machine messages, television news reports, and NPC dialogue with excellent voice acting. A very cinematic, emotional (and linear) experience.

6.7   Modern Classics and How They Tell Their Stories

- **Call of Duty (Infinity Ward, 2003).** Written by Michael Schiffer. A panoramic view of World War II from the perspective of an American paratrooper on D-Day, an English special forces commando, and a Russian tank commander. There's no narrative, other than the history of the war itself, but the sense of place, history, and world are authentic, detailed, and very well established. The story is told through cutscenes, scripted events, conversations with NPCs, mission briefings, and actual newsreel footage.

- **Doom 3 (id, 2004).** Written by Matthew Costello. Basically, the same plot as the original. Besides the usual cutscenes and scripted events, there are hundreds of text, voice, and video messages on PDAs and laptops between lab workers, administrators, and security personnel. Also, there are video booths that offer news, corporate propaganda, visitor information, and technical data about the base. Because virtually none of that information affects the actual gameplay, you can read or watch as much of the story as you are interested in. Or ignore the story and just kick hell-spawn bootie.

- **Half-Life 2 (Valve, 2004).** Written by Marc Laidlaw. A sequel to *Half-Life*. Once again the player is Gordon Freeman, an MIT graduate who knows how to handle on automatic weapon. Like the original, *Half-Life 2* has virtually no cutscenes. The story unfolds in real time through gameplay, and once again Gordon Freeman is a silent protagonist. The breakthrough facial animation helps to create a lot of emotion and depth for the NPCs.

- **F.E.A.R. (Monolith, 2005).** Written by Craig Hubbard. Brings together elements from contemporary Japanese horror films like *The Ring*, John Woo action flicks, and classic shooters like *Doom*. The player is part of a strike force called First Encounter Assault Recon, investigating an experiment in psychically controlled cloned soldiers that went, once again, horribly wrong. The game startles the player with very effective scares and surprises, using eerie sound effects and nightmarish, cinematic cutscenes. The story is told with NPC dialogue, radio communication from headquarters, and the voice and image of an antagonist who communicates telepathically.

- **The Elder Scrolls IV: Oblivion (Bethesda, 2006).** Quest design by Brian Chapin, Kurt Kuhlmann, Alan Nanes, Mark E. Nelson, Bruce Nesmith, and Emil Pagliarulo, Erik J. Caponi, and Jon Paul Duvall. Additional writing by Ted Peterson and Michael Kirkbride. The player is a former prisoner who becomes involved in the battle to stop a Daedric Lord from conquering the mortal plane. *Oblivion* is an FPS with RPG elements located in an open world. Every side quest is a story in itself. All consist of a large amount of dialogue and conversations with NPCs. The player can choose his responses, which in turn affect the relationships in the game. You can start and stop quests at any time, pick up or ignore the main story. It's entirely up to the player. The game world is filled with hundreds of books, filled with lore and information on magic and religion, history and politics. Some connect to specific quests; some simply add to the atmosphere. There are also cutscenes and scripted events, a world map, and a great deal of text. *Oblivion* is ground-breaking in terms of game writing and story. It melds an open world with a satisfying narrative in a way that had only before been done in straight RPGs.

- **Bioshock (2K Boston, 2007).** Written by Ken Levine. Additional writing by Paul Hellquist, Alexx Kay, Joe McDonagh, Susan O'Connor, Emily Ridgeway, and Justin Sonnekalb. Considered a spiritual successor to *System Shock 2*, it's another great FPS/RPG. Set in 1960, the story takes place in a vast underwater city, Rapture, built in the 1940s by a visionary named Andrew Ryan. With Rapture now in chaos, the player explores the mystery of what caused this bold utopian experiment to fail. The world is lovingly detailed and deeply immersive, a perfect example of using environment to further the narrative. The story is told with text, cutscenes, scripted events, NPC conversations, and radio contact from a mysterious ally/antagonist. As in *Doom 3* and *F.E.A.R.*, there are numerous voice recordings that delve into greater detail if the player is interested.

- **Call of Duty 4: Modern Warfare (Infinity Ward, 2007).** Written by Jesse Stern. Unlike the previous WWII-themed titles in the series, *Call of Duty 4* is set in the near future. The story concerns a conflict that involves the U.S., the U.K., Russian ultranationalists, and terrorism in the Middle East. It's told from the perspective of a U.S. Marine and a British SAS operative and is set in multiple locations around the world. As a player, you truly feel like you're in the middle of a huge Hollywood action movie. The characters are well-drawn, and the plot has many surprising twists and turns. Visually, it's extremely cinematic, and the voice acting is spot on. The story is presented with text, dynamic cutscenes, scripted events, NPC conversations, and radio contact from headquarters. The narrative is linear, but the action moves so quickly and the individual levels are so large that the player rarely feels constrained by the boundaries of the game world.

- **Portal (Valve, 2007).** Written by Eric Walpole, Marc Laidlaw, and Chet Faliszek. A first-person shooter with no shooting. Portal is a witty, sophisticated action/puzzle game where the player plays a test subject at Aperture Science, a secret weapons research facility. Using a device that can create inter-spatial portals that can teleport the player through walls, floors, ceilings, space, and even time, the object is to solve puzzles, getting from point A to point B without being killed by GlaDOS, the endlessly cheerful and clearly insane computer running the test. The narrative is simple and told through text, voiceover, and song. By the way, the cake is a lie.

6.8   Storytelling

Stories in games can have several levels, before even stapling a genre to them. The first two styles of narrative (gamespace and empathic) can exist separate of one another. The other two (supporting and independent) actually require the first two to exist, for reasons made clear shortly.

- **Gamespace narrative.** If narrative in an FPS has one basic and overriding goal, it's to facilitate the exploration of gamespace. The story provides the player with reason and motivation to complete objectives, slaughter enemies, and finish the game. Many games do not venture beyond this level of narrative simply because it's the only one that the FPS itself needs to survive.

  This style of barebones narrative is there purely to provide some motivation in relation to the character's actions, but it also exists to supply context for the conflict. Essentially, it answers the who, what, where, why, and how of the game.

- **Empathic narrative.** Other games are able to go deeper than the gamespace narrative, further providing elements to humanize the characters or the situation. In many ways, this secondary storyline not only gives the main character emotional resonance, but it also motivates the player to act. The empathic narrative uses the protagonist as a reporter, a witness to record the effects and drama of the story, investing the player in the eventual outcome. The player wants to succeed because he sees, first hand, the tragedy or the glory. The goals of the character become the goals of the player—what Susan O'Connor points out as a connection with mirror neurons.

In a game like *Half-Life 2*, seeing the world subject to a fascist alien regime is motivation enough to want to fight them. It's empathic narrative because it inspires the player to feel connected to the character, to the world, and to its fate.

- **Supporting narrative.** These types of narratives are often side stories and mini-arcs associated with the main storyline. They may help flesh out the world, enhance the mythology, or even provide story elements that can't be casually dropped into the main arc. Here, characters might exist for the sole purpose of imparting information through exposition, providing humor, or enlivening the world.

  Another technique that uses supporting narrative is one where the story's themes, motifs, and moods are played out through secondary arcs. These support the central elements of the story, whether it's to show the effects of current events as played out during the game, or the dangers of allowing matters to continue unimpeded. Regardless, supporting narratives should always tie back into, and support, the main storyline whether as mirror, as warning, or as beacon.

- **Independent narrative.** Independent narratives add flavor or additional content to the world, and nothing more. Certain elements may contribute to the main storyline, but frankly, the game won't live or die on the strengths or weaknesses of these stories.

6.9   Linear versus Modular Storytelling

At its most basic, FPS story falls into two main categories, linear and modular storytelling. Linear storytelling is closest to the narrative experience found in books, television, and movies, where the story progresses along a set track and deviating from those rails is rarely possible. Modular storytelling, on the other hand, is a "new" storytelling technique unique to video games. The player can explore the world more freely and follow the storyline at his own pace.

Linear Storytelling

Linear narrative is any storytelling technique that forces the player to follow the storyline. The story could be set along one set of rails where the character must either succeed or fail (thus ending the game), or it may incorporate failure conditions where the narrative branches off to another set of conditions.

Regardless, the advantage of linear storytelling, although eschewed by purists as a cinematic convention and not a video game one, is that the writer can create a more focused storyline. Stories of this nature usually use the gameplay narrative and sometimes the empathic narrative to formulate their plot, but rarely the supporting or independent narratives.

In linear stories of any type, the storytelling is more focused, and the events more immediate. There is a definite sense of pressure, and even the environments are narrower. This style of tale is better able to build suspense, and it can carry the action along with the pace of a cinematic nail biter. In essence, linear storytelling is generally best suited for high-intensity storylines and action-packed games. Call it the Roger Corman school of scriptwriting, where every ten pages has a love or action sequence to keep the audience involved and interested.

Modular Storytelling

Modular narratives are a unique way to present story, because they allow the player to explore the main narrative at his own leisure as well as enjoy a number of side stories. Modular narratives can be used in sandbox and free-roam games like the *Elder Scroll* series or *Deus Ex*, where the world and its tales are more open for exploration.

To start with, modular narratives are often stories that encourage players to explore the environment. They are told through moments of discovery and connecting the dots. The basic story is set, so even if the player never ventures from the guide rails of the central story arc, he still enjoys a rich experience, but an even richer narrative awaits those who explore. While this style definitely uses the gameplay narrative, it also relies more heavily on the empathic, supporting, and independent narratives as well, all in the name of fleshing out the world.

Modular narratives are often the stories of an entire setting, and not just the protagonist. It's focused on more global events, with the hero as witness to the happenings of the world. It's more about building emotions like suspense and mystery than pushing the player down the steep slope of action on one ski.

6.10   A Guiding Hand: Staying Inside Your Head

Narrative in an FPS is a tricky thing, especially when more companies are eager to keep the immersion quality high by locking the player inside the character's skull. This can be problematic when cutscenes are usually the chief way of dousing the player with story and game-relevant information. That said, there are tricks to shuttling the player through the yarn without relegating him to the role of passive observer.

Before diving into these methods, however, it's important to note that each technique is strongest when interlaced with the other methods. Think of it as reinforcement or layering the story so that more than two things point to the same clue; it's important since any of these techniques alone can be missed by players rushing through scenes and environments. In fact, it's best to relate information through more than one sense, meaning that if one cue is played out aurally, the supporting cue should be visual.

These methods may also help parse out information over the length of the story. Information dumps are nothing more than heavy-handed exposition, and it's often better to use these events to continually feed the player small packets of information so that each fact becomes a relevant event on its own. Remember that moments of exposition in an FPS can be like applying the brakes to the story's flow. Do it too much, and you risk spinning out of control.

- **Seeding.** Clues are rewards for the observant. They tell their own story about the scene through resources in level design. The most obvious, for example, are things like encountering dead bodies in *F.E.A.R.* or a destroyed location in *Halo*, either of which speaks of a firefight or a massacre. Naturally, the clues might be more subtle, but they should say something of whatever event brought the character to said location. They should be a reinforcing element to the mystery, not the only way to fact find.

- **Signposts.** Signposts are deliberate ways you might lead the player character somewhere (and further along in the story). They are nudges on where the character should go, be it as obvious as HUD markings and map flags, or as subtle as the banter between NPCs. They also reinforce the imperative of the plot, and they remind the player of what he may have forgotten. *Portal*'s wall graffiti, which guides Chell through the level, is a fine example of this.

- **God's voice.** Many FPSs use a commanding officer, guiding intelligence, or some other ally to provide the mission objectives. This technique establishes character through repartee, and more importantly, the person responsible for God's voice is there to help interpret the clues, add more pieces to the puzzle, and vocalize the player's thoughts. God's voice is probably one of the single most important techniques in navigating the player through the game in real time.

- **In-game events.** Scripted events allow the scriptwriter to move events forward in-game without breaking the action. At their most obvious, they might include explosions that cut off corridors, helicopters dropping in with more enemies, or NPCs running in all directions as in *Rainbow Six: Vegas*. They are cinematic as hell, they pump up the adrenaline, and they accelerate the story while keeping the player involved. They also drive home the fact that unlike movies, games are all about being inside the action. They allow players to legitimately participate in the story.

- **Dynamic cutscenes.** Some games lock the character into a cutscene but still enable him to move around or act. In this case, the cutscene is like a theatrical set, and it allows the writer to create special moments within the game because the player is literally both captive audience and participant. Both *Rainbow Six: Vegas* and *Half-Life 2* use this technique.

- **Inner voice.** Inner monologue, better known as the prickly pear of games, is a legitimate technique made viable by hits like *Max Payne*. Nothing gets you into the personality and thought process of the protagonist like inner voice.

Still, this is a very tricky approach because it can easily devolve into film noire melodrama or hard-boiled hackneyed.

6.11   First-Person Characters: Identity Crisis Central

Most non-game narratives, be they cinematic or fiction, rely on the main character. The protagonist is the spine of the story. It's about his life changing because of events that become the focus of the movie or novel; the conflict comes from the character trying to return to his normal life or (at least) a better one. For good stories, the character changes as a result of his ordeal. Now here's the crux: in FPSs, the main character is invisible because we don't see his face often, and almost as seldom hear him speak. And the protagonist is rarely afforded much of a personality to begin with, so where does that leave the notion of character in a story? More importantly, how does that impact the story?

In video games, character growth seems to have been replaced by the character's coolness factor. What can be said about the histories or personalities of Master Chief or the Marine in *Doom*? Tough isn't the breadth of someone's traits; it's simple wish-fulfillment for the player. The situations have likewise become nearly extraneous to the character's personal life. Events exist as puzzles or obstacles for him to overcome, but there's little stake in the protagonist's private affairs.

While "art" might demand that the protagonist has more substance than what is normally found in an FPS, the fact is that video games must experiment with the mold because the main character is a fusion of art, animation, gameplay mechanics, and personality. And to experiment with the mold, you must understand the advantages and disadvantages of having a silent, obscured hero.

Advantages: I Wouldn't Do That

Most people relate stories of their gaming experience with one simple pronoun: "I."

> I flipped over his head and blasted him.

> I beat the game on Extra-Hard.

> I shot him in the face.

> I'm dead.

There is no distinction between what someone accomplishes as a character and as a player. While this is true of all styles of video games, FPSs are the only genre where you and the character are "virtually synonymous." And in many ways, you aren't in the character's head so much as the character is you. This creates an interesting situation for writers since developers seem to deliberately strip the character of personality and voice. Nothing gets the player more into the head of the character (physically) like an FPS; thus, developers are worried about alienating the player by having the character act in a way that the player disapproves of.

So, where does that leave the writer? Once you understand that the main character serves as the player's vehicle, you can actually play on that to the game's advantage instead of treating it as a limitation. At the cost of character development, you can create a story directed at the players themselves, in some ways turning a first-person shooter into a second-person narrative. The player becomes the "you" that the game refers to, and you can then appeal directly to his motivations. The advantage here is that this sets the player firmly inside the shooter, giving him greater personal stake in the story and a half-degree separation between player and game environment. More importantly, the emotional investment is based on the individual player and not the dictates of the game's developer, what's called player agency.

F.E.A.R. and *Breakdown* use this to the best effect by turning the main character into a tabula rasa or blank slate through amnesia. The player is free to imprint himself onto the character.

Disadvantages: Faceless or Voiceless Characters

Now the disadvantage of a faceless, voiceless character is easily evident as well. Would *Halo*'s Master Chief and *Metroid*'s Samus come forward? Stripping the character of face is done for technical reasons, but developers often take it to the next step in an all or nothing gambit. If the player can't see the character's face, then there's almost nothing there to empathize with. And since we can't empathize with a faceless character, why stop there? Why not eliminate personality entirely or replace it with an easily understood archetype? Take that a step further and you might as well eliminate the voice.

Now, would *Half-Life*'s Gordon Freeman, *Portal*'s Chell, *Doom*'s Marine, and *Bioshock*'s Jack please step forward next? Stripping the character of voice is often a technical choice, simply because the player can't actually see who is speaking. More importantly, he can't see himself speaking unless the dialogues occur in a third-person-view cutscene. In first person, this can be cheated using radio communiques, for example, but in normal in-game conversations, having the protagonist contribute to a conversation may confuse players who are trying to place the disembodied voice.

That's not to say that all developers use this approach, but upon depriving the character of one characteristic, mainly his face, developers often take the next step in slapping him behind a mask or robbing him of voice. In many ways, it's an all or nothing approach, mostly slanted toward the nothing.

The decision to remove face and voice is almost always the lead designer's, producer's, or creative director's decision, meaning the writer is forced to adapt to the situation. This doesn't work when you need to interject character development or empathy for the hero's plight. The protagonist must have a personality in these instances; face is therefore important toward garnering empathy for the protagonist and his plight in the game, and voice is necessary for imparting personality.

Allowing the character to speak or be seen can help in developing the characters using traditional methods, but should neither of them be available, then there's another trick the writer can use. And that's implied personality.

Implied Personality: Personality through NPCs

As mentioned previously, an FPS may put you in the head of the character, but it doesn't invite you into the character's mindset. That's where NPCs come in and why they're so crucial to building personality.

NPCs are more than just information brokers; they actually help establish the character by defining the boundaries of the protagonist's personality. Using a trick from such shows as *24* and *Heroes*, the main character is sometimes defined by the personalities of those around him. They might exist to profile a character's conviction (we know the protagonist is against torture because NPC X advocates it). They might exist to warn the hero of pursuing a certain path (the protagonist is in danger of going down the wrong path because NPC Y already took that road). They might even exist to act as the embodiment of an emotion or ideal (NPC Z is the hero's conscience or his faltering conviction).

In games where the hero is often faceless or voiceless, NPCs provide crucial information, but they can also help define the protagonist's personality by displaying those traits that the hero possesses but cannot exhibit himself. Think of the NPCs as mirrors or autonomous personality aspects of the main character. In-game, they are a type of mirror neuron meant to connect the player to his character.

6.12   Technical Considerations

After all is said and done, the limitations of the game itself may be the limitations of the story, hence, "The medium is the message." The obvious biggie is that the story has to adhere to the confines of the game engine. For in-game cutscenes, it means the models and characters can't do everything you want them to do in the script. What if animation didn't account for the characters sitting down? What if the art department didn't build a vehicle whose doors could open? What if the face mesh shows no emotion when the NPC is supposed to be terrified? All these are important limitations to telling the story, and sometimes the principal hurdle in crafting a narrative.

Using CGI for cinematic cutscenes is one storytelling tool to circumvent the limitations of the game engine. CGI, however, has limitations of its own, the most significant of which is cost. On projects where the purse strings are drawn tight, the game may not be able to afford CGI. Or the creative director refuses to have any third-person scenes, just to maintain immersion. Or the CGI is only slated for the opening and climax of the game. In other words, writers shouldn't rely on CGI for whatever reason, unless the game has already budgeted for it.

In short, part of writing for games is understanding the technical limitations facing the game itself. It means talking to the different departments concerning their restrictions. This means animation and AI for the breadth of character movement and NPC reactions; this means level design to understand which level assets are available on any given map; this means modeling and art to know how objects react.

Writing for FPSs means working closely with other teams, because they affect your story on dozens of minute levels.

6.13   Writing for the Multiplayer FPS

There are many FPS games that are strictly multiplayer. *Counter-Strike* and *Counter-Strike: Source* are the most popular, but there is also the *Battlefield* series, *America's Army*, and, most recently, *Quake Wars*. The vast majority of single-player FPS games also come with a multiplayer component: *Halo*, *F.E.A.R.*, *Call of Duty*, the Clancy games, *Unreal Tournament*, the *Soldier of Fortune* series.

Multiplayer FPSs require a different kind of writing. It's very specific, less to do with character and story and more to do with creating the world and enhancing gameplay. As a new multiplayer level (or map) loads, often there is text describing the player's objectives (what you need to capture or who you need to guard). Often there will be static images to help explain what needs accomplishing. In the new *Team Fortress 2*, there are witty black-and-white 1960s style "educational" films that tell the teams what their objectives are and what they need to do to win.

There are also in-game menus that need to be written, like for load-out screens where players must choose weapons, equipment, or character classes. In the afore-mentioned *Team Fortress 2*, there are nine different classes to play. Each is delineated with a little description.

This type of writing is not simply informational. It helps to create the world, the atmosphere, and the setting. Whether it's a sci-fi game or a WWII shooter, the player wants to feel immersed in the game's universe.

Voiceovers are another method used to direct, aid, and immerse the player. Like text, you can use them to help create the tone, the world, and the setting. They can be the forceful, clipped commands of a captain or a sergeant ordering his soldiers (teammates) forward. But there is also room for commentary and humor. Some of these voiceovers are scripted into the game. When a player strays to the edges of the map, the voice of God can direct him back into the game or the next objective.

Player-activated voiceovers also have a large role in multiplayer shooters. There are two basic categories.

Commands

Many of the newer games come with in-game voice chat capability, but there are also standalone voice chat programs that are used specifically by gamers. Teams-peak and Ventrilo are two of the most well-known. This chat capability is used to promote teamwork as many FPS multiplayer games are team-based and require well-coordinated teamwork. If someone doesn't have a microphone (or prefers not to talk online), there are also pre-recorded commands from which to choose. The player can use these to help direct his teammates. In *Counter-Strike: Source*, some of these include:

- "Take the point!"

- "Regroup!"

- "Follow me!"

- "Fall back!"

- "Need assistance!"

In each case, it's a way to quickly communicate to teammates and coordinate play. Usually, each side will have slightly different commands, voiced by a different actor or even in a different language. In *Battlefield 2*, there are American, Chinese, and Middle Eastern forces. Each side voices their commands in their own language with English text, Though there is an option to hear your commands in English as well.

Taunts

The original *Unreal Tournament*'s deathmatch taunts were legendary. They were so popular that an enterprising hacker created a voice mod for *Counter-Strike*, using the very same taunts. "Headshot!" "Burn baby!" "You suck!" Taunts are any voiceover that are non-gameplay related. They build atmosphere and simply make the multiplayer experience a little more fun. A lot of modders created their own taunts for use in both *Unreal Tournament* and *Counter-Strike*. *Team Fortress 2* has different taunts voiced by each character. They have cheers, jeers, and battle cries, to name just a few. The Heavy Weapons guy has an Austrian accent like that famous body builder and former movie star. The Scout sounds like he's from Brooklyn. Writing taunts can be a lot of fun and deceptively difficult. There is a lot of room for creativity and invention and character creation.

6.14   Political Controversy

Video games in general, and first-person shooters in particular, have been accused by certain cultural critics, politicians, and criminal defense attorneys as being murder simulators or trainers. There's been talk of censorship and the outright banning of certain kinds of games. This kind of controversy isn't unique to video games. At one time or another, movies, comic books, rock and roll, and hip hop have all been accused of leading to the lowering of morals (especially of young people) and the general degradation of society.

This is common when a new and popular art form comes to the fore. The older generation doesn't partake, often doesn't understand, and decides the activity must be unwholesome, immoral, and dangerous. Other countries have even been stricter in regulating standards pertaining to simulated violence in games. Many games have been altered or outright banned because of violence and even because of how a country or demographic is represented in a game. Game writers need to be aware of these controversies because it can directly impact their work.

There have been no studies that directly link video games to actual violence. In fact, a 1999 study by the U.S. government didn't find a direct causal link between video games and aggressive tendencies. A 2001 review in the *Journal of Adolescent Health* came to the same conclusion, as did a 2005 Swedish National Institute of Public Health study.

A lot of the critics mistakenly believe that most video games are designed for children, and that's where much of the concern comes in. But according to the Entertainment Software Association, the average American video game player is 33 years old. Ironically, the violent crime rate has significantly dropped since the introduction of first-person shooters. This is according to the U.S. Department of Justice's Bureau of Statistics. Clearly, video games haven't made the world a more violent place. In fact, the number of homicides perpetrated by adolescents and young adults is half of what it was before the advent of the original PlayStation.

In response to this controversy, the Entertainment Software Rating Board (ESRB) was established as a way for parents to know which video games are appropriate for their children. The system includes age recommendations and content descriptors. According to the ESA, in 2005, 49 percent of games sold were rated E for Everyone, 32 percent were rated T for Teen, 15 percent were rated M for Mature, and 4 percent were rated E10+ for Everyone ten and older. You can find the ESRB's Game Ratings & Descriptor Guide at http://www.esrb.org/ratings/ratings_guide.jsp.

When a writer is hired to work on a new FPS, he needs to know the intended rating the developer and/or publisher is going for, as it will directly impact his dialogue, characters, and situations.

6.15   The Future of First-Person Shooters

From *Doom* to *Doom 3* to *Crysis*, the technology for making first-person shooters has advanced exponentially. With the advent of DirectX 10 video cards, we have almost reached the point of photorealism. The PlayStation 3 and Xbox 360 are designed to work with HDTVs. Both have the most powerful CPUs and graphics processors ever put in a game console. The physics, the graphics, and the sound have all reached new heights and will continue to do so, but the underlying narratives in games haven't really changed. Some of the very earliest adventure and RPG games still have some of the best stories. The challenge is to make the stories, characters, and narratives in FPS games as bold and inventive and powerful as the ever-improving technology. In 1910, movies were no longer a sideshow novelty but were not quite an art form. Games have reached that same stage. The technology is here. So is the audience. It's time for writers with vision, ambition, and talent to take FPS stories to the next level.

7

Writing for Real-Time Strategy Games

Stephen Dinehart

7.1 Genesis

In 1992, a company started by Louis Castle and Brett Sperry, then called Westwood Studios, released a game titled *Dune II: The Building of a Dynasty*. The gameplay was in the epic style of traditional wargames past like those from publisher Avalon Hill—specifically their game *Dune*. *Dune* allows up to six players to select a race, build a stronghold, and attack their opponents for resources and power. The object of the game is to seize opponents' strongholds. This is only possible with a player-driven strategy of economics, military, religion, and treacherous diplomacy. The *Dune II* video game also had one primary innovation. Rather than the turn-based systems of the Avalon Hill games, *Dune II* is meant to be occurring in "real time," that is, without turns.

The real-time elements centered around three major activities: building and up-grading units and strongholds, managing and gathering resources for military and industrial needs, and, finally, combat with opponents. *Dune II* is unofficially the first real-time strategy (RTS) game, though it did have one predecessor, a little-known ti-tle called *Herzog Zwei* in which the player commanded individual units in an effort to destroy his opponent's base.

Wargames give the player vast agency in the direction of armies on battle maps. The game type arguably has its roots in the ancient Indian board game of chatu-ranga, but the rebirth of wargaming came when it was first defined as a pastime by the infamous H. G. Wells in his book *Little Wars*. Published in 1913, the book contains the description of a basic rule set for wargames waged with miniature sol-diers on a parlor floor (it is available for free on the Web). In RTS games, such as *Dune II*, it is as if H. G. Wells' *Little Wars* had come to life for players, not in the parlor but on the screen. This perspective is neither third person nor om-

Figure 7.1. *Company of Heroes.* © 2006 THQ Inc.

nipotent. It is a multitude of perspectives, a strange space above men but below gods.

Without attachment to a central perspective, the player is free to manage and direct a seemingly live wargame strategy system. Now called real-time strategy (RTS) games, this video game type has been in constant evolution for the almost 20 years since its inception. Like the entire game industry itself, RTS has evolved from a graphics and cinematics standpoint, yet it has also seen a slow evolution in story-telling.

What is most interesting from a storytelling standpoint is the perspective, or seeming lack thereof. The games seem to have little to do with the stories of individual characters. They exist somewhere between second person omnipotent and third person.

From the inception of the game type, the stories for RTS where all essentially war-based. Even first-generation RTS titles like Blizzard's groundbreaking 1994 fantasy RTS game *Warcraft: Orcs and Humans* were nevertheless about war. The natural competitive ludic nature of RTS is somehow rooted deeper than the game type itself. Stories from mankind's earliest days seem to revolve around war and power struggles. Unless they are creation myths, most stories about early civilizations center on struggle—a competitive moment in time showing who defined history. This is even reflected in our language, as the primary players in a story are called "protagonists," from the Greek roots *proto* meaning "first" and *agoniste* meaning "competitor." In that, the RTS game type is the ultimate dramatic fantasy, allowing the player to be an epic protagonist on the scale of Alexander the Great or Churchill.

Developers of RTS, in creating these virtual domination fantasies, seem to be caught in a strangely reminiscent competitive game, attempting to conquer one another perpetually to define the RTS game type.

7.2   Evolution

In the years that followed the release of *Dune II*, the battle to "one-up" each another ensued. Resource types, unit types, new races, better artificial intelligence (AI), it was all a bit of a mechanic's shop. 1997 saw the release of a game called *Total Annihilation*, arguably the birth of second-generation RTS from a mechanics standpoint. It wasn't until the next year that storytelling would see second-generation content, with the release of a well-known science-fiction title, *StarCraft*, from Blizzard Entertainment. The storyline was epic in nature, covering three eons, or episodes, which dealt with the rise and fall of three races. Though at first blush not more than an evolved *Dune II*, what was most interesting about *StarCraft* was the fact that playing through the entire single-player game required the player to assume control of three very different sides in the conflict. And each episode of gameplay reinforced the abilities of the race to which it was ascribed.

The next year, 1999, a little-known Vancouver developer, Relic Entertainment, released its launch title *Homeworld*. Though in play mechanics the game built on the foundation of RTS, it created a new expectation for an engrossing storyline. Since then, RTS evolution has centered again on technology, as evidenced by Blizzard Entertainment's 2002 release, the ever popular *Warcraft III*, and Ensemble Studios *Age of Mythology*, being works that crossed us culturally into third-generation RTS. Stories and battlefield realism were becoming key to the RTS experience, and fans wanted more.

In 2006 and 2007, Relic Entertainment became one of the top RTS developers, with the release of *Company of Heroes* and *Company of Heroes: Opposing Fronts* (*COH*), games akin to Avalon Hill's *Advanced Squad Leader*. *COH* brought the RTS game type to a new level of realism with tactical gameplay and dramatic story previously unseen in the RTS genre. With top-notch multiplayer and single-player design, riveting storyline, rich characters, and the beauty of the game engine Essence, *COH* created a new standard by which to measure third-generation RTS.

As the RTS game type crosses into the fourth generation, game makers would be apt to study what makes an RTS storyline and how to better craft it. I have had the good fortune to work on and around a few of the largest RTS franchises to date, *Command & Conquer*, *Lord of the Rings: The Battle for Middle Earth*, *Warhammer 40,000: Dawn of War*, and *Company of Heroes*. While at Relic Entertainment, THQ's internal development studio, I held the position of Narrative Designer, releasing my

Figure 7.2. *Company of Heroes.* © 2006 THQ Inc.

first title in the *COH* franchise in 2007. The standalone "Opposing Fronts" was released to much acclaim by fans and critics. This chapter is a guide to how I wrote and designed the award-winning storylines for this World War II Real-Time Strategy franchise.

7.3   RTS Narrative Structure

RTS is a very different beast from the first-person or singular third-person perspectives in most other genres. How do you tell a cohesive story that encompasses many perspectives? This question has been answered in part by the history of RTS storytelling mechanics and its evolution, but there is much more work to do.

The Westwood RTS game *Dune II: The Building of a Dynasty* used simple stills, animation, and text. Somehow the player believed he was playing the "Harkonnen" race. Harvesting spice felt good, everything was fun, battling for resources, evading sandworms, and conquering your enemy. The entire gaming experience has become more vivid since then, but that is not all. The devices are more refined, and the gameplay has evolved, all lending to better experiences for the player. RTS games of yesteryear and today still share one thing in common with most other video games, the combination of linear cinematic sequences and non-linear gameplay that create a cohesive experience for the player.

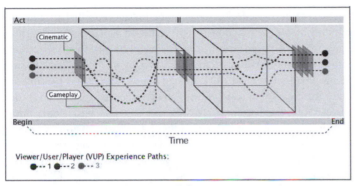

Figure 7.3. Viewer/user/player experience paths.

The interactive narrative as perceived by the player (see paths 1–3 in Figure 7.3) would let him think his path or "story" was "correct," when in fact it was a montage created by his own natural flow of play through a sandbox system. That is not to say that the experience is designed without attention to linear narrative progression. In an RTS game, the player is invited to play with "toys," inside of maps, to accomplish specific goals related to story and gameplay.

Multiplayer narrative is usually left up to the players to construct on a meta level as they maneuver their units in strategies against each other. Cutscenes are usually not presented in a multiplayer game, so the only dialogue conveyed to the player consists of non-linear unit responses to commands. In the interactive system of an RTS, a player encounters two primary types of narrative spaces:

- Cinematics.

- Gameplay.

Cinematic sequences act as choke points, that is, all players must pass through them in order to advance. During a cinematic sequence, the data (as presented) is fixed, so if the total sum of cinematic content within an RTS were to play out in succession, the narrative would be rendered linear and non-interactive, becoming then some form of machinima. Dividing the cinematic segments into interactive "sandboxes" allows the database of art, sound, and play assets to be navigated and experienced via the player's path choice. In this, the experience of database navigation will vary from player to player, and experience to experience, both in the cinematics and the gameplay. Database narrative refers to narratives whose structure exposes the dual processes of selection and combination that lie at the heart of all stories. Particular data—characters, images, sounds, events—are selected from a series of databases or paradigms, which are then combined by the player, through action and thought, to generate specific stories.

If the game allows the player to interject his own story without heavy-handed dictation, a much more rich experience will be had. As any good filmmaker would tell you, some of the best devices are empty mysteries, filled in endlessly by the subjective mind of the viewer. The system relies on a player's own cognitive ability to create meaning and purpose within moments, each piece then woven together by the human mind in a consistent narrative. That is not to say this is an easy task, but that if a well-crafted montage of cinematics and gameplay is presented, the mind lends itself to the creation of story. This is an act every living person can understand; one's life is in fact a database narrative. In this day and age, people digest a lot of media, be it on the TV, computer, or handheld devices. Consumers of digital media constantly move in and out of moments with varying perceived limits to agency. This symphony of seemingly random events is compiled together in one's mind, creating a linear experience through which modern man seeks meaning and purpose.

7.4   The Primary Storyline: Single-Player Campaigns

RTS single-player campaign writing has more to do with tightly interweaving a story with the gameplay content than with voices for the particular units. It's here that the epic story arcs commonly associated with the RTS game type are created. The rise and fall of nations, races, worlds, and empires seem to be the focus for RTS, not to say that more couldn't be done. The sky is the limit. In the broadest sense, RTS is about simulation, tactics, and eye candy; many stories could be applied.

The single-player format is more akin to traditional screenplay writing due to its more linear nature. Traditional screenwriting formats and related supporting software should suffice. The script usually exists in two parts, non-interactive sequences (NIS) like cinematics, and gameplay. Non-interactive sequences act as traditional linear story moments that return the player to third person. In *Company of Heroes: Opposing Fronts*, we began with two such scenes (see Figures 7.4 and 7-rts-5), which carry the player from observer in the cinematic mode to commander in gameplay. The convention is also used at key moments during, and book-ending, single-player missions as a way to carry the stories of NPCs forward throughout the campaign. In these cinematic sequences, the player is rarely addressed, though some RTS games do suggest the player is a commander of sorts, either ascribing some avatar character to the player, as Prince Arthas of *Warcraft III*, or using the second person, as the video-driven sequences of *Command & Conquer*.

Cutscenes must then in some way transition the player to a particular perspective for interactive sequences, or gameplay. The question is, what perspective is appropriate for the game design? Is this a moment in the game for third-person omnipotent god-like powers or a limited second-person control? In some cases, the player is corralled into a smaller perspective by design, letting him control individual hero characters for effect during particular missions, like Frodo in *The Battle for Middle Earth*, or squads such as "The Royal Scots Engineers" in *Company of Heroes: Opposing Fronts*. The writing must facilitate this transition in voice and tone. Non-interactive sequences are meant to connect both story and gameplay in a meaningful moment before, or after, the player is called to tactical or strategic action. While they might

Figure 7.4. *Company of Heroes.* © 2006 THQ Inc.

have the support of "in-game" narrative events, these linear moments are where primary characters, whether on or off the battlefield, are shaped.

Non-player character (NPC) and player character (PC) avatars are used in RTS, like any other game story, as a means to communicate with the player and create drama. Due to the unique circumstances found in RTS, i.e., rampant virtual death, the use of representational protagonists wasn't seen until the hero characters (HC) of third-generation RTS. The introduction of HC inevitably brought a third-person role-playing game (RPG) "lite" experience along with it. Hero characters "level up" and provide a traditional central character, or protagonist (primary competitor), around which to construct a story. The problem is they tend to die, and in ways developers can't easily predict. Needless to say, the death of a primary protagonist can prove a big problem for a story. To overcome recurrent death on the battlefield, explanations had to be created. In the case of *Warcraft III*, temples were woven into the tapestry of the command structures and used to "summon" heroes back to the battlefield in the event of "death." It is for this reason that in *Company of Heroes* and other RTS games the primary antagonists and protagonists take center stage in non-interactive sequences and during gameplay fade into the "background," living perhaps only in speech, in an effort to maintain the suspension of disbelief.

Enjoy the War while you can, Wolfgang, the peace will be hell.

Figure 7.5. *Company of Heroes.* © 2006 THQ Inc.

Character_X	State	Modifier1	Modifier2	
British Commando	Move	Low Health	In Combat	Moving under fire!
		m1	m2	Dialogue line 2
	At rest	m1	m2	Dialogue line 3
		m1	m2	Dialogue line 4
	Attack	m1	m2	Dialogue line 5
		m1	m2	Dialogue line 6

Character_Y	State	Modifier1	Modifier2	
Fallshirmjager	Move	Low Health	In Combat	Vormarsch!
		m1	m2	Dialogue line 8
	At rest	m1	m2	Dialogue line 9
		m1	m2	Dialogue line 10
	Attack	m1	m2	Dialogue line 11
		m1	m2	Dialogue line 12

Figure 7.6. The RTS non-linear dialogue script format.

7.5   System Responses: Non-linear Interactive Dialogue

Non-linear interactive dialogue, or unit speech, which some may call "barks," is the substance of multidimensional arrays. The unit speech scripts (see Figure 7.6) are long lists of lines that refer to the state of the NPC, vehicle, or unit on the battlefield. For each unit, there is a separate script. Depending on the expected use of that unit during gameplay, it receives its own line count. The speech here acts as a multidimensional array navigated by the user based on actions and unit states. How will a player know the voice of NPC X versus NPC Y? Well-cast voice actors help, but a good writer should maximize the potency of his writing by working to create character continuity through literary voice. The lines as written can be played in any order, hence creating affinity or contrast in literary voice. This is essential to maintaining character continuity and differentiation. It helps inform the player whom they are listening to or hearing from.

Unit speech line counts can add up quickly. For *Opposing Fronts*, we had over 50,000 lines of speech. Think of it as a larger palette of speech that is navigated by the player based on his actions in-game. The production and audio departments can decide how much record time is needed or allotted, in which case editing for the best lines prior to the recording session never hurts. Also be aware that lines often come back from record with unexpected reads, unless the writer has the good fortune to be on-site for the record. Everything needs to be in the script. The format seen in Figure 7.6 is a barebones version of a typical non-linear unit response script. Here, "character" refers to a particular unit on the map, be it a tank or a soldier.

7.6   Putting It All Together

An RTS writer's final deliverables are the campaign screenplay, individual single-player mission scripts, and system speech scripts. The campaign screenplay is a readable version of the campaign, with gameplay segments written in brief. The mission script resembles the unit speech script, in that it contains a list of events (see Figure 7.6). The events in mission scripts are linear. The event blocks contain trigger descriptions that indicate how and where a line, or set of lines, is to be played. Here it is necessary for the writer to work hand-in-hand with the individual mission designers to ensure the palette of audio provided satisfies the needs of their design.

They key to integrating non-interactive sequences with gameplay lies in well-executed audio and visual transitional elements. Non-interactive sequences must be used in fluid balance with interactive sequences. Some people may call for the death of non-interactive sequences as if we could just throw them out due to their non-interactive nature. The argument is to be had that they are outdated, but in RTS games, exposition has always been a key player in indoctrinating the player to the universe as authored. The writer needs to work closely with the lead designer to make sure the video game screenplay integrates tightly with the vision of the game as played. Good writing can make these narrative transitions even more fluid and almost seamless to the player. The final scripts, as delivered, should contain all of the gameplay and individual storytelling elements themselves with indicated transitions.

Good writing is almost transparent. It lives contained within the works of audio and gameplay designers. It is there from the primordial stew that is RTS development, a game type that the world, however niche, has come to love.

Real-time strategy games are a compelling game type, one that requires custom writing solutions. Providing those solutions in an accurate manner requires an understanding of the interactive system, or RTS game, as a whole. From video game screenplays, to arrays of non-linear dialogue, each piece must tightly interweave in a narrative concinnity to create a rich sense of game story. Like all things today, RTS evolves at an almost exponential rate; the game type is ripe for innovation. As fourth-generation RTS comes to be defined, excellent writing will prove to be an increasingly valuable asset in creating believable battlefields and continually epic drama, for what is competitive conflict without character and the drama that arises out of the pursuit of domination?

8

Writing for Sports Games

Maurice Suckling

8.1 "He Shoots... He Scores!"

A whole chapter on this? You cannot be serious!

Can there really be much more to writing on a sports title than commentary, tutorials, maybe some character comments, and some on-screen text? (And when you look at something like *Wii Sports* tennis, you don't seem to even need any of that!)

Well, often there isn't any more to it than that. And that's because nothing else is needed—because anything else wouldn't help the game. Sports are essentially physical activities, so it follows that the core gameplay experience is about replicating or simulating these activities.

However, even delivering commentary, tutorials, character comments, and on-screen text requires research—each sport has its own glossary, and you can bet the people playing it know their double faults from their in-swinging yorkers, their curve balls from their linebackers, and their crossover dribbles from their step overs. If you get hired to work on a game and you've played the actual sport for any length of time, the glossary could well be second nature to you. But sometimes you'll have to board the research bullet train and learn lots quickly—go see matches, fights, games, races (or whatever the right term is for the sport in question) and try to take in as much as you can. If you don't, the gaps in your knowledge will soon be exposed. Take a voice recorder, take a notebook, and listen to what the crowd says—and if you go to a soccer match in the UK for the first time, don't be surprised if you can't use any of it if your game is supposed to go out with an E for Everyone rating. But you take my point—get yourself out there and research it. Watch it on TV, too—the chances are the kind of commentary you're being asked to write is supposed to echo the kind of excitement and involvement that comes from the TV pundits.

In addition, even in delivering fairly straightforward writing requirements you may also find yourself being responsible for deciding on, or at least hitting and writing to, a tone of voice. Is your soccer game *FIFA 2009* or *Sensible Soccer*? Is your tennis game *Mario Tennis* or *Virtua Tennis*? Are you making an officially licensed Olympic game, or is it *Asterix at the Olympic Games*? Not every sports title plays it "straight" and is designed to feel like you're watching it on TV. There's a difference between writing for *NBA: 2K7* and for *NBA Street Homecourt*. While the atmosphere of the first is closer to that of watching the game on TV, the latter is closer to the atmosphere of—well, more impromptu street games.

If there's not much word count to get your teeth into, then you need to make sure every word counts—that it either helps convey instructions or helps build the tone of voice of the game (ideally even instructional speech and text is an opportunity to deliver tone of voice)—and makes it consistent with the rest of the game everyone else is building. (Of course, when you're working with a large word count you should still make sure every word counts.)

You may also have to consider other factors such as settling on UK or US spelling and UK or US cultural references. Is it hockey or field hockey? Is it football, or is it soccer? Is it a goal line or an endline? Are they midfielders or linkmen? Is it half-time or intermission? This is far from complicated stuff to settle on in itself, but if you don't get this sorted out with producers and designers beforehand, you might find yourself wading through several hundred thousand words of text trying to rectify it all.

8.2   Extra Time

Occasionally you get sports titles with stories of some kind in them, like *Let's Make a Soccer Team*, and that can require a little extra thought over and above the usual commentary–tutorials–on-screen text requirement. In that particular game, the story was very light and was handled by designers, and my role (and my company's role) as designated writer on the project was to localize the already-written English. Even though the text was already translated, we found that it didn't sit right to just polish the English when we had soccer players talking in changing rooms about playing the violin in the evening and going to the opera. In the UK, this topic of conversation doesn't match our expectations of what archetypal English footballers talk about in changing rooms. We therefore rewrote instances like this to have players talking about going to see a band, or going to the cinema instead. (We avoided the obvious temptation to have them talking about gambling or three-in-a-bed hotel room trysts.)

8.3   Sports Games and Sports Management Games

A distinction should also be made between those games that are sports and those that are sports management. When you're writing for a sports game, it's likely that capturing the atmosphere of live games—from the pundits, the players, or the crowd—is your most essential task and the one that requires the most research to get right. If you're writing a sports management game, your most essential tasks are likely to be capturing the required tones of management speak and the relationship between managers and players, execs, media, and other coaching staff.

8.4   A Whole New Ball Game

However, just because sports titles have traditionally been about commentary–tutorials–on-screen text doesn't mean they'll never change. There have already been sports games that don't just set out to simulate a sport as it already exists, or as we generally experience it as players or witness it as fans. *NBA Ballers* is a basketball game, but it lets players take a character they create from rags to riches and to compete, one on one, against pro players to be the ultimate champion.

There are also games, like *Def Jam: Vendetta*, that are actually full-on sports-story hybrids—games that give players a sport to play but also hitch them to a story to provide the incentive to keep playing them. Not just in sports games, but in all games, the narrative drive, the compulsion to know what happens next that a good story can offer, can be an enormous incentive to keep playing and keep doing something that is essentially repetitive—and can make it feel as if you're progressing and moving toward something, not just repeating the same tasks over and over. (Of course, some games provide a number of other incentives, either separately or collectively, giving players unlockable power-ups, moves, equipment, minigames, etc., but often games use all of these elements in combination with a story to give the player as many reasons as they can to keep playing the game and coming back for more.)

8.5   2K Case Study: *Don King Presents Prizefighter*

By way of demonstration that there can sometimes be far more to writing on a sports game than many might imagine, I thought it would be interesting to present a case study on a game I worked on last year with Marek Walton, one of my colleagues at The Mustard Corporation. In its original design, this boxing game comprised the following elements, all of which came with a requirement for dialogue, text, or both:

- commentary

- tutorials

- on-screen text

- a story

- mini stories

- training games

- girlfriend games

- trash-talk games

- classic fights tutorials

- media games

- fight announcer

- pundit voice

- referee

- crowd

- promoter links

- agent messages

- trainer advice

Many of these elements will be self-explanatory. I'll pick up on a few of the less obvious elements to give you a sense of what was involved.

Mini stories were distinct from the main story in that they were self-contained pockets of story relating to a particular fighter, setting up a particular game incentive for the player; "KO this guy by round 3 just using your left hand and protect your right side," for example—not that that precise example was ever intended to be used.

The misogynistic-sounding *girlfriend games* were, in fact, an idea that was going to allow players to try their hand at talking to the ladies that like to talk to boxers, and by successfully conducting a conversation and choosing the right words to say as they gauged their date's body language, they could hope to leave the bar, restaurant, or wherever the meeting took place with a new, more intimate fan—all of which was intended to have a benefit for the player by giving them the equivalent of a morale boost (which might then have had a counter-effect of them having spent less time in the gym).

I spent about a week writing six girlfriend games, with six different girls, all with their own kinds of personalities. This material was among some of the most difficult and head splitting I'd ever been asked to write. Each game had to follow a procedure a little like a rally in tennis, lasting at least 17 "shots." The girl would "serve" a line, and the player would choose from one of three "returns." Each return would score either negatively or positively on one or more attributes (which would be different in each girlfriend game, according to what qualities that particular girl found attractive). And each return would generate a different kind of response from the girl and would consequently lead to a different kind of "service" line. If you're finding that hard to follow, don't worry—that's precisely why my head was splitting.

In fact, Table 8.1 shows the first four "service" lines of one girlfriend game. Bear in mind that you have to ensure that the game still plays through logically and that

	Lisa Ann Jackson	FUN. HUMOR. FAME.						
Line Ref	Her "service" Line	Player's choices	Player's reply	Her Reaction	FUN	HUMOR	FAME	Links to
1	This is awesome hooking up with you	Be easy going	Yeah. It's cool.	(giggles)			pos	2
		Be keen	Yeah - you are looking hot!	(giggles)	pos			3
		Be blunt	So, you put out on a first date?	what? (confused)				4
2	I can't believe you wanted to see me	Tease her	Well, I got punched pretty hard in training - so that's probably why I agreed.	(laughs)	pos	pos		3
		Charm her	Who wouldn't want to see you? You are smokin' hot!	(giggles)	pos			3
		Impress her	I can't take out a new sports car without a pretty girl next to me, now can I?	(giggles)	pos	neg	pos	3
3	So...you like this bar, huh?	Be direct	I like you.	Right!	pos	pos		5
		Be mysterious	That depends.	Oh, right...			pos	5
		Be positive	One of my favorite bars - right here!	OK			neg	5
4	Is that...is that a joke?	Be apologetic	Yeah - course it's a joke!	Hah! You got me!			pos	5
		Be serious	No, I was being serious.	Huh?		neg		5
		Be confused	Um, I dunno.	Err, right...		neg		5

Table 8.1. The first four "service" lines from a girlfriend game in *Don King Presents Prizefighter*.

every line has to be appropriate no matter which of the multiple paths through this game the player takes. In development, we wrote 3 × 17+ responses for six different games with different attributes, and each line actually made sense.

For anyone familiar with boxing, or at least the pre-fight media events that are such an occasion in the sport, they will be less puzzled by what the *trash-talk games* comprised. The original intention was to have six of these, but that got reduced over the course of development. Each game comprised five exchanges, allowing players to match button configurations on screen (think *Dance Dance Revolution* with your fingers) and by getting them right to score some morale points over their opponent (which have an impact on the ensuing fight). Players can try to match the standard button configurations for a Normal Response, or they can gamble and go for the faster, more difficult configurations for a Good Response. If they fail at either, they deliver the Bad Response, and they find themselves on the receiving end of the battle of wits.

Table 8.2 shows the first exchange of one of the trash-talk games (as it was written during development, not as it necessarily finally made it into the game).

Media games are very simple games that offer players a choice: to raise their public profile by doing things like ads, or to hit the gym. Raising their profile has certain benefits in the ring—increased support from the crowd, which has a real impact on the players' "morale." But then again, hitting the gym has benefits too. And the players must decide which benefit they most need and which one they can most do without. These games can also allow players the opportunity to conduct pre-fight media workouts. These are similar to the training games (hitting the correct button configuration combinations)—if you get them right, you get a boost to your morale in the ring. Get them wrong and that morale takes a dip.

Promoter links and *agent advice* dovetail into the broader story, making the characters feel more alive and a greater part of your life as a boxer. In these scripts, the promoter encourages, cajoles, criticizes, or instructs the player, telling him which fighters he'll face next, or how many of a batch of fighters he needs to defeat to progress. *Agent messages* are related to the media games, in so far as the media games are fed to you by your agent, and the messages you get from your agent give you a sense of how your career is progressing and how the wider world is becoming increasingly aware of you (or not).

In addition to all these elements, and the complexity of some of them, there is a story in this boxing game, and even this is not as straightforward as you might expect.

Early on in development, it was far from certain that the story would follow a rags-to-riches model. Matthew Seymour, 2K's Executive Producer, had spent a number of months wrestling with this issue prior to The Mustard Corporation's involvement, looking for viable alternatives. It was only after a number of different approaches were experimented with, with a variety of outlines and treatments and many further discussions, that it was felt that a rags-to-riches story was definitely the way to go.

Montell Bennet is earnest, easily riled and easily wrong-footed in conversation

Question 1

Bad Response	Normal Response	Good Response
Opening Line		
	Journalist: This is your biggest fight yet. So how're the nerves holding up?	
Exchange 1		
Player: I dunno...I guess...	Player: I got a lot of respect for Montell, but don't feel nervous.	Player: Nervous? You serious? I'm King Kong and I'm feeling on song!
Montell: Let's hope you punch better than you talk!	Montell: You'd better have a dump truck's worth, kid. I play for keeps!	Crowd laughs.
Exchange 2		
Player: Oh...and...um...I can...errr...	Player: Most nerve-wracking thing about Montell's his agent!	Player: See Montell's got an Achilles heel; runs from his toes to his nose.
Montell: This conference started yet?	Montell: And even she can send your loud mouth south!	Crowd laughs.
Exchange 3		
Player: You readly for me,..I mean,,,ready - I meant ready...for me.	Player: You ready for me, Monty? I mean you really ready?	Player: Monty's just a teddybear - so I'm just gonna tickle him under his chin a couple times.
Crowd laughs. Montell: (laughs)	Montell: Yeah, I'm ready.	Crowd laughs. Montell: Oh yeah?
Finisher		
	Larry Easton: Next question...	

Table 8.2. The first exchange from one of the trash-talk games in *Don King Presents Prizefighter*.

Eventually a consensus was reached that rags to riches worked as a boxing story because no other kind of story was as good a fit with the success paradigm that a sports world offered, especially boxing. As the player progressed, got better, and took on more serious competition, that was, in its own right, a story—a shift from one state of affairs to another. Therefore, we decided to hook the story to the clear shape the paradigm of "from zero to hero" that the sport itself already provided for us.

At this stage, the writers set about working with the designers on the game structure. Again, this game might defy expectations, when you think there must be no real complication to the structure of a fighting game—win and you progress, fail and you don't. But a number of ideas were seriously discussed with regard to structure and what progressing really meant. At one stage, the idea was presented that victory in the story mode meant the choice to fight one last fight: success would mean access to the on-line world, but failure would mean the permanent death of your character. As you'll probably have gathered by the lack of consternation and outrage in the reviews, this didn't make it into the game.

In fact, as you may already know if you've taken a look at the game, there is more to progressing than "win a fight, get the next one." We decided on a "batch structure" that allowed players the choice of fights from each batch. In early batches, they need to win two out of four fights to progress. Players can take a look at their potential opposition, read about them, hear what the promoter has to say about them, then back out altogether if they want. In the middle batches, players need to win three out of four fights to progress. In the final fight batches, players need to win all four fights, but they can still choose the order in which they wish to tackle the fights.

Meshed within this structure were key fights that the player had to win to succeed, and these key fights were always linked to the story, forming pivotal plot points, moments of reversal or revelation that helped to drive the story on and helped to make sure it was still intricately linked to the game itself.

Yet even when the kind of story shape was agreed upon and the structure started to take shape, there was still a desire within the development team in general, and from Matthew in particular, to find something special in our approach, to find some way of opening up some distance between our story and the master of all boxing rags-to-riches stories: *Rocky*. This was how the idea of presenting the story in a documentary form got born, and it was Matthew himself who delivered the solution. The verisimilitude that would be generated from a documentary format would help us get players to care about the characters who—given the limited on-screen time we could give them and the kind of story we were dealing with—were essentially cast as archetypes with clear story functions. In documentary form, a viewer would accept that a character wasn't functioning in a usual dramatic context, with his own story arc and his own complex desires and conflicts. In the script, we were able to subsume these elements of character within the nature of their relationship to the central character, a character the player himself gets to create at the start of the game.

The verisimilitude was further reinforced by 2K securing a number of real personalities from the world of boxing: Don King, Larry Holmes, Ken Norton, Samuel Peter, Joe Calzaghe, James Toney, Nicolai Valuev, etc. And these people wouldn't just be CGI likenesses—they would be talking to camera, and not playing parts, but playing themselves. As writers on the project, Marek and I found ourselves writing the documentary with the intention that the player never really thought about there ever having been any writers. We wanted the story to really feel like a documentary, so we set out to write it in such a way that it looked as if there was just a director with a film crew, an editing team, and all the people in front of the camera. When it came to writing the actual script, it became apparent that this was different from dramatic writing we had handled in the past. Instead of the key events in the story being carried by dramatic action, they were carried by dialogue, the antithesis of "show don't tell" and potentially a disaster waiting to happen. What could be more boring than hearing people talking about things that had happened some time in the past?

However, we realized we could use techniques from prose writing and combine them with the way we cut the footage. In this way, we could create disputed testimonies, and present some "witnesses" as more reliable than others. We realized this was a way to create dramatic tension, to wait and see if someone was telling us the truth or not—and to find out, we'd have to listen to more of the right kind of people. Who were "the right kind" of people? Only by paying attention to what they said and how other people within the documentary responded to them could the viewer know. Documentaries often have these moments of disputed testimony. All we did was replicate this effect and "turn it up" higher on characters we wanted the player to have antipathy towards. Or we "turned it down" on characters we wanted the player to feel connected to. We would turn it up by having one or more characters strongly disagree with a statement. We would turn it down by either not calling the statement into question or by having one or more characters echo the same view.

In our script, the "there's no smoke without fire" adage was always true. If a character was to say, "I'm not one of those people who only thinks of themselves," the implication was that they were far more likely to be exactly that kind of person than someone to whom it would never have occurred to say those words in the first place. Everything a character said carried with it an implication of allegiance or selfishness, of his state of mind, or of some kind of relationship to other comments on the same topic. In this way, we were able to construct a script that, although carried in on-camera interviews, was built by invisible strings of tension between witnesses as they agreed or disagreed with each other as, almost imperceptibly, we tried to build a story and move it through the gears of each act toward a climax and resolution.

This documentary format also simultaneously helped support the decision to tell a rags-to-riches story as well as supporting the decision to let the player create his own character. With a documentary format, we were able to present to the player the sense that it was himself (or at least his avatar) that the documentary was all about, that it was his exploits that merited documenting.

The fights, the training, the media games, the trash talk, the mini stories, and the girlfriend games had always been designed to be cast in a present tense, as the player worked his way toward the points of the documentary that charted his own developing career (apparently in retrospect). But in several lengthy discussions with Mario Van Peebles, who was also enlisted on the project as a story consultant, further developments were made as we decided to add another element to this essentially retrospective timeline of the documentary. We found opportunities to dovetail the timelines together, moments where the documentary filmmakers appear in the present time zone that the player fights in and does everything else interactive in.

As it transpired—and as is often the way with development—not all of these elements made it through to the final published game. But just seeing the scope of what lay in wait for us as writers may give you cause for pause before assuming that when a developer asks for a writer on a sports title, all they want is a bit of commentary.

8.6   Techniques

So how do you handle these kinds of elements and things in a game you've never encountered before? Well, here it is in 5 easy steps:

- **Clarify the brief.** Make sure you're clear about what you're being asked to do and when you're being asked to deliver it by. What's the tone? Who are the characters? What's, ultimately, the desired experience for the player? What are the time frames involved, and what are the critical resources available? Then go back and ask what the desired experience for the player is. And try and keep the answers you get from designers and producers in your mind for the length of the time you're working on the project.

- **Research.** Do your research. Make sure you at least understand what it is that people who enjoy the sport would be expecting to see in a game.

- **Understand triggers.** With speech and text that's closely tied to interactive elements, it's critical that you understand what the triggers are, i.e., what is it that a player does that can provoke a response you're being asked to find words for? Unless you understand the context of the action, you can't write the words that make sense in that situation. Talk to programmers, talk to designers, and make sure you understand what a player can do and what responses can give rise to consequences in the game.

- **Provide samples.** Even if the material is relatively straightforward—e.g., commentary or crowd responses—it's a good idea to provide samples as you begin working on the material. If you're heading off in the wrong direction, it's not a painful journey to return to the starter's blocks and rewrite 10 or 20 sample cells. It's a long walk back after writing 90,000 words that don't really do what they were supposed to do. Not only that, but you've also given yourself a whole lot less time to rewrite them.

- **Coordinate with design.** Linked to the point above is to always coordinate with designers—and everyone else who helps shape what you're doing. Things will change over the course of development, and you need to know what's being cut, what's being added, and what the feedback is (what it means, and why it means what it says) so you can deliver the next drafts.

8.7   "The Ref's Going to Blow Up!"

Writing for sports games can be a pretty thankless task. Get it right in a game people don't like and it really doesn't matter what you did because it's unlikely anyone's ever going to know. Get it right in a game people like and they carry on playing it, quite possibly blissfully unaware that a writer was really involved at all (the pundit says the kind of thing pundits say), and that keeps the player locked into the world of the game. (Or maybe you've done a good job with the writing, but there wasn't enough memory space to provide all that many samples, so the player's heard the same stuff repeated so many times he decides to mute the sound after 20 minutes.)

On the other hand, get it wrong and you pull people out of the experience and on goes the mute for the sound, or they're left to struggle through obscure text.

Providing you bear the five steps above in mind, as a rule, sports games won't be the genre that will tax your writing brain the most, and it's not the genre most likely to be constantly pushed to find dramatically different kinds of gameplay experiences. However, there are exceptions to every rule, and every so often a game like 2K's boxing game will present itself to you and knock your preconceptions to the canvas, presenting you with such a fresh set of writing challenges that you'll feel as if nothing you've done before has quite prepared you for it. And, in fact, you'll be glad of that—because it's one of the real virtues of writing in this medium.

All material relevant to the game Don King Presents Prizefighter published with kind permission of 2K Games. All rights retained.

9

Writing for Simulator Games

David Wessman

9.1 Planes, Trains, and Automobiles. . .

. . . and ships, spacecraft, tanks, tractors, and other vehicles: an overview of simulator games and how they differ from other sims and simulations. The Wiktionary definition of "simulator" is: "Anything which simulates, but especially a machine or system which simulates an environment (such as an aircraft cockpit) for training purposes."

A simulator "game," therefore, is a simulator that is enjoyed primarily as an entertainment product (however complex and realistic it may be as a simulation), and the genre is typically understood to describe those games that feature a more or less authentic simulation of one or more vehicles that the player controls as his primary avatar in the game. By this definition, driving and racing simulations should be considered simulator games as well, but driving and racing games are featured in their own chapter.

For our purposes, simulators are not to be confused with other types of simulation games that focus more on strategic play that rewards strong organizational and resource management skills. These include "sim" games such as *The Sims*, *SimCity*, and *Pharaoh* (sometimes referred to as God games) and sports and business focused titles such as *Baseball Mogul*, *Madden*, *RollerCoaster Tycoon*, and *Capitalism* (normally considered sports and/or strategy games, not simulators). It should of course be noted that with any genre definition, these divisions are somewhat arbitrary and subjective. There are definitely games that blur the distinctions between one type and the next.

The best-selling simulator games of all time are probably the *Microsoft Flight Simulator* series that focus on civilian aircraft from small planes to jumbo jets rendered in sufficient detail to pass FAA flight certification tests! For the average gamer, it may seem strange to consider the franchise as really being a game at all, but *MS Flight Simulator* does support combat and racing, and there are many third-party extensions. The majority of simulator games involve combat vehicles of some sort, no doubt due to the compelling fantasy of being a modern-era hero battling for supremacy in a high-intensity, kill-or-be-killed, may-the-best-man-win arena.

During the late 1980s and throughout the 1990s, simulator games were one of the dominant genres of computer games, but by 2000, sales of simulators were in decline. Today simulators are a small but not insignificant segment of the market. Few AAA games are released in any given year, and there has been a decided shift toward more "arcade" style flight models and complexity. Part of this is explained by changing demographics (a larger more diverse audience with different interests) and partly by a general shift toward console gaming. There is also the inherent limitations of console hardware (gamepad-type controllers are simply not suitable for modeling the range and complexity of a real aircraft's controls). Where realistic controllers are used, simulator games typically lack the "under-the-hood helpers" of most games and tend to have literal rather than relative or simplified controls. The complexity of simulator games is itself a steep barrier to entry—it is quite difficult to master a realistic simulator. Most people simply have trouble thinking in three dimensions and so are unable to develop the situational awareness required to succeed at such games. Unsurprisingly, these factors weigh heavily in publisher decisions regarding what types of games to fund.

Outstanding Simulator Games

- *Ace Combat 6*
- *X-Plane 9*
- *Silent Hunter IV*
- *Flight Simulator X*
- *IL-2*
- *Freespace 2*
- *MiG Alley*
- *MechWarrior 4*
- *Longbow 2*
- *TIE Fighter Collector's Edition*
- *Falcon 3.0*
- *M-1 Tank Platoon*
- *Secret Weapons of the Luftwaffe*
- *Red Baron 3D*
- *F-15 Strike Eagle*

9.2 Know Your Audience: Who Plays Simulator Games and Why?

The game mechanics of a simulator game are focused on controlling the vehicle, and the main appeal of playing the game is (usually) simply that—by mastering a virtual representation of the relevant vehicle, the player enjoys the fantasy of being a fighter pilot, a race car driver, or a submarine captain. Simulators are inherently very detailed and complex and typically require an extensive training mode to teach new players how to play. As noted above, this is a major aspect of what makes them attractive to certain fans of the genre, though it also limits the potential size of the audience. Most simulator games attempt to broaden their audiences through option settings that let the user determine the degree of realism. More casual play is provided through an "easy action" or "arcade" mode with simplified controls and relaxed physics.

Hardcore fans of the genre are generally fascinated with the technology portrayed and are often quite knowledgeable about the performance characteristics, history, and use of said technology. For this audience, "realism" is often of paramount importance, and they are highly critical of inaccuracies. For them, mastering such games should require above average performance in a number of skills: situational awareness, eye-hand coordination, multitasking ability, quick wits and coolness under pressure, perseverance, and attention to detail. They revel in the *agon*[1] and *fiero*[2] that such games afford and take pride in the development of elite abilities. They are not, as a rule, terribly concerned with story and characters, and they may even find it distracting.

More casual fans, while also loving the sexy hardware and the heroic role-playing, are not so dedicated to mastering the deeper complexities of a "realistic" simulator. They prefer an easier, more accessible game (though they still value skill-based gameplay) and are far more tolerant of foolishness and fakery as long as the result is fun and looks cool. In fact, "looking cool" is probably one of their top concerns. This audience doesn't care so much about accuracy of the simulation; they just want a lot of action and excitement and cool explosions. They are more likely to appreciate some story and characters, but what they consider "good" is usually rather predictable action fare that features strong characters, rather than actual character development. The hugely successful *Wing Commander* series is testament to this approach.

It's worth noting that most hardcore simulator games are developed for the PC because of the greater input capabilities and interface depth afforded by keyboard, mouse, and specialized peripherals. In fact, hardcore fans typically invest in specialized peripherals such as HOTAS (hands on throttle-and-stick) and rudder pedals to further enhance the perceived realism of the experience. The limits of the typical console controller preclude such complexity, so there are very few hardcore simulators available for consoles; such vehicular combat games as there are tend to be

---

[1] Conflict, struggle, contest.
[2] An Italian word for the feeling of personal triumph over adversity.

arcade-style shooters rather than true simulators. Notable exceptions include *Steel Battalion* and *Ace Combat 6*. Both games could be purchased with custom hardware that supported a more "realistic" control scheme, though only *Ace Combat 6* has sold in sizable numbers (but not in the hardware bundle version, which costs $150—apparently today's gamers are unwilling to spend that much on a peripheral unless it's to pretend to be a rock star!).

What this means to you as a writer is that story and character are typically secondary to the information you convey about the craft and the missions. This isn't to say that mission briefings, in-game communications, and cutscenes don't call for compelling and dramatic writing, just that some players will be annoyed if they feel storytelling is getting in the way. Your writing must be focused and tight, and it must be packaged in a way that maintains the player's willing suspension of disbelief. A lot of the writing will be of a more technical nature—a pilot's manual, for example, detailing the technical specifications and procedures for operating the craft. Since there is usually a tutorial section to teach players the game's controls, be prepared to write extremely detailed step-by-step instructions to assist players over the initial complexity of the game. In fact, the good news for writers is that simulator games typically include quite extensive manuals printed on actual dead trees, though this is becoming rarer.

You will be held to a higher standard of factual accuracy in any game based on real-world vehicles, especially drawn from historical settings. Even when working with an entirely fictional setting such as *Star Wars*, many fans demand a high standard of perceived accuracy. Regardless of the setting, if you're not already knowledgeable about the topic, do your homework!

When I started working on *X-Wing*, it was just to set up and lead an internal test team. Since knowledge of World War II air combat was one of the ways I'd demonstrated my value on the test team for *Secret Weapons of the Luftwaffe*, I decided to learn everything I could about space combat as portrayed in the *Star Wars* films. Mastery of the relevant subject matter provided an essential foundation for the writing I was to do later when I joined the creative team as a mission designer.

Since George Lucas had taken inspiration directly from films about World War II air combat, it was natural that the flight combat engine that Larry Holland had developed for his WWII air combat classics would serve as the foundation for the *X-Wing* series. It also made sense to use WWII for inspiration in mission design as well, particularly the carrier battles of the Pacific theater. This was reflected in the details of missions, the military organization of the fleets and their fighter wings, the tactics employed, as well as the rationales given for them in the briefings, and even echoed in the communications content and style during a mission.

For example, there was a U.S. Navy ace named John S. Thach who developed an aerial combat tactic that became known as the "Thach Weave." I wrote it into the game as the "Wotan Weave" and instructed would-be starfighter pilots in its execution. Another example is the pervasive corruption, paranoia, and self-destructive in-fighting within the Imperial military. This was directly inspired by the historical accounts of Nazi Germany and Imperial Japan and became one of the main themes in *TIE Fighter*.

9.3   Structure

Simulator games often use a linear structure with a sequence of missions that must be completed in the order they are presented. This structure is well-suited to standard narrative conventions, so it does not present any special challenges. However, many simulator games attempt to break free of this with different structures. Some use a branching structure where the outcome of certain key missions determines which branch of missions will follow. Most games that try this end up with the various branches still converging toward the same finale, however. Considering how difficult it is to come up with one good ending for a story, it's not surprising that there are few attempts at stories with multiple endings! Also, there is the sad fact that most players do not play games to completion, and even fewer will replay a game to discover any alternate story paths—thus this extra work is largely unappreciated and therefore a poor use of development resources.

X-Wing used a linear structure, and the dev team decided to try something a little different for *TIE Fighter*. Rather than have all 34 story missions play in a strict sequence, they were divided into seven "battles" consisting of four to five missions each. The battles were arranged in a three-tiered structure with four battles on the first tier, two on the second, and one on the third. Players were allowed to start with any one of the first four battles, and if they got stuck on a mission, they could start another battle, returning to others as desired. The battles could be completed in any order, but to open up the second tier, all four first-tier battles had to be completed. Similarly, on the second tier, players could start with either of the two battles but had to complete both to gain access to the final battle. Players were free to play the battles in sequence, but it wouldn't hurt the overall story if they didn't because each battle was essentially a short story that could stand on its own.

In *X-Wing Alliance*, we returned to a strictly linear structure, but we added a feature allowing players to skip up to three missions over the course of the game. This was in recognition of the fact that many players will find a particular type of mission too difficult (even at lower difficulty settings) or just not their kind of fun. Rather than force a player to succeed on a mine-clearing mission, for example, they could take a pass on it and continue the game. Obviously, this necessitated a bit of finesse regarding the storytelling in order to maintain continuity.

Another structure is what is sometimes referred to as "hub and spoke." There is a central hub (typically represented as a home base) around which there are a number of spokes that present different missions or sequences of missions. There is little or no constraint on the order that players complete each spoke. It's a small conceptual step from this to an open-world structure in which there isn't even a central hub but simply an open environment where the player engages in missions as they choose, depending on what they've discovered. These present obvious and significant challenges to traditional narrative storytelling.

Yet another structure is something called a "dynamic" campaign, in which the player's performance on each mission determines what the next mission will be like. Dynamic campaigns are very difficult to implement well, and there are few examples. Typical approaches are to generate missions algorithmically, or to have a number of mission templates that can be chosen from (with some degree of procedural modification applied to make the outcome of previous missions influence subsequent missions). Players feel like they are actually fighting in a campaign that can have a natural feeling of ebb and flow that does not play the same way twice. This is great for replayability but extremely challenging for game writers trying to tell a story.

9.4   Scope

In general, the writing for any game involves the following areas:

- **In-game.** During gameplay; this includes mission briefings, radio messages, etc.)

- **Cutscenes.** Non-interactive cinematic sequences.

- **Game manual.** Game installation and operation.

- **Packaging.** Game description and features.

- **Website.** Primarily a marketing tool for most games; may be quite extensive and include community support.

- **Other.** Sales and marketing materials such as ad copy, sell sheets, etc.; many games also have a strategy guide written during the end of development so that the book can be available when the game hits store shelves)

The following sections focus more on the specifics of writing for simulators and how this differs from other types of games.

9.5   Story? What Story?

Simulators are not usually known for their stories and character development. Such story as may be provided is usually just a thin excuse for the action. A notable exception is the *X-Wing* series, particularly *TIE Fighter* and *X-Wing Alliance*. Delivery of the story occurs primarily in the mission briefings and the messages the player receives during the missions.

One should also carefully consider the tone. Will the story be played straight, with respect for the deadly seriousness of the subject matter, or light-heartedly with a gung-ho enthusiasm for the sheer excitement of things? On *Blood Wake*, we began with a more serious story and chose an almost stilted Victorian-era tone to the script.

Over time, it was decided to go with a lighter, more contemporary tone, and the entire script had to be rewritten accordingly.

Setting

Every writer knows the importance of setting, and establishing it as quickly as possible. If the game has a real-world historical setting, the writing should be as factually accurate as possible. If the setting is anything else, then it can be as fanciful as desired but should still maintain as high a level of internal consistency as possible. This helps sustain the all-important suspension of disbelief and affords deeper immersion into the game world.

One of the fun challenges of a fantasy or sci-fi setting is in naming things. You can be as creative as you like, as long as it sounds right for the game world. With the *Star Wars* games, we were allowed a great deal of creative freedom, and I have to admit we sometimes got a little carried away. At one point, I named a series of freighters after other game studios, but spelled strangely or backwards to disguise the source. I even used the backward spelling trick to get my wife's name on a Calamari Cruiser, and later as an entire star system!

Backstory

The backstory for a simulator game is similar to that for any style of game—its purpose is to provide additional depth by including the history of the main characters and other elements of the main story. Pieces of the backstory can be delivered anywhere in the game or its ancillary materials.

Characters

For many historical simulators, the player character is notional at best. He may not even be mentioned by name! Instead, he is referred to by whatever "call sign" has been assigned to him. If the player character is more fully developed, it will be entirely fictional, though it may be based on a real person or an amalgam of real people. Often the only real characters are the simulated craft.

In non-historical simulators, the player character may be more fully developed. This will depend largely on how important story is to the overall game. The more story there is, the more the characters must be developed.

Other prominent characters typically include the player's commanding officer(s), his wingmen and/or crew, as well as support personal (ground crew, mechanics, armorer, etc.). Opposition characters are typically faceless and nameless, though there are exceptions. One common practice is to include the enemy leader(s) and/or enemy "aces." For more story-driven games, it is essential to develop a good nemesis for the player.

Some of the more arcade-style games even go so far as to include such things as enemy pilots speaking to the player in their own language. The assumption is apparently that the fans are too stupid to realize that the combatants would not have compatible radio equipment, but is anyone dumb enough to think a German pilot would let you know that you'd hit him...in English?

In the *X-Wing* series, we had the luxury of being able to draw on a stable of great characters, and we were able to introduce as many as we needed. Some of the major characters like Luke and Han Solo appear, but only as people the player would occasionally cross paths with or hear reference to. A big exception was in a series of missions I created for *TIE Fighter* where the player got to fly as Darth Vader's wingman. I was thrilled with the task of writing lines for Darth Vader, but I must have gone a little too far into the dark side because I was instructed to tone it down. Apparently, I'd written lines that were too disturbing to listen to even if they were coming from the ultimate personification of evil!

We always strove to create strong player characters, and for the first two games, we worked with author Rusel DeMaria to produce novellas about these characters as a way to introduce them to players and set the context for what would unfold in the game. For *X-Wing* he created Keyan Farlander, and for *TIE Fighter* it was Maarek Stele. We later used these same characters as the voice of the official strategy guides. Rusel provided additional story interludes while I and fellow mission designer David Maxwell wrote semi-official sounding "after action reports" to serve as detailed mission hints.

Plot

Plot is generally where things get a little tricky. Writers like to follow familiar story archetypes and structures—the old hero's journey in three acts, please. This doesn't necessarily fit an historical situation, but even for a fantasy or science-fiction scenario, the need to keep the gameplay varied and interesting may require a more flexible approach. From both a story and a gameplay point of view, you want a nice mix of mission types: all-out attack, desperate defense, harrowing escort, harassing strike, blockade breaking, search and destroy, stealthy reconnaissance, etc. The story needs to provide a rational fit to an ever-changing sequence of combat scenarios.

For *X-Wing*, we actually built most of the missions before we ever seriously thought about the story. One day we just realized that we were going to need one, so we started thinking about what would make sense using the missions we had. As the story took shape, it revealed gaps in our catalog of missions and suggested some changes to existing missions. The last missions that we built were specifically designed to support the story we came up with.

In all subsequent games that I worked on, there was at least a rough outline of the story before we started building missions. In every case, we tried to evolve the story and missions together to ensure that they supported each other. I believe the key to success in this effort was that the game design and writing were either done by the same people, or by a closely knit team working together. If you're not a designer/writer, then try to ensure that the writer is embedded with the designers as part of the design team.

A general note on pacing: if your story involves a military campaign, then it should have a natural ebb and flow reflecting the changing fortunes of the combatants. In the *X-Wing* games, each campaign of 4–12 missions had its own flow of increasing tension until a decisive engagement. This was echoed in the flow from the first campaign(s) to the last climactic battle. Of course, we expected to produce expansions and sequels, so we always left a few things unresolved and sometimes ended with cliffhangers.

Pacing is also important to think about within each mission. Try to grab the player's attention right from the first moment with something dramatic, mysterious, or surprising. This can be a battle already under way, an unexpected appearance or absence (bad intel), or a sudden change of loyalties.

Cinematics

Cinematics, or cutscenes, are typically used to deliver parts of the story that cannot be portrayed well in other areas of the game. That said, the more action-oriented the game is, the less interested the players will be in extended cutscenes. Keep the scripts as short and concise as possible; sixty seconds or less is a good rule of thumb.

Avoid the temptation to script talking heads. This was something we did too often in the *X-Wing* series. That said, the more action-oriented a game is, the less interested the players are in extended cutscenes. Except for the intro and finale, keep the cutscenes as short and concise as possible; 60 seconds or less is a good rule of thumb.

Mission Briefings

Mission briefings are an essential part of the writing for a simulator game. This is where you will have the most room to develop the story, but be warned: many players will skip right through them! These players are only interested in the action, and they'll rely on the mission objectives to tell them all they really want to know (as displayed in the pause screen, or within a window of the HUD).

The big picture. A good mission briefing explains the scenario, the situation—how the mission fits in the context of the greater struggle. It's a good idea to begin with a brief call back to the previous mission and to end with a foreshadowing of what will come after this mission is successful. It also provides the player with a clear idea of what his objective is. What are the win conditions and loss conditions? What is the player trying to achieve or avoid?

Who's coming to the party, and what are they bringing? The mission briefing should also describe the order of battle for both sides—what the player can expect in terms of friendly support and enemy opposition. Avoid using specific numbers when describing the order of battle, particularly of the opposition forces. Give yourself and the mission designers some wiggle room for difficulty adjustments. For example, don't say, "four X-wings from Red Squadron will intercept three Imperial corvettes near Hoth." Instead, try something like, "Red Squadron X-wings will intercept a small flotilla of Imperial corvettes near Hoth." That way, if the designers decide they want it to be three X-wings versus two corvettes or two X-wings versus four corvettes, you won't have to change the line. In some cases, you can go even further and take out specific craft references. The previous example would then become, "Red Squadron will intercept a small force of Imperial starships near Hoth."

It's okay for the mission briefing to be wrong. This provides a nice element of realism—the proverbial "bad intel" can afford a nice dramatic surprise and/or darkly comic moment. Use this technique very sparingly, however.

Spoiler Alert

One of the most memorable missions in *TIE Fighter* is one in which Maarek Stele (the player character) is ordered to clear a minefield using an unshielded TIE Interceptor. The briefing suggests that this will be an opportunity for the player to demonstrate his remarkable skills. The truth is the commanding officer is corrupt and has determined that the player is likely to blow the whistle on him, so this is his way of getting the player out of the way. For the player, this isn't really a suicide mission at all (very difficult, but not impossible). During the mission, the twist is that as the villain finishes revealing his knowledge that Stele is no longer loyal to him, he orders the player's wingmen to attack him!

Always be cognizant of the fact that the mission designers are the ultimate authority on what the briefing needs to convey (at least they should be, in my opinion.) In all likelihood, they will be the ones who write the first drafts of the mission briefings, and it will be your job to improve upon and tighten their writing.

Mid-Mission Communications and Messages

The messages the player receives during gameplay are perhaps the most important part of the writing for a simulator game. The player can easily become overwhelmed by events during a mission, and the right information conveyed at the right moment can make all the difference. Even more so than the mission briefings, it is essential that you work closely with the mission designers to get this right. Messages received during the mission are also your primary opportunity to increase the drama and emotional impact of the events occurring during the mission.

However, there is a huge caveat: the player's attention is going to be elsewhere. All messages must be as concise as possible. When we made *X-Wing*, there was no recorded voice during missions, and the screen resolution was a mere 320×200, so messages were limited to about 80 characters. The last thing the player wants to do in the middle of a dogfight is read a message, let alone a string of them. Of course, nowadays voice is expected, but it can still be distracting to listen to when you're trying to avoid getting killed. Since a vital message can easily be missed, most modern games maintain a message log that can be reviewed while the game is paused.

Mid-mission messages can generally be categorized as follows:

- **Mission-critical messages.** As the name implies, these are messages the player must receive. They convey vital information about mission progress and can include warnings about damage to a ship the player is trying to protect, or about the imminent escape of a vessel the player is trying to destroy. They may also be used to alert the player to a change in mission objectives.

- **Instructional messages.** Usually restricted to training and tutorial missions, these messages guide the player through the use of their craft, or the employment of some tactic.

- **Story messages.** These messages are used to deliver additional story information, i.e., further background on characters or the situation. Avoid the temptation to trigger too long a sequence of these. If you absolutely must, then remember the 60 seconds max rule for cutscenes, i.e., don't expect the player to sit through more than a full minute of conversation over the radio and be happy about it. If you have to do this for story reasons, then be sure to work with the mission designers to ensure a respite in the action. Whenever I had to accommodate such a situation, I tried to ensure that the player was at least flying toward something interesting.

- **Background chatter and "barks."** These messages constitute "filler" material and include such lines as "I'm hit!", "Good kill!", "They're everywhere!", and "Stay on target!" While they aren't critical, they certainly provide color and a sense that there are other people all around the player. You'll want to write as many variations as you can think of, and I recommend recording as many different takes of each line as possible. This is to minimize the risk of too much repetition since these lines are likely to be triggered frequently. A nice feature we included from *TIE Fighter* onward was a "verbose" flag for each line. That was used by a feature in the options screen that allowed players to control how many radio messages they would hear.

- **System status messages.** This is another category of essential information but one not necessarily to be recorded in voice. These are messages used to confirm changes to various systems and include things like "shields at 50%," "hyperdrive damaged," and "target acquired."

- **Win/loss messages.** As you would assume, these are messages that are triggered when the mission is won or lost. A win message should be congratulatory and stroke the player's ego. Ideally, it should provide a concise recap of what the mission objective was. For example, "Well done, Alpha 2, you stopped the Rebel attack and eliminated over half of their forces!" A loss message should explain why the player lost, and this can be achieved by simply describing the loss condition. For example, "We have failed the Emperor! The Rebels destroyed our base and escaped with most of their forces!"

Debriefings

Debriefings are the bookend to the mission and serve to answer the question, "How did I do?" They should provide a recap of what the mission was about, what the player has achieved, and how it all fits into the greater campaign. They can also be used to foreshadow the following mission(s).

TIE Fighter had separate debriefing screens depending on whether the mission was won or lost. If you failed the mission, then the debriefing would provide a more detailed breakdown of what you were supposed to have done, and you could restart the mission. If you needed it, you could click through to an additional page that would provide tactical advice on how to beat the mission.

This (and the fact that we added difficulty settings plus cheats for invulnerability and unlimited ammo) had the unforeseen consequence of eliminating the need for the official strategy guide. The *X-Wing* strategy guide had been very successful, and based on that a large number of *TIE Fighter* books were ordered by retailers. When they didn't sell as expected, the publisher demanded the return of some of the money they had paid us for writing the book!

In *X-Wing Alliance*, we introduced yet another method of story delivery that was unusual for a combat simulator: email. The player character, Ace Azzameen, would receive messages periodically that would provide deeper looks into his personal relationships and expand on his background.

Gosh, There Are an Awful Lot of Controls to Memorize!

Tutorials and training missions present a special case requiring variations on all of the previously described sections (briefing/debriefing and mid-mission communications). The main difference is that you should assume that the player has never played one of these games before and that you're going to have to do a lot of hand-holding. There's nothing more discouraging than firing up some cool new simulator that you've heard so much about and find that you can't figure out how to do anything! The writer's responsibility here is to work especially closely with the designers to write step-by-step instructions that teach the player how to operate the controls.

When it comes to tactics, a good AI wingman/flight instructor is invaluable because the NPC cannot only tell the player what to do, but he can be scripted to show the player by example.

Note that some games forego any training missions and rely instead on providing a basic overview of the controls and how they work in the game manual. Needless to say, it is absolutely essential that the information presented in this case is completely accurate!

Technical Data

Once again, we are reminded that simulator fans are fascinated by the hardware. They are gearheads, and they love to know all the technical details and performance characteristics of their chosen vehicle. Hardcore fans will have already memorized much of this data. They have little tolerance for factual errors, so be sure to get it right!

One of the first bugs I reported as a tester on *Secret Weapons of the Luftwaffe* had to do with the altitude a German fighter was flying at. I had specifically chosen an American fighter with a ceiling of 42,000 feet because I knew that the highest any of the German planes could reach was 39,000 feet. I discovered that the game would automatically spawn enemies a few thousand feet above the player. The fix was simple, but if no one on the development or test team had caught it, we sure would have been embarrassed when the fans did!

Following the release of *X-Wing vs. TIE Fighter: Balance of Power*, there were heated debates among the fans over the true size of the Super Star Destroyer portrayed in the game. Depending on the reference source, it was supposed to be either 8 km long or 16 km long. Since a careful viewing of the relevant scenes in the movies demonstrates clear inconsistencies in scale (the shots having been composed for dramatic visual effect, and evidently not with overly much concern for continuity or "realism"), the developers went with the smaller size due to limitations with the game engine. Judging from some of the arguments, though, you'd think some fans believed the movies were a documentary series!

Where this can get a bit tedious is when you have to make up a bunch of plausible-sounding techno-jargon. I got myself in a bit of hot water over some placeholder text that was in a hidden file in *TIE Fighter*. Working well into the wee hours I got a bit loopy and thought it would be funny to say things like, "techno-jargon for fanboys with no life" and "still more techno-jargon for fanboys with no life." Not surprisingly, some fans were insulted by this and called for the head of the person responsible! Don't do that.

9.6 Conclusion

Simulator games are among the most challenging to design and to play. It should be no surprise that they are challenging to write for. You face some unusual constraints and expectations but can still be creative and have fun. Your audience tends to include a higher percentage of gamers who know something about the vehicles and settings, so you really have to show respect for the material and demonstrate that you know what you're talking about. This may require some serious research, but you should find that research a rich source of inspiration for characters, situations, and themes.

As most combat simulators are set in a war, they are solidly grounded in one of the most dramatic environments possible. Few settings but wars afford the opportunity to show the best and worst that humans are capable of. From vicious brutality to selfless heroism, and from senseless tragedy to blackest comedy, you will have no shortage of opportunities for deep emotional impact. Simulator games put the player in an exciting, heroic role, and the writing should support and reinforce that. Just don't forget to show some love for the hardware!

10

Writing for Driving Games

Maurice Suckling

10.1 "I'm a Game with Cars In It. What Kind of Game Am I?"

There are a lot of games with cars. It depends whose figures you use over what term and in what parts of the world, but games with cars could be said to account for roughly 20% of the games people play—a huge proportion. It's possible to slice and dice this body of games up in a variety of ways: simulations and arcade games, games with characters (*Driver*), games with car tuning (*Gran Turismo*), games on roads (*Formula One*), games off-road (*WRC: Rally Evolved*), games in cities (*Crazy Taxi*), conventional racers (*Ridge Racer*), underground racing (*Juiced*), "no-rules" racing (*MotorStorm*), sandbox games with cars—or you could call them RPGs with cars— (*Grand Theft Auto*), and so on. Many games fall into more than one category—it just really depends where you decide to put your knife in to divide up this pretty vast cake.

For the purposes of this chapter, I'm going to break them into three categories. These are not categories you will usually find consumers thinking in terms of, nor the categories execs, producers, designers, programmers, or artists will generally be thinking in terms of. But this being a book for writers, this is often the way writers tend to think. For a writer working on a game with cars in it, there are essentially three types of game:

1. A driving game with a story.

2. A driving game without a story.

3. A vehicle-related game with a story.

There's an overlap between all three, which could be represented by Figure 10.1. However, this chapter is going to take a look at writing for the first two kinds of

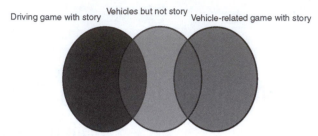

Driving game with story   Vehicles but not story   Vehicle-related game with story

Figure 10.1. Types of games with vehicles in them.

games. Although perhaps not immediately apparent, there is a fundamental difference between the first and third categories. In writing a story for a driving game, a
writer generally has to consider ways of directing that story in such a way it feeds
directly into driving-related activities. Or, another way of putting this: the writer is
constantly looking for ways to link the story to a reason to get in a vehicle and do
something, preferably to do something that can only be done in a vehicle, something
that wouldn't make anywhere near as much sense to even attempt without a vehicle. In this way, driving missions effectively become the "plot points" around which
you're looking to build your story. These "plot points" are sometimes linear, such as
in games like *Driver 2* and *Driver 3*, and sometimes they are "pot-based," optional,
but unified by theme, as in games like *Driver* and *Driver '76*.

The essential difference between this and a game that has car-related action and
has a story is that the writer isn't always looking at driving elements—often termed
"missions"—as being "plot points." In these kinds of games, a vehicle is a tool,
something to use if it's helpful but not something the writer must necessarily always
look to incorporate. In a driving game, the player has to be coaxed by the story to
get behind a wheel with a reason. Or, if the player is always locked in the vehicle,
the story needs to provide additional incentive to stay with certain characters and
complete certain passages of gameplay. If the story doesn't create a situation in which
the player is going to drive, then there is no game—one *must* feed into—or feed
off—the other.

Not only that, but the writer is usually looking to find ways of stringing a number
of car-based missions together with the minimum amount of story between them.
As a rule, the more car-based missions you can "run off" the same part of story the
better.

A game like *Crackdown* can work just as well without the player always getting
into a car. In fact, sometimes it can work even better and be even more satisfying as
an experience when, instead of setting off on a chase, you realize you can circumvent
the whole episode by shooting someone at range beforehand.

The difference is that cars are a means to an end in a game like *Saints Row*—
they're something, as a player, you use and abuse as a situation requires. As a writer,
this means, design permitting, your story can meander in and out of vehicle-related

set-ups and motivations, with a primary concern that the motivation you instill in the player is to get him to see the world as an arena for his ingenuity. The world is the hero in these games.

But in a game that is fundamentally about driving, you must get the player into a car or the designers will take you out to the parking lot, lie you down, and drive backward and forward over you until the message sinks in. In driving games, it's the car, or the bike, or the driving experience that's the hero.

Writing for each type of game requires its own skills and approaches. I have no doubt that a number of these skills are essentially transferable. Although I maintain these categories require a different mindset for the writer, I don't think that one is necessarily more problematic than the other. Trying to link everything back to being in a car is a thin tightrope to walk for a 40-hour gameplay experience—but then again, freedom is its own curse.

Essentially, I'm making the point here that games like *Grand Theft Auto*, *Scarface*, and *True Crime* are not truly driving games. In terms of writing, they actually have more in common with RPGs with a more interactive and physics-endowed world.

10.2   "Delivery for You! Where'd You Want It?"

When it comes to driving games, writers can be asked to deliver all kinds of elements, often some or all of the following:

- Instructional speech and text, outlining mission objectives, also hints and minigame objectives.

- Tutorial speech and text.

- Mid-mission speech and text.

- Main story scenes.

- Character profiles.

- Linking in-game cutscenes.

- Pedestrian and NPC city speech.

Exactly what you might be asked to do, with what priority, and quite what the requirements for each element will be will inevitably vary depending on the studio and the project.

I would think most of these elements are fairly self-explanatory, but I'd like to pick up on a couple of them. *Mid-mission speech and text* is the dialogue and on-screen text spoken and delivered to add "flavor," "character," and "tone" to the game. It is distinct from the instructional speech and text in so far as its function isn't necessarily to clarify the player's objectives—it's often primarily to help with the pacing, rhythm, and excitement of the game, while also making the world and the characters in it feel more "alive." A writer will not always have the opportunity to employ this—you either need a player character with one or more passengers, a radio or phone buddy, or a player character who monologues, or even a narrator voice over the top of the game experience.

Likewise, *linking in-game cutscenes* are not always used. Sometimes the mission design may necessitate a break in the game action, perhaps to change from one vehicle to another, or to explain a shift in the motivation, say from chasing to being chased. On such occasions, a writer may need to employ a linking in-game cutscene. In essence, this is much the same as any other cutscene—except that it's even more critical to write the scene as efficiently as possible, and it must explain the shift in mission objective. (In older games, this kind of scene would also very rarely—if ever—be an FMV. In more contemporary games, there is often less distinction, with FMV being used less frequently across all cutscenes in any case.)

As for *pedestrian and city speech*, this tends to break down into two sub-categories: player-triggered and idling. Idling speech is what you hear when you go near NPCs—near enough to overhear, but not in such a way as you interact with them. Player-triggered speech can be a "conversational response," which could be tied to any number of samples either randomly or sequentially triggered, or it can be a "sensational response," i.e., running away when you try to run them over—cue screaming, yelling, and lots of "argghhs." While writing script for this latter sub-category will never be the most exciting thing you'll do, the occasional gem can keep you entertained long after it first mutated in your head in a desperate attempt to find another way of delivering an "argghh." One such gem—which I can't take credit for as a writer, and only a very partial credit for as a voice director—came from a voice actor ad-libbing her way through a Chinese-American woman's lines in which she found a car in her supermarket. Having seemingly exhausted every scream and yell either of us could think of, she delivered the memorably fierce admonishment, "You bad driver!"

10.3   The Sports Cars

From the writer's perspective, the shiny, eye-catching part of the job is often the story. This is where the writer will tend to feel he can contribute the most, where he can help shape the game experience with the characters and plot.

If you're working on a driving game with a story, it's this element you ought to tackle first—not necessarily to script level, but at least to outline and treatment. Once you get approval on the various outlines and treatments, they will be your compass for how to approach the whole game with regard to tone of voice and character.

At the same time as developing outlines and treatments, you need to be getting your head around the game structure. The game structure is the foundation you build your story structure around; it's the structure that tells you where you need to get your characters into vehicles. Sometimes the motivation will be dictated by the kind of mission, and sometimes your motivations in the story will shape new mis-

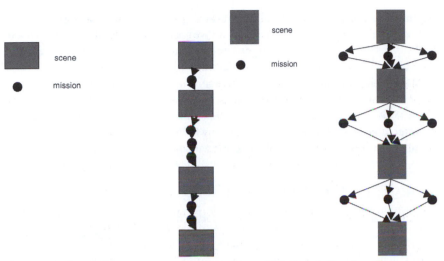

Figure 10.2. Sample linear story structure diagram.

Figure 10.3. Sample "pot-based" story structure diagram.

sions. But only after working closely with the designers can you generate a diagram that represents the skeleton of your story.

Sometimes designers will ask for a lot of input from you at this stage. Sometimes they won't, and they'll show you the structure they're working to and ask you to fill the allotted story sections with the appropriate content. It usually works out better when there's a degree of give and take at this stage, with a structure developing alongside the content. In these situations, a designer can find he's making contributions to the story, and the writer making contributions to the design. Once a story context is developed, it can be a tremendous aid to sparking design ideas.

Once you have something that might look like Figure 10.2, or perhaps like Figure 10.3, then you'll have a structure to bind your story around. There are more structures you could employ beyond these, including ones where there is "no scene" as such, but the story is wholly subsumed within the game action, or where narrative tracks are determined by selecting different characters, or where branching and semi-branching narratives are employed, etc., etc., but these two are intended to serve as simple examples. Figure 10.2 shows a wholly linear approach, one scene feeding into one (or more) mission. Figure 10.3 shows what I call a "pot structure," allowing one scene to "feed" a whole pot of missions that can be attempted in any order by the player, but they are all unified by the same motivation or objective—for example, "take out the bad guys," or "do all these jobs and make enough money, then come back and see me."

I find creating a structure diagram essential, because I can't finalize a treatment until I have a structure in place, and I don't ever like writing a script until I have a treatment in place. It would be like trying to organize D-Day by saying, "Everyone turn up on the south coast of England, and we'll ship you to France soon as we can find some ships. Oh, and bring some weapons, and—while I remember—a map," then hoping it all works out.

Developing the structure in tandem with the treatment and character profiles before beginning the script strikes me as no different from the approach to take when in working in other genres. What is critical in conventional driving games, however, is just this: every scene must directly help explain why the player is in a car (or on a bike, etc.) and why completing the gameplay will move the story forward.

10.4   The Other Cars on the Road

A writer might be tempted to see the "non-story" contributions he makes to a game as being secondary to the "sports cars." "Non-story" contributions can often be summarized as the stuff that's in-game. If you look at the bulleted list above, it's everything that's not the main story scenes—with the character profiles work straddling both the story and in-game requirements.

But in terms of workload, these "other cars on the road" generally consist of more than 50%. And in terms of the way players experiences the game—understanding what they're supposed to do, or hearing people shout as they dive out of the way, making the world feel populated—this is the stuff players generally care about the most. (And if they don't, there's something seriously wrong with the game.)

Players generally spend around 95% of their time in the game outside of the story's key scenes, which means that 50% of the writer's workload—the non-flashy, unglamorous part of what he does—is actually the most important.

However, the key skills of a writer are still essential even in the "non-story" parts of the game—the game itself. In fact, the biggest contribution you can make to a game and the experience of playing it can often result from the characters and tone of voice you help develop.

Creating characters and shaping tone of voice are core writing skills, and even more than the script, it's in these areas that you really leave your fingerprints on the game. The character outlines you develop (which can then be translated into a 3D form by artists and animators) and the tone of voice you help shape through your outlines, treatments, and script are the most enduring ways your presence is felt.

A series like *Mario Kart* may not have story, but it has characters and a tone of voice. Whilst most games in the series display no credits (at least in Europe), for sure there was at least one person (probably several) working on every title who was employing the fundamental skills of a writer as the characters were conceptualized and the feeling of the game world began to take shape.

Not all driving games have characters, and those that don't will often not turn to a writer to help with the tone of the game; however, even in these instances, it's not unheard of for writers to become involved and to become part of a development team because of the ideas they bring, ideas that designers can sift through for their gameplay applications.

For those games that do include characters, the characters can become the face of the game for marketing and can be an essential way in which one driving game differentiates itself from other driving games. Imagine *Diddy Kong Racing* without Diddy Kong. It's the same code and the same game mechanics, but an essential emotional connection between the player and the game disappears.

So don't downplay the importance of writing up character profiles, and be aware that most documents you create are actually helping to generate a palette for the tone of voice—even a brief synopsis you write on the story for the team during development is an opportunity for you to cast a certain kind of light on the feel of the game. Many other people are creating documents over the course of a development cycle, but as a writer, you have an obligation to try to make your documents not just functional but also evocative of a tone of voice—an attempt to cast in words something of what it might feel like to experience the game when it's completed, thereby helping to give a sense of direction, a sense of what everyone is aiming at. (Of course, if you're required to write a functional document, to explain story structure, or the production process, etc., then don't add "writery touches" just for the sake of it.)

10.5 The Right Kinds of Cars for the Right Kinds of Roads (or Dirt Tracks)

It's a general point, and one that will have been raised elsewhere in this volume, but nevertheless it's important enough to warrant restating. The kind of dialogue, the kind of in-game speech and text, the kind of characters, and ideas that you generate as a writer are all determined by the brief, by what kind of game the developer is trying to make. There is a vast amount of difference between writing for 1920s US East Coast gangsters and writing for 1970s French traffic cops. So read books, watch movies, and think about the era you're working in because one driving game is very much not like another driving game—and the chances are, as a writer hired to work on one, the main reason why you've been hired in the first place is to make sure that it isn't.

10.6 Hybrid Cars

However, for all that I've said above, driving games are in flux as developers are looking for ways to create different kinds of gameplay experiences. This means the essential distinction between story and in-game won't always work the same way.

Can story be immersed inside the whole game world, without players feeling they're clearly crossing over the boundary between interaction and the story they're being told? How can this story-seeding be realized? What techniques need to be developed to achieve it?

Driving game with story   Vehicles but no story

Figure 10.4. The future of driving games?

What do you do with the camera when the story is being told but you don't want to stop the game?

Can a structure be developed that allows a player the freedom to choose the missions he wants in the order he wants and yet still allows for the linearity a story needs for it to develop?

How do you handle multiplayer modes in conjunction with a story in which each player can direct the course of his own story world?

These are questions for a different chapter in a different book, but in reference to my earlier diagram, it seems we are increasingly seeing a desire from developers to move the circles closer together, perhaps blurring the distinction between those driving games with story and those without (see Figure 10.4).

So, if designers look for increasingly non-linear ways of implementing story into games, writers will be called on to find new ways not only of telling stories but also of stage-setting stories, creating the environments and conditions under which stories have the potential to develop without dictating their precise course—rather like the way primordial soup had the potential for life but came without any clear instructions on what to do with it once it developed. All of this generates its own set of problems, with its own set of potential solutions. Game writing never has stayed in one place for too long in any case.

11

Writing for Horror Games

Richard Dansky

11.1   Defining a Horror Game

Trying to figure out what exactly falls into the category of "horror game" can be, well, scary. Is it a game that features traditional monsters like zombies (*Dead Rising*, *Stubbs the Zombie*) but that otherwise has standard or comedic gameplay? Is it a game that features no monsters whatsoever (*Condemned: Criminal Intent*, *Manhunt*) but that features the standard horror trope of being stalked through a dark space by a killing machine? Is it the subgenre referred to as "survival horror" (*Resident Evil*, *Silent Hill*), which tends to mix old-fashioned adventure game puzzle solving with monsters and action sequences? Or is it some mixture of all of the above?

Horror games are actually an odd fit in the world of video game characterizations. Most game genres are defined by their play styles or content. *Rainbow Six* is a tactical shooter because the central play mechanic is based around shooting people and the play style is based around engaging the enemy tactically. The latest incarnation of *Madden* is a sports game. The *Sly Cooper* series are platformers, and so on.

But then there are horror games, which are defined not by their play mechanic but by the mood and emotional effect they intend to transmit. The point of horror, after all, is to frighten, and a horror game is one that is created with this goal in mind. *Dead Rising* may use traditional horror elements (zombies in a mall, thank you George Romero), but the focus of the gameplay is on slaughtering your way through masses of the undead with CD cases, sporks, and clothing racks, not the soul-freezing terror that a real mall full of walking corpses craving human flesh would invoke.

By the same token, "horror" tends to get reduced to a descriptor in games of other genres that utilize horrific elements. *F.E.A.R.*, for example, is chock-full of creepy supernatural badness, but since its primary play mechanic is firearms-based, it gets referred to as a "horror shooter," as opposed to simply a horror game.

What that leaves, then, are survival horror games and, to a lesser extent, adventure games with horrific settings. Writing these games calls for specific techniques, both because horror's genre conventions are so strong and because sustaining a tone of tension and fear throughout a ten-hour plus play experience is not an easy task.

11.2   Limitations and Conventions

Because horror games have been around so long, they've developed a series of conventions that serve as boundaries and guidelines. Understanding what these time-honored—or perhaps hoary, nitre-encrusted, and ancient—rules are can help save time that might otherwise be spent reinventing the suitably horrific wheel.

Tight or Locked Camera Work

One of the unspoken rules of horror games is that the player avatar does not control the environment. They are constantly off-balance, reacting to the world with imperfect knowledge. One of the ways horror games emphasize this is through the use of tight or locked cameras. Giving the player long camera ranges can, when combined with firearms, allow them long firing sightlines, which gives the player better control of the space. Fixed cameras only permit the player certain angles of view, which allows the game to get monsters up close and personal before they appear onscreen. When those monsters appear, they do so in startling fashion, reinforcing the shock and horror of the conflict. And since most monsters are the biting/tearing/rending type, using the camera to allow them to get close renders them more effective and thus more threatening.

Long Bits of Exposition

This is handled in more depth elsewhere in the chapter, but horror games generally come with lots and lots of backstory. Some of this is genre convention, as the player expects to spend gobs of time digging through the arcane secrets of the world. Some of it is simply because there's generally a lot of information to transmit in horror games and thus a variety of means of getting it across—conversations, cut scenes, in-game artifacts, etc.—is necessary to keep the player from feeling like they have to take notes.

Characters Wandering Off by Themselves to Get Eaten

In general, secondary characters in horror games tend to meet gruesome ends, often abruptly. There's also a strong subset of secondary characters whose sole purpose is to go mad and/or betray the main character at some point, possibly offering exposition in the process. A good many of these end up monsterbait as well, but the overall convention is that secondary and tertiary characters are sometimes used more as plot devices than as actual developed characters. That's not to say this is entirely a bad thing. After all, there's no better way to prove that the monster is, indeed, monstrous than by having it chow down on a hapless sidekick or two. But it is a genre convention that can easily slip into parody or cliche if not watched carefully.

11.3 Defining What Needs to Be Written

The writer's first goal on a horror game is defining what actually needs to be written. In large part, this consists of figuring out, in conjunction with the rest of the team, what needs to be done to support the horrific nature of the game: how many in-game artifacts are needed to support the gameplay, how much character design needs to be done, how much backstory needs to be written, and so forth.

It's always a good idea to start with the world backstory and integrating that with the gameplay so that the secret history supports the features. If the game's central conceit involves a body-switching mechanic, the story needs to support and emphasize that by building a world wherein body-switching is believable and consistent. If the horror is something that suddenly mutates allied NPCs into monsters, then the world needs to provide an explanation for why and how this happens, in a way that matches the gameplay.

11.4 Mood, Tone, and Atmosphere

Then again, the setting needs to match the gameplay for pretty much any game. What, then, makes writing a horror game special?

The answer is fear. The writer on a horror game has an added responsibility. In addition to supporting gameplay, creating an engaging story, and writing good dialogue, the horror game writer must help create and sustain a feeling of fear. And that means working with mood and tone in a way that can be different from other games. Military jargon and modern weaponry are generally what's needed to define a tactical shooter in the minds of the audience; keeping a mood of fear going in a game can be sometimes a little trickier.

Setting and Backstory

In addition to working with the game, the backstory and setting need to support the possibility of fear. That means more than just creaky architecture, fog, and deserted streets. It means building the possibility of bad things happening into the space and the context. The history of the horrific events of the game needs to be supported, so that there's a solid answer to the question "Why is this happening here, of all places?" Silent Hill used to be a "sacred place," Innsmouth is the closest town to Devil's Reef and the Deep One colony beneath it, and so forth.

Saying Enough—Or Too Much

Horror thrives on understatement. E. B. White's famous statement about dissecting a joke—that it's a lot like dissecting a frog; you may understand what makes it tick, but you'll end up with a dead frog—also works for dissecting scares. Say too much and the threat's dimensions become known; known threats can be planned against, countered, and fought on an even level. The point of horror is that the enemy is not understood and not defined, that it cannot be faced as though it were a normal form of opposition.

In practical terms, this means figuring out what the player needs to know at any given time and giving them that, but no more. Additional mood or flavor material can be useful to reinforce the game's tone, but providing too much information can be deadly. It engages the analytical part of the player's mind while shutting down the visceral response, exactly the opposite of what a horror game should be doing.

11.5   Character

The Hero

Someone always has to save the day, or at least try to. Building and writing a horror game protagonist means figuring out who the hero is, why he's particularly suited to be the hero, and why he's not headed for the hills at the first sign of alien slime infestation.

Getting the job.   Why the hero is the hero is an important question. "Wrong place at the wrong time" is a popular answer, but it's rarely enough to serve as a strong motivation. After all, lots of people can be in the wrong place at the wrong time when there are monsters afoot, and most of them end up getting called "victims." The hero needs a special reason he's the one who's on the scene and who can survive long enough to provide some reasonable gameplay. Whether it's military or police training (*Resident Evil*, *Cold Fear*), psychic/magical powers (*Siren*, *Eternal Darkness*), a seriously good camera that turns out to be effective against ghosts (*Fatal Frame*), or superior knowledge of the situation (*Necronomicon*), there has to be an aspect of the hero character that allows him to act effectively when the rest of the world can't.

Character rationale.   There also has to be a reason the hero is the hero and isn't running for his life instead of kicking monster butt. Any sane character, after all, would get the hell out of town after the first zombie attack. Building a believable hero means building a reason for him to stick around.

The rationales for staying in the horror zone can be broken up into three rough groups: doing it for themselves, doing it for someone else, or doing it for the world. The last is the easiest to understand but also the broadest. It usually comes down to, "If I don't save the world, no one will." This also covers the more military style of horror game, whereby the hero has been ordered into the danger zone and it's his job to stay there. While saving the world is a noble and understandable motivation, it's also a fairly generic one and doesn't do much to individualize the protagonist.

More interesting is the notion that the hero is there for someone else. There's someone that the hero has to save, protect, resurrect, or otherwise take care of, and that person is the real reason they're in the danger zone. Leon Kennedy in *Resident*

Evil 4 is a perfect example of this sort of hero. He's there to rescue the President's daughter, when otherwise he'd probably be calling in an air strike on the spooky Spanish village infested with parasitic monsters.

Finally, there's the horror protagonist who's doing it for himself. This can be either a positive or a negative motivation. In some cases, the protagonist can be after power, an ancient artifact, or his own salvation. The latter works well with a "ticking clock" scenario, whereby the hero has been infected or otherwise tainted by the horror and only has a limited time to save himself before suffering a hideous fate. Conversely, the protagonist may be drawn in because of fate, family history, or destiny, in which case what he is drives the character's action. *Eternal Darkness: Sanity's Requiem* provides a good example of this style of character motivation. No matter which character the player is currently controlling, they're all tied into the same accursed bloodline that ties them to the action.

The Creature

The key to almost any horror game is the monster. Without a monster, you've got something else entirely. That doesn't mean that the definition of "monster" needs to be a narrow one; there's a lot more out there that's monstrous than just Frankenstein, Dracula, and Boo Berry. The term "monster" is a loose one, meaning "the supernatural or unnatural antagonist(s) the hero faces." In practical terms, that covers everything from mindless zombie hordes to tentacled horrors to berserker robots to unfeeling serial killers.

With that in mind, defining the monster is one of the most important tasks a horror game writer faces. Because it's a game, it's highly unlikely that there will be only one monster. After all, if there were only one critter to face, fight, and defeat, odds are that it's going to be a pretty short game. Instead, that leaves the writer helping to craft an entire hierarchy of beasties, figuring out what they're doing in the game world, and establishing why it's scary.

What does it want? Monsters have needs, too. A key ingredient in making a monster believable and interesting is giving it objectives that make sense. In some cases, this is simple—zombies like tasty brains. In others, it's a little more difficult, and establishing what a monster might want to do can be the difference between a successful, memorable creature and yet another tentacled target.

The obvious answer to "what does the monster want" is "to eat the hero character," but that's too glib a response to be meaningful. Besides, pretty much all game monsters want to eat the player, so setting a particular creature apart is going to require more than that. One successful approach involves turning the game narrative around and looking at it from the monster's perspective. In other words, if the boss monster were the player avatar, what would its objectives be? Working that down the line for each of the lesser creatures—even if it eventually ends up as "reproduce and feed" or "obey the Master's will"—helps tremendously in making sure the monsters act and speak in a way that is believable and consistent. If they're working toward something, instead of just reacting to the player presence, they become characters instead of furniture.

And the most memorable monsters in books, games, and movies have always been characters who've communicated their maleficent desires clearly, even if they've never spoken a word.

How does it communicate? Speaking of which, that brings up the question of how the monster communicates. Good old-fashioned speech is a reliable standby, but it doesn't necessarily work for a creature that doesn't have a face. On the plus side, establishing how a creature communicates and integrating it with the beast's motivation can go a long way toward providing a unified experience for the player that's that much stronger and scarier. In other words, the monster's means of getting its points across should reinforce what those points are and what the monster is, not reduce it to a mundane threat to be identified in terms of how many bullets it can take.

So, an Elder Thing from beyond space and time may work better if its means of communication isn't simple dialogue but is instead something like blasting its unholy thoughts directly in the player avatar's mind, or causing letters of blood to appear on the wall (or in the character's flesh), or speaking through an obviously possessed, tormented mortal victim. The method of the message should match the monster.

Hand in hand (in tentacle, pseudopod, or other appendage) with that should be monster voice. Just because a monster isn't the hero doesn't mean it can't or shouldn't have a unique voice, one that helps define and characterize it. This may seem like common sense, but it bears repeating—a resurrected sorcerer from the fourteenth century is unlikely to refer to something as "straight bangin'," while putting compound-complex sentences into the mouths of cannibalistic sewer mutants is probably going to come across as jarring. Writing monster dialogue also needs to take into account anatomy—something speaking through a mouthful of jagged fangs is going to sound different than a suburban kid with expensive orthodontia—and the critter's mental capacity as well. Making sure that the dialogue fits the monster—its form, function, and construction—supports the monster's role and effectiveness in conveying horror.

What makes it scary? All of this leads to the big question about a monster: What makes it scary? A monster that's not scary might as well not be a monster. There has to be something about each monster that makes it memorable and frightening, or else it's just a placeholder.

The best monsters are the ones based around exaggerated characteristics. That's a fancy way of saying that they have a human or animal characteristic that's taken way too far, or a couple that are combined in a way that Ought Not To Be. For example, take the werewolf, which combines animal ferocity with human intelligence—a mix that shouldn't be. There's also the classic B-movie zombie, which just keeps coming in defiance of how the human body is supposed to operate. Bear in mind that these characteristics don't just have to be physical—the hyperintelligent serial killer who spouts off the protagonist's life story and 16 ways to kill a man with a spork is just as monstrous, just as much an exaggeration as the Giger-esque nightmare that stalked the decks of the *Nostromo*.

Identifying the characteristic or characteristics to blow out of all proportion is one essential part of making the monster scary. Along with that, however, is making sure that its actions, moves, words, and appearance match and support that base wrongness. That's where the job of monstermaking becomes collaboration with concept artists, animators, designers, and the rest of the team, to make sure that all of the elements to produce a good scare are all available and incorporated.

11.6   Plot and Payoff

Narrative, particularly the payoff of the narrative, is key in horror games. If the payoff at the end doesn't match the buildup throughout the game, then the letdown is tremendous and the ultimate effect of the game suffers irreparably. Horror works by continuously ratcheting up fearful tension past the point where it is comfortable, ultimately leading to a (hopefully) scary release. There's a reason the monster is less effective if it lumbers out in Act I, Scene I. The stage needs to be set properly. The ominous hints at its true nature need to be delivered. Its hapless victims need to be displayed. Evidence of its presence—creaking floorboards, distant cries, vague glimpses in the distance, fuzzy video footage—need to ratchet up the player's tension level to where the actual appearance of the monster is a form of relief, a chance for the player finally to act. If the buildup exceeds the release, then the player is disappointed. If the release exceeds the buildup, then the player is unprepared and overwhelmed. In either case, tuning the scenario is vital.

Making Sure It's Scary

There are people in this world who are terrified of, among other things, the number thirteen, standardized tests, and pickles. In other words, what's scary to one person— or the writer—may not be scary to the audience at large. Since fear is such a tricky emotion to generate and sustain, it pays to double- and triple-check the response to the writing, in order to ensure that the scary is really there.

Originality versus Homage

Using classic horror tropes and figures has drawbacks as well as benefits. The main benefit is that everyone knows how, say, Dracula works and who he is, and so the writer can get straight to the point without having to waste a lot of exposition on who the guy in the opera cape with the bad overbite is supposed to be. On the other hand, drawing on that knowledge means actively engaging the player's knowledge base, instead of the character's, and this can break the player's immersion immediately. They've seen it before, they know how it's supposed to go, and as a result, they're thinking about the last time they saw that trope instead of thinking about the game.

Even individual sequences or character names can be a double-edged sword. On one hand, they can bring with them strong positive connotations and the intimation of shared knowledge between player and game. On the other hand, if they're handled poorly, it's easy to have the player decide that the writer's lovingly intended homage is really a cheap knock-off.

Ultimately, it comes down to whether the writer can come up with a concrete reason to be using that particular homage. If you can say without hesitation or regret that there's something that using Dracula adds to the game by virtue of his being Dracula and not any other vampire, then go for it. If not, it's best to think again. Mind you, the benefit that is brought can be as simple as giving a little something extra to the educated player who knows where a particular reference came from without distracting the players who don't, but it must be something. Otherwise, it doesn't bring anything to the fear quotient of your game and potentially subtracts from it instead.

Establishing the Monster—And the Threat

If the game's going to be scary, then something in it has to do the scaring. That's the monster's job, and it's the writer's job to demonstrate how threatening that monster really is. A large portion of this involves leaving evidence around of just how nasty the threat can be. Partially devoured corpses, messages smeared in blood, screams that are abruptly cut off—all of these are tried-and-true techniques. Recorded evidence works well, whether it be the radio relay from the soldier who's hopelessly fighting the monster or the surveillance video that shows the critter's handiwork in suitably blurry imagery. All of these serve the same function—to show how dangerous the monster is. If the player doesn't believe the monster is a threat, then he's not scared of it, and the game's horror will be lost.

Reveals and Pacing

It is impossible to talk about tension without talking about pacing. The rate at which information is revealed—or scares are doled out—is the heartbeat under the floorboards of any good horror game. Too fast and it gets frantic, spinning out of control. Too slow and it's a lifeless hulk. A good technique for establishing a solid pace is outlining. Sitting down with the mission flow and figuring out what reveals need to be made when allows the writer to divvy up the information leading to those reveals and to realize how much time there is to get them out there. That allows not only for doling the information out at the right time but also a way to check on the right amount. The target should be just enough to keep the player moving forward, except after a major find or victory. At that point, information can be used as a reward. Whether it's a dying threat from a defeated foe or the trove of documents it was guarding, a reveal is a useful reward to give the player. Furthermore, it's one that can be given without fear of affecting game balance. Learning more about the world may help the player solve puzzles or understand the game better, but it doesn't jack up his combat percentages.

11.7 Exposition

Almost by definition, horror games have plenty of exposition. There's much that needs to be explained—the nature of the threat, where it came from, how to stop it, and usually a ton of world-building that goes along with it. Furthermore, since a great many horror games are built with backstories that go down the centuries, there's the weight of those ages' worth of words to consider as well. The clever game writer will be able to deliver this exposition in a way that entices the player to go forward and seek out more, using it as a reward for successful exploration of the world and conquest of enemies. Otherwise, the risk is that the player will drown in a sea of names, made-up magical references, and ill-communicated warnings, all of which will become nothing more than reference.

The most important thing to remember about exposition in a horror game is that it should be there for a reason: to guide, reward, or assist the player. A secondary reason for it is to provide mood, tone, or depth to the world, but paying heed to these needs without seeing to the primary ones results in a game that's unfocused, diffuse, and not very scary. Focusing on what the exposition is there for can help rein it in and prevent it from maundering all over the real action.

How to Deliver It without Boring the Player

Exposition always needs to be delivered well. Dropping it on the player's head is going to get it skipped, skimmed, or ignored. Instead, it needs to be doled out in appropriate-sized chunks, in ways that are appropriate for the game, and at appropriate times within the game narrative.

It also needs to be delivered in ways that are appropriate for the game's tone and setting. Faux Old English works very well for some games, but in a *Resident Evil*-style mutantfest, it's anachronistic and inappropriate. Keeping the tone of the exposition in line with the visuals and the player expectations helps the message get across better.

In addition, there's also a need for the writer to do his research, and there's nowhere bad research shows up more starkly than in expository passages. Research isn't just actual factual stuff (though that's vital); it's also the game world and bible information that needs to be conveyed properly. It's one thing if a character is lying in his journal or infodump; it's another entirely if the writer screwed up in a way that the player can't defend against.

What Needs Delivery and What Doesn't

Above all, this also means that the exposition needs to be viewed in terms of how it's useful to the player and not be used to show off how bloody clever the writer is. Shoving the entire backstory of the haunted castle/mutant-infested laboratory/ancient backwoods town full of star-spawn down the player's throat just because it was written and someone thought it was clever is bad game writing. The information that gets handed off needs to go through the filter of "what does the player get out of this," and if there's no good answer to that question, then it should be shelved.

When to Deliver It and How Much at a Time

Pacing is exposition's éminence grise. An awful lot of explanation can be doled out if it's done in such a way that the player doesn't realize he's being given a lecture. As a general rule, shorter bits of exposition are better than longer ones, and tying them into player actions means they're more likely to be received well. The pages from an ancient diary will carry more weight if the player takes them off of a revenant's corpse after a hard-fought battle instead of picking them up randomly every 15 feet.

Part and parcel with that is making sure that the content the player receives is appropriate. That doesn't mean that it has to be "on the nose," one-on-one instructions on how to beat the next monster. Rather, it means that what comes across should be useful and relevant—maybe not always immediately, but in such a way that the player will be able to use it without endless slogging through his journal. If necessary, this can be reinforced with dialogue or inner monologue—the standard "Hey, I'll bet that is what the old guy with the lizard head was talking about" affirmation, though hopefully done with more originality and less Scooby-Doo.

11.8   Dialogue

Horror game dialogue is hard to write. In many cases, the writer is trying to transmit over-the-top emotions like terror, megalomania, and unthinking devotion to soul-devouring cosmic entities whose mere names are sufficient to inspire endless Lovecraft-derived gibbering. All of these can be difficult to write without sounding completely goofy, overwritten, or derivative.

An additional challenge is writing effective disbelief. If everyone in a horror game believes that there's something nasty in the woods, then it's a short step to arming the local citizenry and taking care of the lurking critters en masse. But horror games don't work that way. There need to be plenty of civilians who don't believe in the monster in order to move the discovery-style plot along, no matter that the player knows there's a monster because he's seen it on the cover of the box, and if he doesn't get the monsters he paid for, he's going after the developers with a sock full of nickels.

Conversely, there are horror games where The Whole Town Is In On It. In that case, the player knows that the NPCs know something but has limited means to extract the information, and the writer runs the risk of having the endlessly evasive dialogue these characters spout turn tooth-grindingly annoying. The fourteenth time a player hears, "Ye'll be larnin' soon enough, heh heh heh" from the creepy innkeeper with the bulging eyes and fish-scale rash is about the thirteenth time too many.

And so, the challenges in doing horror dialogue are simple to see but difficult to overcome. Provide sufficient information to the player to allow them to keep advancing, while supporting the mood and tone and not having your characters come across like morons.

Keeping It Punchy While Delivering Information

Punchy dialogue and horror often fight against each other. Because there is so much to explain in most horror games, the dialogue can get overstuffed. Overstuffed dialogue, in turn, can wreck the mood of horror that the writer is trying to deliver. If the player has to sit back and listen for too long, they lose the intensity of fear that leads to a good horror game experience.

The risk is always to try to pack too much information into any given line. This can be a mistake; too much information is, well, too much. A better approach is to list out the information that needs to be doled out and to give a maximum of one to two points per line. Trying to cram in more than that is self-defeating, as the useful information gets lost. "The creature is an unholy blood-drinking spawn of Vlad Dracul himself, and only with a wooden stake through the very heart will you lay the beast to rest!" is one way; "It's a bloodsucker. Pack your stakes and aim for the heart" is another, more effective one.

How to Deliver Fear

Delivering fear is in large part allowing the player to scare himself. Telling the player how scary something is—how horrifying the monster, how dangerous the situation, how mind-blowing the insanity—ultimately ends up as a challenge, one the game will always lose to the player. Instead, the writer should seek to engage the player in a cooperative agreement with the player to scare him, encouraging him to allow himself to believe in and discover the horror himself. After all, the player wants to be scared. That's why he bought the game in the first place.

So instead of announcing that there's a titanic hell-spawn underneath the house, it's better to hint at something strange going on. Having some characters deny the strangeness helps, as do the disappearances of helpful characters, the refusal of others to talk about what's going on, and references to legend or history as opposed to straight-out "on the nose" description. A creature that is described in detail is not a monster; it's a problem to be assessed and solved. A shadowy presence lurking in the fringes, to be discovered slowly and at the worst possible time, is much more likely to be genuinely frightening.

How to Make the Character's Actions Seem Believable under the Circumstances

It goes without saying that characters in horror fictions of all sorts seem, in many cases, to be unbelievably dumb. After all, they do things like voluntarily offer servitude to genocidal monsters who want to wipe out all humanity, ignore the mounting evidence of monster activity to say, "But that's impossible!" right up until the moment they get chomped on, and go down in the basement alone, often right after having had sex.

This is true, and yet it is the writer's responsibility to make sure that characters don't seem dumb, even when they do dumb things.

The best way to avoid having characters look stupid is, of course, to avoid having them do stupid things. This may not be possible, though—the plot or gameplay may necessitate someone wandering into dark areas with only a sputtering flashlight and a six-shot revolver, or reading from a book of ancient evil, or striking a deal with a demon lord who's obviously going to renege at the earliest opportunity. And if that's the case, then the stupid action needs to get cast in context that makes it look at least a little less stupid, if not outright understandable.

The best technique for doing so lies with strong character-building, particularly in the area of motivation. The first question anyone ever asks when a character does something egregiously dumb is, "Why did they do that?" The smart writer has a ready, believable, and accessible answer. If he's really on his game, he's answered the question before it's asked through the character's dialogue and previous actions, so that it seems completely believable and the question never comes up at all. If the character is prone to wandering around in dark places by his lonesome and scoffing at stories of monsters, establish that he's a long-time skeptic and that none of the other stories he's been told have ever amounted to anything. That way, the character's action is more believable, and the player gets a little frisson of schadenfreude for having known better.

Avoiding Cliché

Familiarity breeds contempt, and it's hard for things that you have contempt for to frighten you. The cliches of the horror genre, then, are deadly to true horror and should be avoided at all cost. These include, but by no means are limited to, the following.

- Bad imitation Lovecraftian chanting, usually with an eight-to-one ratio of consonants to vowels.

- Vampires with Transylvanian accents.

- Zombies who groan "braaaaains," unless they do it ironically.

- Cackling mad scientist infodump loaded with a double helping of pseudo-science natterings.

- Ancient evil demonic overlords explaining exactly how ancient and evil they are (bonus points if they somehow work in Atlantis, Lemuria, Mu, or any other piece of subaqueous real estate).

And so forth.

And yet there is a reason things like this become clichés, and that's because on a base level, they serve a useful purpose. Zombies (of a certain sub-species) do like brains, and this gets the point across. Lovecraftian chanting, at least in the original, emphasized the otherworldly nature of what was going on, and so forth. But just because it worked then doesn't mean that it works now. Instead, the best approach is to find the underlying reason for the cliche and attempt to come up with another method of producing it. Mindless repetition of old-school stuff will rarely produce new thrills.

11.9   In-Game Artifacts

One of the staples of the horror game is the in-game artifact. Diaries, voicemail messages, ancient tomes of nameless evil—they're all integral to the genre. By this point, players expect to find them and to find them useful sources of information. In practical terms, this means that the writer on a horror game can expect to have to write not only the game dialogue but also a positive raft of supporting documents. On the bright side, these in-game artifacts provide text-only room for the writer to really stretch out and go wild. They're often pure writing with few limitations, a rarity in game development.

Diaries

Diaries in all their many forms are the most venerable form of in-game artifact in the genre, going straight back to horror's literary roots. Most in-game diaries show a pattern of discovery, followed by increasing madness, until a final, shrieking conclusion that's often ended mid-sentence. The implausibility of this aside, diaries also provide an excellent method of providing plenty of information wrapped in flavor text.

Writing diary entries is in large part a matter of voice and pacing. The voice of the diary's in-game author needs to be consistent and believable, while the pace at which the diarist—and thus the reader—uncovers the horror needs to be carefully monitored.

Note that diaries don't just have to be diaries. They can be lab notes, log entries, patient observations, or any other form of serial narrative that serves the same purpose.

Ancient Tomes of Evil

An ancient tome of evil is another standby of the genre and is typically trickier to write than a diary, in large part because the temptation to go over the top is much greater. An ancient tome of evil serves as an authority, a primary source on whatever horror is skulking about, and it usually comes encrusted with age and pseudo-archaic phrasing. Again, the best way to write one of these books is to outline what exactly it needs to communicate and then build the framework of the artifact around that.

11.10   Conclusion

Perhaps the most frightening thing about horror game writing is the prospect of having to do it, and do it well. After all, good horror game writing means establishing and maintaining a mood of fear on top of all of the other tasks of good game writing, none of which magically go away once the horror comes out. However, through understanding that particular efforts are necessary, and by paying proper attention to constructing the unique elements of a horror game, a game writer can help create a sufficiently spooky experience for the player.

12

Writing for Science-Fiction and Fantasy Games

Chris Klug

12.1 Fireball Spells and Ray Guns, What's the Difference?

What *is* the big deal? I mean, why even bother to try and separate these two genres?

The idea for this chapter came from years of being frustrated with (mostly) younger writers who seemingly didn't understand the difference between these two forms of genre fiction. I would work with, say, a freelancer, or I would be interviewing a potential employee, and we'd get talking about sci-fi and fantasy. In those situations, I was mostly working on science-fiction games, so the dissonance was coming from the direction of fantasy-to-science-fiction (as opposed to the other way around). I'd make a comment about the kind of story we were telling, or the kind of style I was looking for, and the applicant would make some sort of comment to the effect of, "That's kind of like what Jordan did in *The Wheel of Time*," or, "I've seen that done well in *The Dragonriders of Pern*," and I'd think to myself, "Why is this person pulling examples from fantasy when we're doing a sci-fi story?" I'd dig deeper and find out that, all too often, the applicant hadn't read a great deal of what I would consider science fiction (Asimov, Heinlein, Niven, Card, Orwell). I remember vividly in 1997 when I was doing a fantasy N64 title (let me repeat that, a fantasy title), the author most often quoted to me as a "touchstone" was Jordan. Now, I don't mean to take anything away from Robert Jordan, rest his soul, but the point here is that many younger fans of genre fiction aren't very well read. I'm sure this would be different today since the *Lord of the Rings* (*LotR*) movies had yet to be released, but hardly anyone in that discussion had ever cracked open Tolkien. So I guess expecting younger readers to know the early greats in any of the genres might be too "old-fashioned" of me. But that didn't explain the ignorance of the distinction between fantasy and science fiction.

If you think about it, the two genres are often lumped together, as in "Science Fiction and Fantasy Writers of America." In fact, right now as I was writing this chapter, I Googled "famous science fiction authors," and the top hit was a list of mixed-genre authors (Heinlein, Hubbard, Orwell, Bradbury, King, Herbert, Card, Vonnegut, Adams, and Tolkien all graced the list; I wonder if all those were gathered at the same cocktail party they would have much in common to talk about; oh, wait, I'm sure that Vonnegut would). However, I believe they are often lumped together *not* because they are similar genres but rather that the audience who reads fantasy is very, very close, demographically, to the audience that reads science fiction. This leads to some people concluding these two genres are just "the same" in theme and structure but parade around wearing a different set of clothing. I believe this isn't true, and I set out to illustrate the differences in those two genres. I believe that not only are the underpinnings of the two genres very different indeed, but also the two are best suited for very different types of stories. And, if they are better suited for different types of stories, the genres are better suited as settings for very different types of games.

However, as I began to dig deeper into this idea, I became much more interested in *why* and *when* these two genres became intermingled. There was a singular watershed event and a particular singular piece of fictional invention where these two very different "streams" were crossed, and while not the intention of that particular author, caused the very problem I discuss herein.

In any event, my observation is that today's young writer tends, on average, to read much more fantasy than science fiction. The proof for this observation is in the marketplace. Fantasy outsells science fiction today by a fairly large margin. If you doubt this, there's an easy way to check my supposition: just wander down to your local bookstore and measure the shelf-inches devoted to fantasy and then measure the shelf-inches devoted to science fiction. Bookstores stock what sells.

It wasn't always this way. In fact, before J. R. R. Tolkien revolutionized the fantasy market in the drug-heavy 1960s, there were hardly any successful fantasy writers at all. I remember searching for these writers, because I was a voracious reader of fantasy in the early 1970s and I scoured the bookstores in the summers of 1973, 1974, and 1975. What I found were scant few, including: Michael Moorcock (most famous for the Elric series, but those were just one of his many Eternal Champion books), Fritz Leiber (inventor of the wonderful duo of Fafhrd and the Gray Mouser), Robert E. Howard (Conan, of course), and the master himself, Tolkien. These were wonderful writers all, and many of my fantasy-reading friends and I devoured every word. We would scour through bookstores together and recommend authors we found. But there wasn't much besides those noted above.

As an example, I vividly remember when Terry Brooks' *The Sword of Shannara* came out, because it was a *new fantasy novel*! Brooks' new work came out in 1977, and its success helped show publishers that fantasy was ready to become more mainstream. Let me just repeat that date: *The Sword of Shannara* was published in 1977. Remember that date, because it is an important year.

Science fiction had been successful for many years before 1977. It was (at that time) more deeply ingrained in the culture than fantasy. There had been successful sci-fi TV series and movies for over twenty years by 1977. *Forbidden Planet*, the film that gave birth to Robbie the Robot, came out in 1956. The original *The Day the Earth Stood Still* was released in 1951. *Flash Gordon* was a successful TV series in 1954. 1954!

Television just echoed the popularity of written sci-fi in fiction at that time. There were many successful sci-fi authors during what would later be called the "golden age" of sci-fi after World War II. Amazing writers such as Larry Niven, Jerry Pournelle, Isaac Asimov, Ray Bradbury, Robert Heinlein, Frank Herbert, Gene Roddenberry, James Blish, Arthur C. Clarke, Frederik Pohl, and Theodore Sturgeon all put pen to paper in that era. Philip K. Dick (*Blade Runner* and *Total Recall*) was writing during this pre-1977 period. *Star Trek* and *Lost in Space* were both on TV in the 1960s. Has there ever been a more influential genre intellectual property than *Star Trek*? Oh, yes, there has.

Man set foot on the moon in 1969, and *2001: A Space Odyssey* was released in 1968 and was a huge success. Science fiction was all the rage in popular culture during this time. People who consumed "genre fiction" consumed mainly science fiction, period. Fantasy was a "geeky" backwater. Fantasy did not appear on television. Fantasy did not appear in the movie theaters. Think about that a minute. No fantasy on TV, hardly any fantasy in the movies, hardly any fantasy in games.

In games, science fiction was well-represented by such titles as *Starforce: Alpha Centuri* and *Car Wars*. *Starforce*, published by Simulations Publications, Inc., known as SPI, was typical. Combat-oriented, strategic in scale, and hard-sci-fi in backdrop, *Starforce* and its spin-offs easily outsold a little-known fantasy game during this time period called *Dungeons & Dragons*. *D&D* became very well-known by 1977, when it split into *D&D* and *Advanced D&D*.

Fast forward to 2008. Newly published fantasy novels outnumber new science fiction books two-to-one. That doesn't take into account sci-fi books that are simply knockoffs of sci-fi movies (I mean, how many *Star Wars* stories can we read, now, anyway?). And, 20 years after the watershed of 1977, in the late 1990s along came *Harry Potter*. There has never been a sci-fi book with anywhere near the impact or success of Rowling's masterwork.

And, in games, there is *World of Warcraft*. 'Nuff said, there.

What happened that caused this sea change? What was this watershed event? Well, my friends, it was a movie released Memorial Day weekend in May of 1977. That movie was called *Star Wars*. I'll come back to why I believe *Star Wars* was such a success *and* why it muddied the water in terms of the sci-fi/fantasy gap in just a bit, but first I want to dig into the differences between fantasy and science fiction.

12.2   What Makes Sci-Fi and Fantasy Different

To reiterate, over the last 30 years, fantasy has overtaken sci-fi as the dominant form of genre fiction. Because of this "mushing," many people now confuse the unique elements of the two genres, and there aren't many who can articulate what makes sci-fi unique. To analyze these two genres, below I list a series of bullet points that summarize essential elements of each. These bullets are based on extensive experience (exceeding 25 years) writing fiction and creating games in each genre type. In addition to this personal experience, I also base my observations on interviews I have conducted with sci-fi authors and consumers and, last but not least, consuming these genres for going on 30 years.

What Is Fantasy?

- Fantasy's roots are in fairy tales. Fairy tales almost always take place in the reader's past, or a supposed "alternate" past. Think about the cliché beginning of a fairy tale: "Long ago in a land far, far away..." Notice the intentional "dreamlike" motif. This dreamlike state is crucial to fantasy.

- Childhood or children play an important part in fairy tales. Following this, many fantasy stories are "coming of age" stories, meaning a journey from childhood to adulthood. This journey may be physical, emotional, or, perhaps, metaphorical. For many of us, our personal ties to childhood are almost all laced with emotion (good or bad). This central use of emotion is a critical element in fantasy. The *Harry Potter* series sits squarely in this type of journey. So does *The Lord of the Rings*. In *LotR*, Frodo and, indeed, all of Middle Earth pass through and away from an age of innocence toward an "Age of Men" as they defeat their ultimate enemy. The Age of Men could be interpreted as an age of "duality" or "reality."

- Because they utilize a child-like motif, fantasy stories are often about the "self" (internal and/or emotional) facet of the main characters, especially the hero. These "self" stories also tend to focus on right-brain issues (self-fulfillment, emotional maturity, love). Many times these values are in conflict with the left-brain qualities. These stories are very, very personal. They are almost intimate in their focus.

- Fantasy often feels soft-edged in tone. The story settings themselves contain softer elements (clothing, colors, use of time and nature).

- Because of the central themes of growth, emotion, and overall softer tone, fantasy appeals heavily to women, and the female demographic is crucially important in fantasy MMOs (admittedly those games have a heavy social component, but even sci-fi MMOs don't have as large a female demographic as fantasy MMOs).

- Fantasy encourages "escapism." These are "fantasies," after all. These alternate worlds, often taking place in the past, which emphasize a dream-like quality, are "escapes" from *this* world and its concerns. This element of escape is crucial in fairy tales, mythology, and fantasy. There is an idea that a hero (or indeed the reader) journeys to this alternate place to learn a lesson about life and then returns to enlighten his community (or in the sense of the reader, himself). This is Joseph Campbell's hero's journey, which is a typical fantasy structure.

This would be a good time to mention very briefly Joseph Campbell's hero's journey. Simply put, Joseph Campbell researched thousands of myths and fairy tales of hundreds of world cultures and discovered that many of these stories had an identical structure. He theorized that these stories formed a "monomyth," meaning a myth that all mankind shared at a deep, perhaps even cellular level. This story structure had distinct phases, as follows: "The Ordinary World," "The Call to Adventure," "Refusal of the Call," "Meeting the Mentor," "Crossing the Threshold," "Tests, Allies, and Enemies," "Supreme Ordeal," "Revisiting the Mentor," "Return with New Knowledge," "Seizing the Prize," "Resurrection," and "Return with Elixir." We will re-address these points later in this chapter.

- In fantasy stories, good and evil are often simple and clearly drawn, and the divisions between them are obvious. White knights versus dark knights. This is in part related to the simplicity of the stories, but it is most assuredly part of their attraction, the conflicts of the world boiled down to their essence, so even a child can understand them. The complexities of day-to-day living are stripped away. The story takes place in an alternate locale where life is simpler.

- Because fantasies are appealing more to the emotional part of the brain than the analytical, they can successfully use our deeper yearnings, including the more primal urges. Fantasy settings are often used in "bodice ripper" stories and can succeed very well in those settings. This just echoes the genre's foundations in the emotional arenas.

- In fantasy, unusual events are explained by using "magic." This magic, whether actual, assumed, or psychological, has its roots in areas traditionally associated with the feminine: psyche, earth, and the elemental forces. One interesting thing: magic is often powered by an internal discipline or force (except, of course, when it is wild and uncontrollable). Both sides of this power source are very feminine in nature, relating to cycles in the feminine. The important point here is this: magic is personal and internal. Magic is "of" the person who wields it.

- Fantasy centers itself on the "why" of things. Motivations. Wants. Personalities. Forces in the fantasy world are rarely out of control, except as a result of emotions (jealousy, rage), meaning that the balance of the world setting is not out of whack unless some wizard or act of some specific person or personal act has set things off.

- Fantasy deals with "monsters." Rarely does the hero need to understand or deal with or communicate with these monsters, but rather they perform the role of gatekeepers or "tests" for the hero, battling him for some prize. While monsters such as dragons are usually portrayed as intelligent, the point of many fantasy stories is to battle these monsters rather than integrate the monsters into fantasy society.

What Is Science Fiction?

It has been said that the typical place to start a science fiction story is to take one natural law then break it, and then ask, "What if?" Faster-than-light (FTL) travel is a classic, oft-repeated example of such an approach, and many stories have been woven based on the idea of, "What if we could travel to the stars quickly in some fashion?" There is a comparison between this kind of "classic" sci-fi, which (interestingly enough), is called "hard" sci-fi, with what has been called "soft" sci-fi. Soft sci-fi is that which is not so fundamentally rooted in the science of it all, but drifts more towards themes and elements of the fantasy story. The *Dune* series of Frank Herbert is often classified as soft sci-fi because it takes place in a star-faring society but with themes that are very fantasy-like. Traditional sci-fi is rooted in the use or breaking of one of those natural laws.

- Sci-fi seems real. Here. Now. It could happen today or tomorrow. Think of the famous "War of the Worlds" broadcast by Orson Welles. On October 30, 1938, Orson Welles adapted the H. G. Wells sci-fi novel and delivered it as a "live" radio broadcast. The broadcast was delivered as if it were really happening that very evening. Even though the novel was decades old (Wells wrote it in 1898), people were taken in and thought the invasion was actually happening. Welles warned people that it was fiction but couched it in the vernacular of a radio news broadcast. Could that have ever happened with a supposed invasion of dragons or trolls?

- When science fiction stories aren't happening *now*, they tend to take place in the future, often using a "future" extrapolating one fundamental change to society. "In a post-nuclear holocaust world, one man takes it upon himself to re-start delivery of the mail," for example (*The Postman*, starring Kevin Costner). Famous sci-fi author Larry Niven made a career for himself by using this "what if" technique, such as: "What if organ transplant technology became perfected and the demand for organs far exceeded the supply? Would society begin to increase the crimes for which the death penalty was appropriate punishment in order to fuel the organ banks?" This question is at the heart of Niven's Gil Hamilton detective series. It is only very recently (in the last 15 years or so, after 1977) that science fiction has begun to delve into the recent past, as in the steampunk genre of stories.

- Science fiction explores the implication of technological change. William Gibson made himself famous by taking the basics of the Internet and extrapolating that technology into his "cyberpunk" series. Gibson even coined the term "cyberspace." One of the things that marked Gibson's work was his almost prophetic understanding of what "cyberspace" would do to entertainment. His vision was similar in this respect to Wells' vision for travel to the moon and outer space. Science fiction is marked by this prognostication into the future.

- Science fiction feels adult. The stories are often complex. Love isn't easy, emotions are conflicted, relationships are strained by the environment or society. *Logan's Run* is the story where overpopulation has caused society to adopt mass suicide at an early age. What is love like in that kind of society? This motif, where simple things are made more complex due to changes in society, are common.

- Sci-fi is male, hard, rough-edged, left-brain, analytical. The current hit TV series *Battlestar Galactica* is viewed as the perfect modern sci-fi. It uses a very limited and muted color palette, documentary-style camera work, and harsh lighting to emphasize the danger to humanity itself as a result of the Cylon War. Over the show's history, in fact, the story has morphed to move more and more squarely into sci-fi territory. The risk of human annihilation has subsided, and the show's writers now focus more on the question, "What does it mean to be human?" as they examine Cylon society. This is a riff on the way *Star Trek: The Next Generation* used the character Data as a foil. Data was an android, and he spent much of the show's seven seasons trying to prove or disprove that he was robot or human, and what it meant to be either.

- Good and evil are blurry concepts in sci-fi, and in fact, sci-fi often takes some liberties with those very concepts. What is evil and what is good are, in science fiction as in life, subject to interpretation and context.

- Science fiction is often about environmental (external) forces or how an individual reacts to an external force. In fact, often the antagonist is the environment itself. In the classic Larry Niven story "There is a Tide," an astronaut is sent on a mission to determine how a fellow astronaut explorer died. The explorer's ship is untouched, but the astronaut himself was ripped to shreds inside his ship. The explorer was in orbit around a neutron star, and the extreme tidal forces reached inside the ship and tore the explorer's body in half.

- Science fiction can often be emotionally cold and unforgiving. Whether this comes from the environment so often playing a role in sci-fi stories or the other way around, it is true. The emotion present in a fantasy story is replaced with deep-thinking analysis.

- In science fiction, there is often a scientific (or pseudo-scientific) explanation for events. All these events are perceived to be somewhat beyond the control of the protagonists, so there is a man-versus-environment feeling to the stories. In fact, in detective science fiction, the plot is often about the uncovering of that plausible explanation which roots the story.

- Philosophy is a viable topic in sci-fi. The stories may deal with the clash between, say, science and superstition, progress and the status quo. What *should* we do to solve our problems? Since sci-fi is often analytical, paths for all of us are presented, wrangled with, and argued over. Science fiction often posits to what may happen in the future, so at stake is nothing less than our future. "If we don't turn away, this is where we might end up." With our children's future up for grabs, the stakes are very high indeed, and arguments get heated. Fantasy, being the past, can certainly teach us lessons, lessons we might need to learn yet again, but those people in that fantasy story lived their lives; we have yet to live ours.

- While fantasy deals with, "What should I do?" science fiction worries about what should *we* (read here humankind) do?

- Science fiction often deals with the *many* as opposed to the *individual*. In Issac Asimov's *Foundation* trilogy, the story centers on mankind's advancements, extrapolating at great length on how mankind grows its galactic empire so large that we lose touch with our history. The scale of that story is humongous.

- Sci-fi worries about how things happen, rather than why. How does society go off the tracks when *Star Trek*–like teleportation actually works? In Larry Niven's *Known Space* series, he wrestles with this idea, positing that if the world were covered with teleportation booths, not only would you be able to commute anywhere you wanted (one obvious fallout), but when an interesting event was taking place, people from all over the world would instantaneously flock to that event, creating riots. That's science fiction at its best, extrapolating a societal change from a technological change.

- Science fiction, especially through the "robot" and "artificial intelligence" motifs, can neuter much of the potential for sexuality. Because in part futuristic worlds are portrayed as "without emotion" or "sterile," romance and sex don't work as well and appear more rarely. It is hard to be concerned about

your sex life when the environment itself is hostile and your very existence is
threatened.

- Science fiction uses aliens instead of monsters. However, these aliens are almost always intelligent and often technologically as advanced as us (if not
  more so), and communication/negotiation/integration is part and parcel of
  the story's main conflict. These aliens are often symbols or metaphors for aspects of the human psyche (Spock of *Star Trek* is a well-known example of this
  technique), and this allows the author to use the "alien" to help him examine our human foibles. In addition to this kind of use, aliens often become
  metaphors for our own human failures and successes in the area of race re-
  lations. Our own historical integration of foreign nationals is played out in
  the pages of the best science fiction. Again, *Star Trek* is a perfect example as
  in the series *Deep Space Nine*, where the Bajorans and their religious beliefs
  were not only deep, complex, and mysterious but related to the very nature
  of time and space. The Bajorans used the wormhole near the space station as
  a means of travel as well as a religious entity. This interweaving of science,
  philosophy, and human societal problems is very much the territory of science
  fiction.

While perhaps the root difference between sci-fi and fantasy is the left brian/right
brain or male/female dichotomies, as you can see by examining the list above, the
stories are very different. One could probably make an argument that while a similar
story could be told in either genre, the angle of attack (the *way* you would tell that
story) should be different depending on whether it is sci-fi or fantasy.

12.3 The Pivotal Role of *Star Wars* in This History

In May of 1977, George Lucas released *Star Wars*. According to Lucas, when he
was planning the script, he had become familiar with Joseph Campbell's work and
his hero's journey structure. Lucas wanted to tell a mythic tale, so he adapted the
structure for *Star Wars*. It has been argued that this use of a classic fairy-tale structure
is the very element of that story that made is resonate with the audience. I'm not
capable of authenticating that argument, certainly, but I do believe that this relatively
unique approach, marrying fantasy structure with a sci-fi setting, made *Star Wars* feel
familiar yet new at the same time. "A long time ago in a galaxy far, far away…" *is*
a fantasy-style introduction. I don't believe that Lucas fully expected to get quite the
bang for his buck with this choice that he did, but I do believe he knew what he was
doing to try and evoke that feeling in his audience. How far it would go, no one had
any idea.

If you take the structure of the hero's journey and map it to *Star Wars*, you get an
amazing one-to-one comparison. Let's take a look:

"The Ordinary World"	Luke and the moisture farm.
"The Call to Adventure"	Luke is invited by Leia to help her.
"Refusal of the Call"	Luke decides to stay instead of going.
"Meeting the Mentor"	Luke meets Obi-Wan.
"Crossing the Threshold"	Luke's aunt and uncle are killed, and he chooses to join the rebellion.
"Tests, Allies, and Enemies"	They meet Han, travel to Alderaan, it is destroyed, they are captured by the Death Star, they decide to rescue Leia.
"Supreme Ordeal"	They all almost die in the garbage disposal.
"Revisiting the Mentor"	Obi-Wan is killed but now can mentor Luke spiritually.
"Return with New Knowledge"	They bring Leia and the plans for the Death Star back to the rebels so they can destroy it.
"Seizing the Prize"	Luke decides to turn off the targeting computer, embracing Obi-Wan's advice to "trust the Force."
"Resurrection"	Luke is about to be killed by Darth, but just as Darth presses the trigger, he is blown out of the sky by Han. Luke then fires his torpedoes into the Death Star, destroying it.
"Return with Elixir"	They fly back, R2D2 is repaired, and they are heroes.

When he combined the mythological structure of Joseph Campbell's hero's journey with spaceships, aliens, and FTL travel, I'm sure Lucas didn't realize the seismic shift he was about to impart to genre writers. Many of the current generation of game writers hadn't even taken a breath before *Star Wars*. Think about what happened here: *Star Wars* uses Joseph Campbell's hero's journey beat-for-beat. This is, and has been for millennia, a fairy-tale structure. This is a structure that has been used for tens of thousands of years of human existence to deliver emotionally laden, journey-into-adulthood stories to clans, tribes, and (in recent centuries) children. This structure has been used to teach audiences about life and how to live it.

In *Star Wars*, Lucas delivered this message: you need to trust your instincts, your *emotional* truth, instead of technology (the "targeting computer"), and only by trusting these instincts will you become a powerful, actualized man. Is that the message of a fantasy story or a sci-fi story? I think this is, historically, the kind of story that has always been delivered in a fantasy setting.

But Lucas brilliantly set the cliché on its head by delivering that message in a setting with spaceships and blasters and androids.

This is why the modern writer gets the genres confused: because George Lucas changed all the rules. But sci-fi and fantasy still need to tell different stories in distinct ways. I just wish young writers would dig deeper and use something besides *Star Wars* as their inspirational wellspring. Perhaps this chapter will get them digging deeper.

13

Writing for Sandbox Games

Ahmad Saad

13.1 Introduction

So you're on a project with a huge team developing the next great game set in a sandbox environment. Sandbox games have great potential to be fun, but what is it that would make them so? What is a sandbox exactly, and how do you write for one? This chapter is meant to go through the basics of what is generally required to write a sandbox game. Keep in mind that this is introductory. The methods included are by no means the only ones that exist, but it should give you a good enough foundation for you to eventually do things your own way.

13.2 Defining the Genre

The Word "Sandbox"

Before jumping into how sandbox games are written, let's explore what the word "sandbox" actually means to us. Conceptually speaking, the word sandbox may conjure up the vision of that square box filled with sand at the local park. As children, the most fascinating thing about sand was its malleability. You can just dip your hands into it and, with a little water, begin shaping whatever comes to mind. The sudden removal of all barriers to sculpting any shape, or even the ability to destroy it, is what makes it so enthralling. You've got a toy that offers full freedom to your play.

The essence is the same when applying the word to a video game. Sandbox games need to offer players the same type of freedom of play. Certain sandbox games don't need to have objectives; *SimCity* is an example. The need for objectives arises when dramatic stories are included. With this insertion also comes the addition of directed motivation. Players suddenly perceive the game through their characters' points of view and are motivated to pursue their interests. Narrative in a sandbox game is basically, in the best case, a story that is shaped by what the player does. In the simplest case, a set story is told in a sandbox environment, where players have

137

complete freedom to alter their surroundings, yet the story still comes through and seems natural vis-a-vis the in-game situation.

13.3   Examples of Sandbox Games

Let's look at some of the past examples of sandbox games. Some of these games demonstrated the different directions a sandbox game can be taken. They are definitely recommended for study as the experiences they present are profoundly unique.

- **Ultima series.** A series of role-playing games originally developed by Origin Systems, Inc. between 1980 and 1999. This is one of the earliest iterations of an RPG played in a sandbox environment while holding firmly to a rich dialogue and storyline. The best example is Ultima VII, with its improved approach to dialogue and general interaction.

- **Grand Theft Auto.** Driving/action series of games developed by Rockstar from 1997 to present. *GTA* sticks to a more streamlined approach to sandbox gaming, yet story is still kept intact and emphasis is placed on action-based gameplay.

- **SimCity.** Developed by Maxis, first in 1989 and last in 2007 (*SimCity Societies*), this is a city-building simulation that gives free rein to players without worrying about plot at all. This type of title is often likened to a toy rather than a rule-based game and probably owes its success to that characteristic.

- **Other sandbox games.** *Baldur's Gate, Gothic, Oblivion, Assassin's Creed*, and *Saint's Row*.

13.4   Structuring a Narrative in a Sandbox Game

The prime difference between a sandbox story and a regular story is in the linearity. Sandbox games are non-linear. Missions usually can (and should) play independent of sequence, allowing the player to pick and choose the story thread he would like to pursue (yet still feeling natural). For the writer, this means a difference in structure, which needs to allow the player the sort of freedom a sandbox game usually demands. I'd really like to deal with some of the prevailing philosophies behind stories and non-linearity, but that is not the focus of this book. In this chapter, I hope to outline a method/process I've found useful in structuring such a story, which hopefully will lead to less confusion on prospective projects. For brevity's sake, we'll need to assume that you already know the basics of writing stories. I'm going to deal with just the aspects of sandbox games that have to do with writing.

Your Approach to Writing

So let's just jump right into things. Hopefully you've spent some time coming up with concepts and writing backstories and character profiles. Now you've got your plot, the entire story planned out on a very large napkin, and it's perfect. It's time to start writing the scenes for the sandbox game. This part depends on how you prefer to write your scripts. Some people like to plan out the number of scenes they'd like to have and write brief descriptions of the important actions contained therein. Others like to go straight to writing the script and see where that takes them. Whichever method you use, you can't reasonably begin making your story into a sandbox one unless you've either got the first draft of the script written or you've planned out the whole story and are confident you won't deviate from what's been prepared. You cannot begin to split the story thread without knowing where it's going to go. This can often produce quests that lead to nothing as the writer failed to factor in the production time constraints and never got to tie up these loose ends before the ship date. So, long story short, you need the whole before moving on to the parts.

In this chapter, I will use the process of visually flowing out stories to really illustrate what makes a game a sandbox one. I can't explain how important it is to visually flow out your story for your game. It'll be immensely useful for you as you continue to explore the various plots, as well as for the team, as members will be able to situate themselves within the project that much faster. In many cases, I've found that producers use it extensively to develop the project plan and assign tasks to everyone concerned. I'll explain how sandbox games differ in writing as we proceed with flowing out a sample game.

Blocking It Out

What you need to do is take your story ideas and start blocking them out into separate events. Chart out your main plot; you'll want to use software like Microsoft Visio or the like, whatever does the job. Be sure to accompany each of these blocks with a page describing what that event is about and what occurs in it. This is a detailed ver-

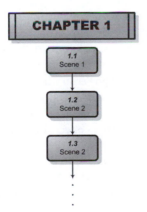

Figure 13.1. Example of a barebones story flowchart. Each block represents a scene that pushes the story forward.

sion of your plot skeleton; with this in hand, you can begin preliminary discussions with your leads or upper management about any changes deemed necessary.

Nothing different so far from ordinary writing, except what I'm trying to point out is that sometimes writers don't bother with producing actual charts. This may be fine in other games, but sandbox games can be huge, and having something everyone can refer to will save immense amounts of time. The manner in which you can access quests in sandbox games also demands a level of organization in the representation in order for things to go smoothly. You may not like doing it, but trust me, your team will thank you or it.

Sandbox Games Depend on Level Geometry

Before further defining the game story chart, there's another important thing to point out about sandbox games.

Since players have the ability to roam where they want in sandbox environments, you will need to make sure your story progression takes that into account. You'll want to distribute story elements as widely as possible in the game world, so the player has a chance to experience all the different areas. This comes with an obstacle, though; typically, game designers are going to lock out certain parts of the map for varying reasons, the least of which being that players may have too much freedom at the start to properly channel their concentration on the fun parts of the game. Find out what those reasons are and, more importantly, what these locations are and make sure that none of your story elements occur in places that are supposed to be locked at that point in the game. The last thing I'd suggest is to really study the map and know all the locations; try to tie each scene to the "sets" that will really produce the kind of emotions you're looking for. In many cases, the map itself can be a good source of ideas, so get your magnifying glass.

Story through Objectives

When looking at your story structure in a sandbox game, a good way can be to look at how it breaks down into objectives for the player. When thinking of the game from the player's point of view, it's important to understand that your primary motivation—what pulls you to action in any game—is completing all the objectives handed out to you. A game story is powerful when what concerns you as a player also concerns your character, so you need to blend your story with the type of missions that have been designed as much as possible, thereby ensuring that those objectives are interesting as well. Look for what concerns the character and what he is trying to accomplish throughout the story. If your story is centered around action, this action should be immediately transferable to the player, keeping his motivation constant and his play interesting and relevant. An objective can be as simple as "defeat your enemy," but the obstacles combined with dramatization will really make the experience a memorable one.

Therefore, what's important to understand in sandbox games is that the story or level architecture aren't really the vehicles to the gameplay—the players are. Players

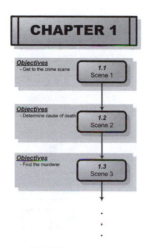

Figure 13.2. Example of clustering scenes within objectives.

must choose where to go and what to do, so it is up to them to keep things moving in a sandbox game. With that in mind, you must understand that the most important thing in driving sandbox games are the objectives given to the player. So, pace the game by outlining the objectives you're giving the player, and look at the level design as the "receptacle" of that objective.

Figure 13.2 is an example of clustering scenes within objectives.

Game designers and level designers will need to give their feedback at this point. It's important that these objectives turn out as strong motivators as well as drivers for gameplay. Make sure to integrate their suggestions into the story as best you can, but keep a tight leash on your plot just the same. This can be a tough situation. There have been many cases where writers and game/level designers weren't able to see eye to eye, so tread carefully. With objectives defined, level designers may now be able to start putting together ideas for what the player actually has to go through to complete these objectives. New ideas may crop up at this point, such as reversals to the objective. This is where some of the best ideas may come out, so be open to the collaborative process.

Fleshing Out the Story

It's now time to further flesh out the sandbox game. This part of the task requires identifying all the different elements involved in getting any of these scenes done. This is a tough part of the job. You may need to work with a game designer as you split up the elements into story and gameplay. I say "split" grudgingly, as the split shouldn't be identifiable to the player. The blending of story and gameplay together is always greater than the sum of the two.

Here are the different elements that you can further split your sandbox game into:

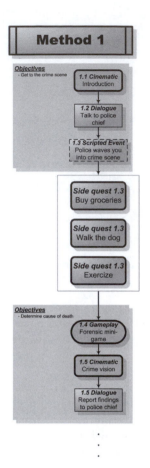

Figure 13.3. The flowchart from Figure 13.2 with further definition.

- Cinematic sequences.

- Dialogue.

- Scripted events (interactive).

- Gameplay sequences.

Figure 13.3 is the same flowchart as Figure 13.2 with further definition.

Plots and Subplots

Let's look at the story for a second without the added input of the player. We're all familiar with plots and subplots; today's movies or television shows usually sport the two in tandem. Simpler—though sometimes deeper—stories usually contain only a main plot, that being the situation the protagonist is trying to resolve. Some movies spend their entire length developing the main plot, while in others, and certainly in many of today's TV shows, a good portion is also spent developing the subplot. The same situation could be said to be true for video games as well. A sandbox game with no subplot is pretty much what we've been looking at so far. It allows players to explore the world at their leisure and choose when to launch the missions. Therefore, a sandbox story can certainly have only a main plot to deal with, but subplots can make it so much richer.

Subplots are useful in that they allow a further look into the story world by showing sides of certain characters or locales that we would otherwise not be able to see in the main plot. They certainly aid in immersing the viewer in the story world, and so too do they accomplish this even more so for video games. Although not required, it is certainly my suggestion that you add a subplot or two to your sandbox world, as the medium is certainly capable of supporting it. As a sandbox world allows players the ability to roam freely in an open environment, it is valuable to your game world's feel if all areas of this world are populated with story-related items to discover.

If you want subplots, think of the secondary characters you've already created and give them their own stories. For the Harry Potter series, J. K. Rowling spent a lot of time detailing out *all* of the characters she had in her world, even giving them their own histories and preoccupations that occurred during Harry's escapades—even though you never heard of them in the books. Think of the opportunities a sandbox game then presents, where the player is now free to choose where to go and actually see and deal with these characters a little more deeply.

Since in the main plot players are able to launch missions at their leisure, adding subplots can then translate into the option of taking on side objectives, or "side quests."

Sequencing Main Objectives and Side Objectives

Your story doesn't necessarily need to flow in a linear manner. Some objectives can be done in any order, but you need to pace the game with the main plot. When structuring story, a little dilemma with adding side quests is figuring out when to make them invalid. The only reason you would want to make them invalid is when the situation in the world has changed, such as the man you were meant to perform a quest for has become your enemy or has died because of a scene in the main storyline. To deal with this, some games "funnel" these side quests between spaces within the main storyline. Therefore, before going on with the main quest, you'll have your chance to do all the side quests you want. But going on with the main story nixes the leftover quests. Other games just keep all the side quests open all the time and won't include any of the characters from the main plot. Alternatively, some games will take stances in between the latter two. You can take whatever position you like;

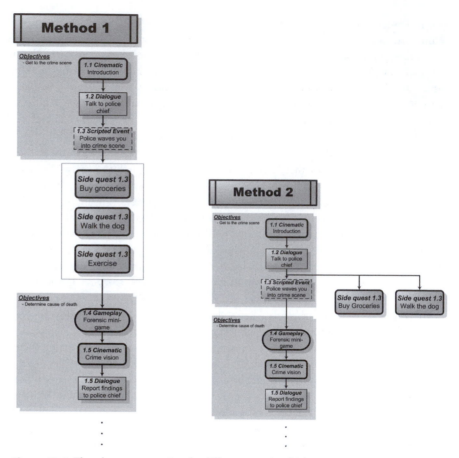

Figure 13.4. Flowcharts representing the different ways in which you can sequence your game.

just make sure you haven't created any situations where a player is tasked to find a certain character he'll never find since the plot saw him killed off already.

Whether you'll be required to conceive of these secondary objectives or not depends on the type of team you're working in. If you're the one doing it, though, remember when doing so that secondary quests are typically less important than main ones, so make sure to tone down the complexity of what you come up with so that all of it stays relatively implementable. No matter what the case is, you will still need to place them in the game vis-a-vis the story.

Figure 13.4 shows two ways you can represent the different methods to sequence your game, and Figure 13.5 shows a hybrid method.

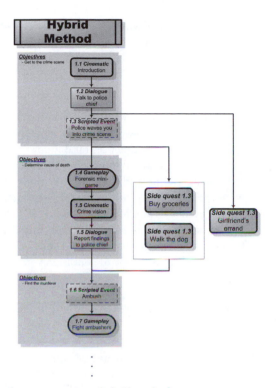

Figure 13.5. Flowchart representing a hybrid method you can use to sequence your game.

13.5 Elements That May Increase the Complexity of Your Sandbox Story

Dialogue Systems

Often, in a populated sandbox environment, players will have the desire to interact with the NPCs that surround them. Other than killing or molesting them, the next thing they'll want to do might be to actually speak to them. If this dialogue has choices within it, this presents a new level of complexity to your work. Not only do you have to write the script for your main story, but you'll also have to determine which characters the player can actually speak to, and if so, you'll also have to create "dialogue trees" for each case. This means you'll have to create different sets of options within the dialogue, and different responses for each choice given. Players will want their choices to actually make a difference, so you'll have to think pretty hard on this, and you'll also have to have a good way of keeping track of all this. Despite the effort, I think the rewards are worth it for the player. Just make sure to study the audience your game is meant for—trigger-happy players, for example, don't like to listen to too much dialogue.

The book *Game Writing: Narrative Skills for Videogames*, edited by Chris Bateman, goes into detail about how dialogue systems work. I highly recommend it as a resource if you plan to implement such a system into your sandbox game.

Consequences/Branching

This is similar to dialogue but on a more macro level. Certain games allow their missions to be open-ended, meaning they allow players to solve them in several different ways. This could also mean different consequences for different actions in a mission. Case in point: You're a cop sent to a classic hostage rescue scene. You can kill the criminal or sneak in and talk him out of it. Killing him effectively removes him from the rest of the game, while sparing him allows him to lend you a hand later on. This is a consequence, and it can even lead to a branching storyline. Consequences have to be kept in check, and the script has to take all the cases into account so that no one forgets to record the necessary dialogue or forgets to code the different cases. Neglecting this may cause plot holes in your game or confusion within the development team.

Things to Watch Out For

Improper Flow (Illogical, Not Dramatic, Too Dramatic)

Sometimes, when there's a multitude of quests and side quests, writers and designers lose sight of the actual flow of the story versus the gameplay. Some events may require a certain item, skill, or any other object that will allow access to further parts of the game, but due to improper sequencing, that item is not available when needed. Other problems could be having too many cinematic sequences versus gameplay, or the other way around. Properly charting out your game and keeping everything tangibly clear can remedy this.

Too Many Consequences

Each consequence you place into the game is something you need to keep track of, as anything unaccounted for could be a game-stopping bug later. If you're going to have consequences in your game, keep them at two to three, and try as much as possible to not make the story depend on them too much, thus making sure your story can continue whether or not there was a glitch.

Story Bogging Down Gameplay

Examples of this could be too much dialogue to go through, or cinematic sequences that are too long, or just too many interruptions on the way to some gameplay. If you're going to have narrative, try as much as possible to have it happen during gameplay, and in no way should it cloud any part of the action. *Bioshock* and *Call of Duty 4* are good examples of this.

Unclear Objectives (Non-Linearity Can Sometimes Lead to Confusing Objectives)

This can come in two forms. First, vague writing can cause players some confusion as to what they're supposed to do. Be very clear with your writing and state the objectives simply. Avoid using metaphors as much as possible, unless it's meant to be a puzzle. Second, as players travel around, they may get caught up with doing side quests for so long that they lose sight of what the main objective of the game is. You'll need to have the objective transmission system remind players, being careful not to annoy them in the process.

Improper Scheduling

All the loose elements in a sandbox game can be hard to keep track of. If you don't have all the elements of your story properly organized, you won't be in a good position to give good schedule estimates. Try using this method of charting out your story and, from there, document each element within it so you always know what is going on in the game. Be thorough with your documentation, thereby enabling you to be thorough with your scheduling.

13.6   Conclusion

I think that more games are going to incorporate sandbox elements into their design from now on. People naturally want to approach the game in their own way, and game structures will eventually have to expand enough to accommodate that. In five to ten years, we may find that the term "sandbox" is not used much to describe a whole genre of game, mostly because it will be more of a norm.

14

Writing for Alternate Reality Games

Wendy Despain

14.1   What's an Alternate Reality Game?

It's not easy describing alternate reality games (ARGs) to the uninitiated. The best way I've found is to explain how I ended up making my first ARG-ish thing and go on from there. So here's how I got into this crazy business.

In late 1996 I found myself in a phone conference with Majel Roddenberry and friends as she laid out the backstory for the science fiction television show they were putting together from some of her late husband Gene's notes. My job was to use the Internet to get this backstory across to fans and interested bystanders, starting almost a year before any video hit the TV screens.

I was baffled at first, but then she explained that the action in the show starts three years after benevolent aliens have made contact with Earth. After convincing the whole planet that they really do come in peace, a small group of humans working closely with the aliens start to suspect that not everything is as it seems.

So, if PR-conscious aliens really had made contact with us sometime around the late 1990s, it was obvious to me that they would put up a website. Everybody else was stumbling over themselves to put up websites for their company, their mother, their dog. If aliens wanted to get a message to the world about how great they were—and control that message—they would definitely have a website. I decided I was going to be their webmaster.

I worked up a site for them, a site for the suspicious humans, a site for the resident hacker who would appear in the show, and a more traditional website to answer questions about the television series.

The alien website featured news stories describing all the great things they had done for humanity. The resistance website asserted that each of these great achievements came with strings attached. The hacker was reluctant to take either side but linked to all these "fictional" websites and acted as a friendly face, someone the audience could relate to. In the beginning, none of the main content on the sites explained that this was part of a promotion for a television show. It simply existed—as if this alternate reality were just the way things are.

If readers took a minute to look closely at the websites, scroll down to the bottom of the page, examine the copyright notice and fine print, they would find clues. We even put the show logo at the bottom of each page linking back to the show's main website.

The sites changed over time—even before the show aired. We added a website for a malevolent mega-corporation (which put banner ads on the alien site) and more clues to the fact that life wasn't as rosy as the aliens claimed. Eventually, the resistance got more organized, and the aliens got more desperate with their PR. We introduced the main characters on the websites before the viewers met them on the show. The hacker joined the resistance.

But this narrative didn't play out separated from the audience. We invited them to "join" one side or the other and interacted with them via email and chat. They played along, with alien volunteers regularly ratting out the resistance fighters and vice versa. They enjoyed acting as if this alternate reality were real, hunting down the mysteries, solving riddles, and joining a vibrant community of like-minded players.

And that's the basic idea behind an alternate reality game. Another example of one of these proto-ARGs is *The Blair Witch Project*, from 1999. There were websites asserting the horror film was real footage produced by real kids out in the woods. Websites featuring the newly minted legend of the Blair Witch linked to websites for the small town where it all started, as well as personal blogs by characters in the movie.

The only element fully fleshed out from *The Blair Witch Project* and Gene Roddenberry's *Earth: Final Conflict* that is now integral to full-blown ARGs is organized "live" events, where players meet up in person to go on interacting as if this alternate reality were real.

The alternate reality game that really got the live element to work was known as *The Beast*, in 2001. It was a game tied to the Spielberg film *A.I.: Artificial Intelligence*, and it featured real-world Anti-Robot Militia rallies in New York, Chicago, and Los Angeles.

The next big ARG, which really solidified the player base and helped the genre gel, was known as *I Love Bees*, a game associated with the launch of the video game *Halo 2* in 2004. In this alternate reality, an artificial intelligence from the future made contact with humans via the payphone network. Players solved puzzles that would lead them to payphones in public places that would ring at a particular time—so people would gather in person near these phones at the appointed time and wait for that phone call where they could talk to—or hear a message from—this woman from the future. It was magical.

Alternate reality games done right allow players to tap into that feeling of "let's pretend" from when we were kids. No peripherals are required beyond players' imaginations and the tools they use every day in their real lives.

The Beast and *I Love Bees* fostered a community of players that has nurtured the genre and pushed forward the art form. Since then, there have been many other ARGs, and not all of them are marketing stunts for more traditional media. Some were purely fan-run for the love of it, such as *Lockjaw* and *Metacortechs*. Other pro efforts have been less marketing effort and more serious social commentary, such as *World Without Oil*, which took the "let's pretend" into an alternate reality facing the final oil crisis. The genre is so new, we're still exploring what the possibilities are.

Some might wonder what a chapter about alternate reality games is doing in a book about video games, but there is a method to the madness. One of the things that sets ARGs apart from street games and performance art is the use of the Internet to not just organize but also play parts of the game. So computers are an integral part of ARGs.

The Web is such a part of our everyday lives now; it's easy to use that malleable medium to tweak reality and create a play space existing right next to day-to-day living. There's no need to set everything else down and pick up a game controller or put on a costume. These games stretch across multiple touchpoints and allow for many points of entry—it could be a Google search phrase, or a phone number, or a snippet of graffiti, or a cocktail party. Clues to the puzzle you're working on may be hidden in TV commercials or films or newspaper classified ads. You can choose to dive in and evangelize your theory with the community, or sit quietly and watch as it all unfolds.

As a writer, ARGs are particularly interesting to me because the one thing that ties together these scattered pieces of gameplay is a cohesive narrative. The overarching story is the driving force, the way forward, and the foundation of trust for players. They need to know that the clues they're finding add up to a coherent solution. They need to know that someone is behind the scenes doing the care and feeding of this alternate reality. Seeing a narrative unfold builds that trust and allows them the freedom to inhabit this play space.

Which brings me to the nuts-and-bolts of how to write for an ARG.

14.2 This Is Not a Game

One of the driving principles behind the design and building of an ARG is known as "this is not a game" or TINAG (pronounced "tea-nag" by most). The basic idea is that everything in the game is presented as "real" and not as a game piece. There's no introduction saying, "If there were an email sent from this fictional character, it would read something like this..." Instead, players are just presented with the email itself—not an approximation of an email, not a summary, not a parody, not a playing card with a quote on it. It's just an email. This is not a game—this is an email this person wrote.

If there's a phone number mentioned in that email, it will function as promised when called. If it's incomplete, it's not because the game developers only wanted to give you the pertinent bits—it's because something mysterious has happened to this complete, real email and maybe you'd better find out what, because the most important bits may have been hidden. This is not a game.

In theory, this also means copyright notices should be attributed to fictional characters, no one involved in the making of the game should ever acknowledge their part in it, and no one should ever have to say, "Hey, come play my ARG!"

In practice, the TINAG principle needs to be modified a bit. It's not a good idea to attribute copyright to people who don't exist. It's not a good idea to lie to the police or your employer. It's not a good idea to keep all your hard work a secret. In fact, presenting people with an elegant "rabbit hole" (à la *Alice in Wonderland*) is one of the biggest challenges in the evolution of ARGs today. But that's a marketing problem, and this chapter is focused on the writing problems. So let's look at what TINAG means for writers.

- **You're not writing help text and barks.** Working as a writer in other game genres may mean you spend all day writing explanations for navigating the on-screen interface, or finding ten different ways of saying, "I've been hit!" When working on ARGs, you spend all day writing emails in the voice of a fictional character, or writing newspaper articles about events that never really happened, or making a corporate website for a company that only exists in your head. It's not just a tweak on writing for other game genres; you have to draw on an additional bag of tricks to get your work done. Which brings me to my next point.

- **You are writing in established forms.** While other game writers complain about having to reinvent their craft every time the designers come up with a new dialogue system, ARG writers can go buy a book about how to write a good business memo. They can take a class on how to write in newspaper style. They can convince a 13-year-old girl to let them read her diary, so they can see how it's done. ARG writers are usually using well-known styles of writing to build puzzle pieces.

- **You have to include clues in otherwise straight forms.** TINAG means you can't put your clues on the face of a deck of cards marked "Clue!" and breadcrumbs for players can't be enumerated in a quest log. They have to be worked subtly into blog posts and banner ads. If you're ham-handed about presenting clues to players, they'll doubt that your overarching story is well thought out and ultimately fun. This is a craft requiring clever writing and the ability to immerse yourself inside your character's minds while holding on to the larger plot points.

- **You have to write in exploratory ways, not just expository ways.** Resist the urge to force-feed the players! Don't give them everything on a silver platter. Make them work for their rewards. If you don't give them anything to do other than read, you're not writing a game of any kind, let alone an ARG.

Leave mysteries. Hint at things and leave the payoff till later. Clicking "next" barely qualifies as interaction. You can do better.

- **Let the players make real choices.** Don't be afraid to use things like branching narrative and user-created content. As a player, it's nice enough to unlock puzzles leading to the next segment of an established narrative, but it's magical to be involved in the shaping of the narrative. Let the players influence who wins and how. Let them participate in the story as integrated characters and not passive audience members. This includes letting them tattle on each other and spy for the bad guys. Embrace that in your roller coaster ride and let their actions have real consequences. Other chapters in this book talk about different ways of planning for interaction in a narrative. Use these tools to plan ahead and let the players have some power. It can be done without blowing up the big-picture plan.

14.3   Evolving Narrative Over Time

One thing I've heard from every ARG developer I've talked to is a reference to the military maxim that battle plans never survive the first encounter with the enemy. Months and months of planning ahead of the launch of an ARG often fall apart when players take routes through the game that were never anticipated. This can have miserable results for both developers and players. However, there are strategies that can mitigate the damage.

- **Build a big-picture plan.** The only way to handle a narrative that evolves and changes before it's finished is to have a big, overarching plan. Things won't go well if you just do the initial setup for the story then wait to see what happens. You'll find yourself needing to generate entire websites literally overnight, and can you be sure you can do that in a believable, quality way? More than once? If you have a general idea of where you're headed in the end, you can manage individual battles in such a way that you still end up going somewhere fun. I usually start my big-picture plan by laying out two plot points—the beginning and the end(s). If I clearly write these out for myself and the rest of the team, we'll all be less likely to get lost. Then I connect those dots with major plot points or event nodes (more on that later) so the path from point A to point B is clear to the dev team, although it should be mysterious to the players at the beginning of the game. Your starting point needs to have several elements that are painfully unresolved so there's somewhere for your plot to go. Players want to feel this forward motion in the story. It helps them trust that the developers will entertain them in some way. It can also help convince the people paying for this game that they're getting their money's worth. For a sample of the way I do my big-picture plans, see Appendix D for a high-level sketch of the plan for an unproduced game called *Starfall*.

- **Great narratives have a beginning, middle, and end.** So should your ARG. The difference is that you should consider—and prepare for—one beginning, a few different middles, and several endings. Then don't freak out when the players figure out how to go forward in a way you didn't anticipate. If you have an overarching plan, if you know where the whole thing is headed in general, you can edit and adjust pre-prepped text to fit the new direction. This is a much more manageable task than generating entirely new, quality text in a time crunch.

- **The players are not your enemy.** But sometimes it will feel that way. There's a distinct danger of falling into the idea that the players are out to get you, coming after every little bit of you, trying to suck you dry. But these are the people you made the game for! This is who it's all about. So don't get trapped into hating them. There are a few strategies for managing this problem:

  - **Embrace the opportunity for drama.** Drama is all about conflict, and if you're feeling like you're in conflict with your players, go ahead and use that to create more drama. Just make sure you don't lose track of the ultimate goal. In this case, "winning" means achieving your established goals for the game, and one of those rarely includes chasing away all your players. Consider getting the players to compete against each other instead of just against you, but also be careful about setting up appropriate ways of being in conflict with other players. Safety of your players is also a priority.

  - **Dodge and weave.** Use the adrenaline to motivate great work. If you're really angry at a player for doing something unexpected or just plain mean-spirited, use that emotion to write the angry memo from the fictional boss that gets distributed tomorrow. Don't write an angry email out of character to the player. Also consider ways to take the players off-guard. If they're being antagonistic, consider responding with compassion and pacifism. It's unexpected and could provide a pleasant surprise for your players.

  - **Take a step back.** Yes, I just hit the TINAG principle pretty hard, but sometimes you need to take a step back and remember that this really is just a game. It's not worth getting an ulcer over.

- **Use "event nodes" with branching possibilities.** When you've laid out your big-picture plan, identify which events are set in stone and which ones are flexible or optional. Consider opening or closing "acts" of your narrative with an event the players have no control over—if there's going to be an earthquake, there's going to be an earthquake, no matter where in your fictional city the players have chosen to put your fictional characters. These solid "event nodes" happen at specified times and aren't dictated by the players, although the players may have an impact on the consequences of these event nodes. If the characters have been chased into the city park through player actions, they survive the earthquake. Still in the apartment? Sorry, that character just died.

- **Make sure every battle you fight is gaining the right ground.** Keeping this strategy in mind, you need to make sure that each "act" in the narrative is headed in the right direction. Don't get too bogged down in side skirmishes. These can be fun sometimes, but they're rarely going to be more exciting for players than the original narrative you planned. It's really hard to do foreshadowing for a story headed off into the unknown.

- **Manage player expectations.** Good narrative takes time. Consider rationing new content on a regular basis—once a week or twice a week or once a month. Don't plan to be "on stage" every day, 24 hours a day. Allow yourself the time to produce quality.

- **Stay organized.** Know exactly what content goes where when an event node is reached. Keep a spreadsheet or a whiteboard sketch and name your files in ways that make sense. (But be careful about where you store those materials. Players have been known to hack websites and find future materials using your helpful file-naming conventions.)

- **Communicate with your team and trust them.** I know some people have tried to do ARGs entirely as a one-man-band, but I don't recommend it. Constructing an alternate reality is a big job, and delegation can make everything better. However, it's essential to keep all of the team in the loop about what you're thinking and planning. Others will be able to contribute good ideas, but only if you include them in the scheming. Communication with the team is even more vital when you're dealing with live interaction with the players. Actors need to be prepped with as much information as you can possibly give them about the part they're about to play and the rules of the alternate reality they're in. Who are the bad guys? Who are the good guys? What side are you on? They need to know everything you can get across in short synopses. They don't have the time for a ten-page treatise on the childhood problems your villain went through. But they do need to know about his ultimate goals, his allies, and his recent victims. When at all possible, use actors who are comfortable with improv and have more than one conversation with them about their role. Take time to practice, and communicate with the whole team about how that actor fits.

14.4   Writing Live—Working without a Net

When I say "writing live," I mean writing when there's no opportunity to edit your work. No opportunity at all. Your first draft goes live as soon as you type it. Some people are natural geniuses and never need to do a second draft. Most people aren't. If you have a good editor, or learn how to edit yourself well, you can greatly improve the quality of writing you put out. This is why you need to prepare as much material up front as you can. It gives you a chance to catch contradictions, improve voice and style, and strengthen connections and clues.

However, there are some cases in ARGs where everything is moving so fast there's no alternative but to write live. In particular, there are chat rooms, busy message boards, and helping out actors who are "on stage" and need help with a line. In these cases, you can't prepare everything up front, but you can do some things ahead of time to make the job less crazymaking.

- **Writing in chat rooms.** The anonymity of Internet chat rooms provides the opportunity for any writer to play the part of any of their characters. It doesn't matter that I'm a 30-something white woman. In an Internet chat room I can be a child, a man, even an alien. I can even be these things more or less simultaneously, having conversations among characters. It takes some practice—and I do recommend practicing this kind of stunt before trying it out on your actual audience—but a writer who really knows their characters should be able to chat for them pretty convincingly. Here are some tips for making it work:

  - **Post your "talking points" above your monitor.** Remember that this is just another scene in your narrative, and every scene needs a purpose and direction. Some of the chatting is there for the pure fun of it, but the fun runs dry if there's no new clue or information conveyed to the audience through this interaction. But it's easy to get sidetracked, so taping a notecard with talking points to the top of your monitor can help you remember to work those all-important clues into your conversation.

  - **Remember to stay in character no matter what.** It's tempting to try chatting in the public chat room in one character voice and at the same time send private messages in your own voice to friends who know your real identity. Resist that urge. If you're sitting in front of an open chat or instant message window, communicating as a particular fictional character, be entirely in that character's shoes. It's far too easy to literally send the wrong message. So if someone tries communicating with you out of character, put off the conversation and do so in the voice of the character you're portraying. You're not being cute; you're preserving your sanity and the quality of the experience for the entire audience.

  - **Consider using multiple machines with character photos attached.** I've never had a large enough team to indulge in letting one writer portray only one character when writing live. It may seem like overkill, but I find it really useful to use different computers when playing multiple parts simultaneously. So when you're sitting at your desktop you're writing for the aliens, and when you're using the laptop it's the head of the resistance fighters. I tape a character photo to the monitors to help reinforce this mental shift between people.

- **Writing in busy message board environments.** Internet forums and message boards are supposed to move a lot slower than chat rooms, but when a large enough number of people are participating in a forum, and the tempers are riding high, ten new messages can be posted while you're writing one. This can get the adrenaline pumping if you're trying to steer or control the momentum and write in a particular character's voice. I use a lot of the tricks mentioned above, but specifically for message board interactions, I also use these rules of thumb:

  - **Use the "quote" function.** Always include at least a snippet of the message you're responding to. When lots of people are posting at the same time, your message may show up in a completely different order than you anticipated. Imagine simply posting, "Yes, exactly!" in response to one player's post, only to discover that while you were typing some other player posted a completely different theory, and your affirmation shows up after that one instead of the correct one. This is easily avoided by using the "quote" function in the forum interface.

  - **Take a step back when you need to.** Sometimes the online community will suck you in to posting to message boards when you've had no sleep for 24 hours, or when you're burned out on a particular character. Live interaction with your players can be intoxicating, but you know what they say about emailing drunk. When you've gone past your limits, the wiser course is usually to step away from the computer and go do something outside for a while. Get something to eat. Connect with friends and family. The alternate reality you've built won't self-destruct entirely if you step away for a few hours. It may feel that way, but really it won't. No matter what the community does while you're gone, you can always fix it. You're the one in charge of this reality after all. And sometimes the players will surprise you; give them a chance and they might take the story to exactly the right place—or a better one than you planned—if you just let them do their thing without meddling.

  - **Know when to ignore.** For every Internet forum there are trolls. For every chat room there are 12-year-old boys who think it's funny to say bad words and get people angry. There are often people who think it's fun to play ARGs by waging a campaign to convince the entire audience one at a time that this whole thing is a fraudulent trick. The best way to deal with all of these people is to ignore them. You don't have to answer every post. You don't have to respond to every leading question. Sometimes it's best to just pretend they're not even there.

- Writing for actors who are "on stage" and need a hand with improv. Any time interaction with the players goes beyond text, the writer can't also be the actor. You can write scripts and talking points and prep the actor all you want, but there will be times when the actors are in the middle of improvising their part and find themselves at a loss for words. The writer can jump in and save the day here, but once again it requires some preparation.

  – Establish a method before you begin. Talk to the actors about ways to work together while they're on stage (on the phone, behind a bar at a party, etc.). This will probably be a new experience for the actor, too, and you want to make sure your live writing will be seen as a help and not additional pressure to get things absolutely right.

  – Don't rely on hand signals. It's fine to have a hand signal so the actor can indicate she's in trouble and could use a line, but don't rely on hand signals to convey the line you want her to use next. Even if you think your hand signals are completely clear, a flustered actor may not have any idea what all the twitching is about. You're a writer. Write. Don't just try to motion to her to cut it short. She might think you mean she should feign death. And even if both you and the actor are fluent in sign language, don't use it in public places. It will be just your luck to have players watching who also know sign language and will catch you manipulating events.

  – Pass notes whenever possible. Pull out a pen and write down exactly the line you want the actor to use. Don't include commentary like, "Say this..." Simply write down the line and use ALL CAPS. Seriously. It's much easier to read quickly and requires less squinting. Just make sure the actors are aware of how this is all going to work before you hand them a note that says, "RUN AWAY!"

14.5   If the Writer Ain't Having Fun, Ain't Nobody Having Fun

This phrase is usually about moms and happiness, but I've found it holds true for writers and fun in ARGs. Writers are sometimes the same person as the designer and producer for an ARG, but in my experience when those roles are separated out, the responsibility still falls to the writer to keep up the fun. A miserable, grumpy writer churns out miserable, broken prose if he produces anything at all. This makes the designer and producer and actors—the entire development team—miserable and worried. A cheerful, enthusiastic writer produces consistently quality work and the occasional gem. This makes everyone else on the ARG dev team excited about the project and eager to see how everything turns out.

And it's even bigger than the internal team. When you're turning out good material, the players are happier too, and everything feeds on the momentum. If the writer is having fun with the game, the game is more fun. So, how do you keep your ARG from killing you? These things work for me:

- **Make sure you're comfortable with the scope and reach of your material.** If the plan calls for writing a ton of fake press releases, and you just hate writing press releases (like I do), reach out and get some help from someone who is more comfortable in that medium. Every writer has strengths and weaknesses. If you're aware of your own weaknesses and can set yourself up for playing to your strengths, you'll have a lot more fun and produce better work. Don't be afraid to admit that you're just not that great at writing X kind of material. Also be aware that creating an entirely alternate reality can require the generation of a great deal of content, and there's never enough time. If you don't confine the scope of the project, you'll be bled dry before it's half over. Make a point of figuring out what content is really important and focus on the essentials for the game to be fun. Sure it would be nice to have a blog for the nephew mentioned in the main character's emails, but if he's not going to play an important part in the plot and gameplay, just say no—and consider cutting the mention of him in the emails, as extraneous details can kill you when players are combing your materials for clues.

- **Give an in-character reason when you need to take a break. Remember, TINAG.** An ARG schedule can be grueling, and if you need to take a break to maintain your sanity or get a root canal, build in a reasonable reason for the writing to go on hold for a while. Don't cop out and just say, "We're pausing the game for two weeks." Make your main character's in-laws show up for an unannounced visit. Break his CB radio. Make the time machine malfunction and send him to an ice age for a week. The players will appreciate the maintenance of the alternate reality and be more forgiving when you return refreshed and ready to have fun again.

- **Get another set of eyes on your work when possible.** It can be very lonely to be writing these materials for a wacky, twisted world. Have your teammates read over your work whenever possible. Get feedback. Make sure you have someone on the team who will shout down your internal critic and keep you going.

- **Don't neglect your timeline and organizational materials.** Once the doors open and the players come in, things can get hectic pretty fast. The big spreadsheet on the wall can quickly get out of date, and all that careful preparation can get jumbled. Build time into your daily schedule to organize yourself and update your big-picture plan. It will help you remember that you're the one creating this alternate reality, you're not just its slave.

- **Enjoy the ride!** You'll hear novelists talk about how their characters take over and drive the story places they never imagined when they sat down to write their magnum opus. The more alive your characters are, the more they'll surprise and delight you. This is part of what makes writing such an intoxicating profession. Don't forget this element of magic when you make your story interactive and allow real people to put their hand to the plot. It's amazing when a character you made up presents you with a new solution to the problem you've set them. Accept the input of players the same way—as gifts to your communal experience of creation. This can be way more fun than writing a novel if you accept what this alternate reality gives you.

14.6 Conclusion

In the end, one of the most helpful principles I've found while writing for ARGs is the acting improv notion of "Yes, and..." I put this phrase up on the wall by my desk when I start working in an alternate reality. The idea is that all the actors on stage improvising together accept what their partners present and elaborate or improve on it. They don't shut them down or mock their efforts. You're on stage with someone who just claimed he's an elephant? Well, you have two options.

1. **You can say, "No you're not. You're a journalist."** This will kill your performance, I promise. It saps your partner's confidence and breaks the collaboration between you. Suddenly one person is in charge, and the other is at their mercy. This isn't fun to watch or participate in. Saying no is deadly.

2. **You can say, "Yes, and I'm a panda bear."** This reinforces your partner's confidence and demonstrates your willingness to contribute and collaborate. It may take you unexpected places, and be way different from what you had planned, but it's guaranteed to be more fun than the alternative.

Alternate reality games are a hot topic. Some people are always saying they're just a passing fad. Other people think they're great but that nobody is doing them "right." Emotions often run high, and we can't even seem to agree on what an ARG is and what it isn't.

In my opinion, alternate reality games are the emerging native form of entertainment for the Internet. Sure, video games can be played on websites, novels can be posted one chapter at a time, movies can be downloaded. But ARGs are something more—greater than the sum of their parts—using all the elements of the Internet age to create a completely new entertainment experience. I have loved watching them develop and being a part of that development—both as a creator and a player.

15

Writing for Serious Games

Sande Chen and Anne Toole

15.1 Introduction

Through Writers Cabal, we have been fortunate enough to participate in projects that fall into the category of serious games. While serious games do not get as much attention as flashy, next-gen titles, they have the potential to integrate video game playing into every facet of society. From university students to health professionals to corporate CEOs to activists, all may use serious games to improve education and productivity or to encourage societal change.

Serious games are meant to have real-life impact. For this reason, writing for serious games can be a rewarding experience.

Our purpose here is not to explain serious games or their markets in depth. If you are interested in learning more about these aspects of serious games, we encourage you to read the book *Serious Games: Games That Educate, Train, and Inform*, by David Michael and Sande Chen.

In this chapter, we will explain briefly what we mean by the term "serious games," and we will discuss the challenges involved in writing for serious games. We conclude with a case study involving our experiences working on Futur-E-Scape's educational massively multiplayer online game (MMOG), *Physics Adventures in Space-Time*, or *PAST*.

15.2 Introduction to Serious Games

While many serious games are simulations, serious games can be of any game genre or hybrid and on any subject. Therefore, all the skills described in the other chapters pertain to serious games. Additionally, serious games may require skills that are pedagogical, instructional, and/or artistic in nature.

What are Serious Games?

Serious games are games that do not have entertainment as a primary purpose. More traditional games repurposed for a serious aim also fall into this category. This serious goal does not mean that the games themselves are dull or serious. On the contrary, entertainment in serious games strongly motivates audiences to learn the topics in the games.

Furthermore, the philosophy behind serious games is to go beyond the shallowness of previous offerings referred to as "edutainment" and instead fully use the medium of interactive games to get players to understand dynamics and relationships.

As such, serious games can be as complex as any hardcore game and even wear the trappings of a fictional context. Whether the serious game is an *Unreal* mod meant to teach Arabic like *Tactical Iraqi* or a training simulation designed to help retail sales representatives, game writers can help make these scenarios more entertaining and compelling.

However, writers should never forget that these are not solely entertainment products. Entertainment must never sublimate the software's primary purpose. If the project management program about aliens in outer space does not help managers become more efficient and productive, then the serious game has failed its "serious" mission.

Who Uses Serious Games?

Several groups are interested in using serious games. An educator may use Muzzy Lane's strategy game *Making History*, which is designed to help high school students understand the causes of WWI. Educators see these games as an opportunity to reach students who learn by doing rather than by reading or listening. Furthermore, the educator desires students to gain a deeper understanding of world history by experiencing the dynamics of world politics. Indeed, one lofty goal of serious games is to revolutionize education in the classroom.

Other organizations, like the military and corporations, are also putting games to good use. Serious games have been used to train doctors, fast-food preparers, and derivatives traders. In the health-care arena, diabetics have been taught to manage self-care, and all sorts of exercise games have been embraced by the public. Religious and protest groups have used games to promote their viewpoints. In addition, new media artists have used games to further artistic expression in multimedia installations.

Serious game developers tend to use whatever game genre best fits the serious game's purpose. *Re-Mission*, HopeLab's game about cancer recovery, is a shooter, while *Peacemaker*, Impact Games' exploration of the Israeli-Palestinian conflict, is a strategy game.

15.3 Serious Games Challenges

Faced with such disparate markets and formats as the ones described above, game writers may find writing for serious games a challenge. However, some commonalities exist across all serious games. Typically, the client will not be a game developer or publisher, and the players will not be hardcore gamers. Furthermore, because of the nature of serious games, a writer may need to interact with subject matter experts who may never have played video games before.

Different Clients, Different Expectations

For years, corporate trainers, e-learning specialists, and instructional designers have penned scenarios and synopses without regard to entertainment. It may be hard to convince clients that a game writer is actually needed. They're reluctant. Will a game writer turn their inoffensive software into a *Grand Theft Auto* clone?

On the opposite extreme, there are those clients who are already gung-ho about video games. They believe that video games will give their projects added pizzazz. They nurse a game writer within. They have lots of ideas of where the story will go, how the game will be, and how it should be written. They, in fact, would not mind writing the whole game themselves if only they knew how to start.

In both of the above cases, the clients are not knowledgeable about the game development process. They may not understand why their serious game does not play like the latest console blockbuster. While it may require more handholding, a game writer benefits in the long run by educating clients about the writer's role in game development. Communication ensures that both sides understand the requirements.

In the first scenario, the game writer could address the reluctant client's concerns by demonstrating an understanding of instructional design or a willingness to work with an instructional designer. In the second scenario, the game writer needs to establish boundaries while still taking into consideration the client's ideas.

The best circumstance for a writer is to be hired by a serious game developer, who then develops the game funded by the non-profit, corporation, or government agency. However, in some cases, a writer is hired directly by those organizations to improve a product. Some organizations have been using serious games for years and thus may be savvy about the process.

Different Audiences, Different Expectations

All games have a target audience. For instance, a game could have a target audience of men ages 15–35, or women ages 25–45. A Nintendo DS game could be targeted to attract tween girls. Serious games encompass these audiences and more, such as the category of products known as "lapware" that targets infants and toddlers small enough to be snuggled in their parents' laps. Furthermore, serious games could be targeted toward specific groups: domestic violence survivors, leukemia patients, resistance groups, political volunteers, and so forth.

While game writers may be familiar with writing for children's products, they may have never written for software targeting non-verbal infants and toddlers. This situation explains why working with a subject matter expert may be a common experience in serious games. In this example, the subject matter expert may be one well-versed in educational psychology or development. If a subject matter expert is not available, then it behooves the writer to thoroughly research the related subject, similar to what a writer would be doing for any writing gig.

If a subject matter expert is not available, reach out to friends and acquaintances with relevant experience. They may give insights. Or take a field trip and really learn about the audience or the subject matter. Writing for people who live in nursing homes? Go visit them. Writing for a game to help oppressed people? Go see a related non-profit for information. Serious games allow for real connections with people and subject matter. After all, one of these games could end up changing a person's life.

In addition to the developer and subject matter expert, the audience may have little knowledge of video games. In this way, writing for serious games may have similarities to writing for casual games. There's no expectation that the audience would be familiar with video game conventions. In fact, it might be best just to assume the audience knows nothing about video games.

Working with Subject Matter Experts

As mentioned previously, working in serious games will generally mean some kind of interaction with subject matter experts. Serious games are often factual, and even those serious games using fiction are based on facts. Games that are mission-critical—a surgery simulator, perhaps—need to be checked and rechecked for factual basis. The importance of facts or proper methodology cannot be overemphasized.

While it is obvious that teaching doctors the wrong way to go about surgery is not a good idea, there are others that may be less obvious. Take a roller coaster simulation. It's a fun activity in *RollerCoaster Tycoon*, but in real life, operating a roller coaster incorrectly could lead to a tragic loss of life. Programs on firefighting, homeland security, gun safety, air traffic control, disaster recovery, and chemical plant management are just a few examples of how proper training protocols could turn a life-or-death situation into a more favorable one. Writing for serious games can be a very serious task indeed.

In these situations, developers use the catchword "engagement" rather than "fun." Engagement suggests interest without inappropriate hilarity. Keep in mind that engagement does not require a writer to keep the game's tone entirely serious. Humor is always appreciated as long as it's not offensive or culturally insensitive.

The amount of interaction with subject matter experts will differ from project to project. In some cases, the expert will work closely with the writer. In other cases, the writer is handed text to read and translate into fun, entertaining gameplay or dialogue. This is not altogether different from situations where writers are looking at storylines in programmer-ese, except that the subject matter expert has no inclination to create a storyline. The subject matter expert's responsibility is to make sure the writer understands what learning objectives are needed in the story and dialogue.

Here is an example of some dry, textbook language you might receive:

Dynamics

A massive object will not have a change in velocity (v) unless acted upon by a net Force (F).

Every force (F1) has an opposite twin force (-F2).

Acceleration (a) is equal to net Force (F) divided by (m).

Velocity (v) is equal to net Momentum (P) divided by (m).

Position (x) is equal to net Work (W) divided by net Force (F).

Conservation Laws: Mass, Energy, Momentum.

As an exercise, you may want to translate this language into entertaining dialogue between two opposed characters.

In most cases, the expert's work is simply presented as information for the writer to know and absorb, not as something to be translated directly into fun dialogue. More often than not, the subject matter expert will be thrilled to provide resources for study, so be prepared to sort through a deluge of information. It will be the writer's job to figure out how and when to weave that information into dialogue or storyline.

When there is limited interaction with the subject matter expert, the writer will have to do research on the side. When there is a lot of interaction, the writer is blessed with a fact checker but will have to decide based on the learning objectives and fun factor how much of this information will end up in the game.

Translating Facts into Fun

As any writer knows, good fiction has a basis in facts. Well-researched facts add to the believability of the scenario, setting, and/or characters. Some authors even pay research assistants to gather this information. When working in serious games, writers have the unique opportunity to work with subject matter experts who may have spent years studying the subject matter.

As was mentioned before, subject matter experts are willing to share their knowledge but are not obligated to create a storyline for the game. That's the writer's job. With direct access to a subject matter expert, a writer should not be afraid to use that expertise. In order to write factual dialogue or a story based on facts, the writer needs to constantly check with the subject matter expert. This is of utmost importance since the serious game will not be judged by game reviewers but by other experts in that field. So, if the writer includes a far-fetched plotline or inaccurate speech patterns in the serious game, it calls into question the validity of the entire game.

When the writer has no access to a subject matter expert for questioning, the writer needs to do additional research to supplement the writing. For example, when working on Legacy Interactive's veterinary simulation *Pet Pals: New Leash on Life*,

Writers Cabal looked up animal rescue stories as well as specifics on animal diseases to supplement the veterinary notes provided by Legacy Interactive.

Example Veterinary Notes Provided for *Pet Pals: New Leash on Life*

Metabolic Bone Disorder is caused by a calcium deficiency. This can be caused by the iguana not getting enough dietary calcium or by factors that cause the iguana to lose the ability to use the calcium that it eats. When the body does not get enough calcium, it takes calcium from the bones causing them to become thin, soft and easy to break. In advanced stages, fibrous tissue will become deposited in weaker bone areas causing deformations. It is important to make sure that an iguana has sufficient UV light, heat and the right balance of dietary calcium and phosphorus to prevent this debilitating disorder.

Dialogue from *Pet Pals: New Leash on Life* Based on Veterinary Notes

Head Vet: Princess contracted a Metabolic Bone Disorder due to a calcium deficiency. Most likely, her illegal breeder didn't feed her enough dietary calcium, so her body took calcium from her bones, making them thin, soft and easy to break. Her bones could have become deformed and she might have died from malnutrition. An iguana needs sufficient UV light and heat as well as the right balance of dietary calcium and phosphorus to thrive. The calcium and fluids you gave her set her on the right path.

As can be seen from the examples in the boxes, translating facts into dialogue can be quite straightforward. With storylines, the process is more complex due to adherence to learning objectives. The following case study illuminates some of the challenges.

15.4   Case Study: *Physics Adventures in Space-Time* (*PAST*)

Introduction

Founded by Dr. Ricardo Rademacher, Futur-E-Scape's goal is to further science education by combining pedagogy with a massively mulitplayer online role-playing game (MMORPG) so that players can experience science firsthand in the virtual world. An avid MMO gamer and physics professor, Dr. Rademacher quickly realized that many physics assignments could be mapped directly to activities in MMORPGs. A group lab assignment could translate into a quest fulfilled by a party. A multiple-choice question could also be incorporated into a quest. Furthermore, a student's avatar could show visible signs of achievement through different clothing and items. Intrigued by this idea, Dr. Rademacher soon obtained government grants so that he could start building the *PAST* game world.

However, it was not until his experience as an unofficial consultant on *Stargate Worlds* that he began to appreciate how a good story would engage students and thus provide a "hook" for the presentation of physics lessons. It was important to him to have students enjoy the experience and not view the game as an interactive problem set. Thus, he brought Writers Cabal (the authors of this chapter) aboard as story consultants to help develop a story that would not only engage university students but also motivate them to learn physics.

Narrative Considerations in an Educational MMO

With this in mind, Writers Cabal set upon the task of defining the world in accordance to Futur-E-Scape's parameters. Despite its prevalence in traditional MMOs, Dr. Rademacher was adamant that there be no player-initiated violence in his world. In addition, because of the reluctance of some educational professionals to embrace game-based learning, traditional tests would have to be somehow incorporated into the game.

These requirements all addressed educator concerns. Any software that seemed to promote violence, however indirectly, would not be welcome in schools. Furthermore, teachers often have to show "proof of learning" through tests and other assessment methods. Most of the traditional educational system is set up this way.

The mandate that there be no player-initiated violence was not as damning as one might think. With the rise of MMOs for children, there are likely to be even more non-violent offerings. This does not mean there can't be an antagonist, only that this would be a different type of MMO. For *PAST*, the antagonist appears as Disruptures, magical rifts in space-time that threaten to tear apart the fabric of the universe.

Merging Pedagogy and Narrative

Developing new IP. Since Writers Cabal's primary concern was player engagement, our approach to developing new IP was not that dissimilar to that of an entertainment product. The learning objectives and lesson plans were important considerations, but they would be integrated once the preliminary backstory was established. Writers Cabal began by proposing several high-level concepts that fit the requirements.

Several of these initial concepts did find their way into the eventual story. For instance, the idea that virtual sports tournaments would be an excellent way to explore physics applications gave rise to the Olympics-styled interplanetary Magical Games featuring archery, soccer, and horse racing. An idea about saving indigenous species that were literally fading or blinking out morphed into a plotline about Disruptures affecting the universe. An epic tale about an apprentice racing to repair a magical rift was transformed into the journey of a star athlete chosen to investigate the secrets of the ancients in order to save the Realms.

Plot. *PAST* is a high-fantasy MMO full of spells and magic. It takes place in the Realms, which consist of human, dwarven, and elven worlds, along with a mysterious land known as Now-Here. From these locales, the player can travel backward and forward in space and time—hence the game's name, *Physics Adventures in Space-Time*, or *PAST*.

Physics is a lost "art" in this world, and its rediscovery is an integral part of the plot. In order to fight the Disruptures, the player travels through time and space to find Ary the dwarf (based on Aristotle), Galy the elf (based on Galileo), and Iza the human (based on Isaac Newton), the legendary experts of this lost art of physics. Ary, Galy, and Iza actually correspond with planned sections of curriculum on introductory math and trigonometry, kinematics, and dynamics. Although the player can ignore the physics component and still advance in the game through guesswork, the player who learns physics will have a definite advantage. After contacting Ary, Galy, and Iza, the player discovers the true nature of the Disruptures.

In the meantime, the Disruptures have increased in frequency, and the magical leaders of the Realms fear they must act now before the situation gets any worse. The player must convince each leader that their plan will actually worsen the problem and destroy the universe! Since each magical leader represents a common physics misconception, the player must then present evidence to combat the misconception.

Now united by the urgency of their mission, the magical leaders and the player look for a permanent solution to the deadly Disruptures.

Merging Pedagogy with Design

The design of *PAST* was very much influenced by the pedagogical concerns. The quest design, too, reflects these concerns. Throughout the story, the player is asked to engage in the scientific method to investigate the Disruptures. Encouraging player analysis and action presents a big departure from previous offerings in educational software that would ask students to read about physics or play a simplified game.

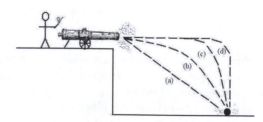

Figure 15.1. This projectile cannon drawing mock-up is based on the Force Concept Inventory test, which measures a student's physics conceptual knowledge. Diagram courtesy of Futur-E-Scape, LLC.

In *PAST*, students would be learning experientially, like in a physics lab. They can explore firsthand the variables that have an effect on a particular problem.

For example, a player who knows how to apply physics would advance quickly in any of the Magical Sports. The arrows and bow in Magical Archery are a 3D virtual replication of the hypothetical "projectile canons" used in traditional physics labs. Switching the variables, like the arrow's mass or the bow's applied force, would make a difference. A change in the angle or position of the bow would, too. In Magical Soccer, players try to kick balls into one of nine goalposts. Students would learn about momentum and impulse as they apply these concepts to the differently massed balls and differently placed goalposts that make up the game.

Finally, as an example of how to combat the Disruptures, the player could calculate how dense of a mass and how fast of a velocity would be needed to collide with the Disrupture to drain joules of energy from it.

Quests. Quests in *PAST* are similar to other fantasy MMORPGs. Players can learn about each world's history, the political situation, and become more adept at spells. At the same time, players also have physics-related quests. Similar to traditional physics lab questions, these quests would involve finding the correct physical parameters to fulfill the mission. For example, if the player wanted to send a message to the top of a castle with a bow and arrow, the player would have to select the right angle and force such that the arrow has the kinetic energy to reach its target. Immediately following the completion of the quest, there would be an optional multiple-choice question for extra loot. To avoid drawing undue attention to the physics-related quests, these multiple-choice questions would appear after story-based quests as well. If the player successfully completes a quest about elves, then the multiple-choice question might ask "Who is the king of the elves?" with a special reward for the correct answer.

Figure 15.2. An example of the quest system in PAST. Screenshots courtesy of Futur-E-Scape, LLC.

Since the quests do in fact cover the same material as the multiple-choice questions, the follow-up questions are unnecessary. However, these multiple-choice questions are part of the compromise needed to allay some teachers' fears. These multiple-choice questions also give a way to track the students' progress in the game. Additionally, students might prefer to see multiple-choice questions as preparation for classroom tests.

15.5   Conclusion

Writing for serious games has its challenges, but the writer who embraces the opportunity to do so can make a real difference in the world. Serious games have real-life impact, and for some writers, that may be just as thrilling as writing for an entertainment title.

16

Writing for Casual Games

Chris Pasley

16.1 Who Is a Casual Game Writer?

Or, even more fundamental: "What is a casual game?" There are countless semantic squabbles among game developers as to the exact definition of what makes a casual game casual, but a widely accepted explanation is a game with a relatively small budget, meant to be played in short amounts of time over several sessions. The majority of casual games are either PC downloads or browser-based Web games (Flash, Shockwave, or other plug-ins), though both consoles and handhelds have begun to embrace the casual gaming space as well.

On a casual game team, the writer is usually the game designer, or the artist, or the programmer—someone who already has a job to do. By definition, casual game budgets are small, and very few independent casual game developers can afford dedicated writers. Often, this can lead to hackneyed, overly long stories, embarrassing typos, and horrible dialogue (when there is any). This isn't anyone's fault. The programmer spent a lot of time learning to be a programmer, not a writer, and any writing that has to be done is often viewed as a distraction or, worse, unnecessary.

So how can an average part-time writer keep the writing a priority, especially when there's so much else to do? First off, by making sure that the scripts, the story, and even the instruction text has its own deadline in the production schedule. The writer has to get the rest of the team on his side, and treating it as an equal task among all the rest is the first step to doing so. It also helps ensure that the writer has a strong motivation to actually get the work done. A game's writing may need to evolve even after this deadline, but having the bulk of the work already done makes including it much less painful.

Another way to convince everyone on the development team that the writing is an equally important job is to create a wireframe flow of the game as it will exist, including all in-game slots in which story will need to be written. Game flows and wireframes are incredibly helpful tools anyway, and making it easier for team members to follow the flow of the game from beginning to end will help show them why if the writing isn't done and done well, the player will have no idea what he's supposed to be doing.

Without polished writing, instructions, and copy (meaning any of the miscellaneous text that appears in the game), a player can be lost and bewildered, rendering all the other work the team has done wasted as the player simply stops playing—especially when you've only got a few seconds to let the game make an impression.

16.2   But *Tetris* Didn't Need a Story!

To story or not to story? Many classic-game faithful often point to *Tetris* when debating the need for story, pointing out that game's success without having even a hint of exposition. Most casual games have their roots firmly entrenched in the 8-bit era, so the argument becomes especially relevant to casual game developers. If *Tetris* doesn't have a story and *Tetris* is a lot of fun, then why should anyone bother?

A lot of flustered writers aside, it's a valid argument. Does a red ball, for instance, that you have to hit against a bunch of yellow squares for points, need a backstory? Does it need emotions? Does the player need to empathize with the ball? There are many who would say that yes, a player does, but they usually mean that the player creates his own experiences with the ball, crafting an individual narrative of his own through play. Not really something a writer can do, is it? Just as in any other art form, there are no ironclad rules. So sure, maybe a ball could have a story, but in general a good rule of thumb is simply to ask if the game has characters.

Games like chess, billiards, or Sudoku don't have characters. They just have rules and implements (pieces, balls, numbers). And they don't need stories to be perfectly fun experiences; the entire game lies purely in manipulating the implements according to the rules to reach a specific game state. The same could be said to be at the foundation of any game, but when an implement has anthropomorphic characteristics, the journey from opening game state to ending game state isn't the only concern. So you beat all the levels in *Super Mario World*. But what happened after that? Did Mario save the princess? Did Bowser get away? Even in games with storylines as minimal as the Mario series, characters can't just complete all the game objectives to offer a satisfying ending. Players need to know what happens to the character, because they've just spent hours on hours empathizing and identifying with our little plumber friend in the red hat.

If a game has characters, it should have a story, or at least a scenario. Scenarios are much simpler and more common in casual games than stories. Take a game I worked on for Adult Swim called *Bible Fight*. It's a simple fighting game similar to *Street Fighter* or *Mortal Kombat*. In this sort of game, it's more than enough to just convey: "Biblical characters fight it out in an unholy tournament." That's a scenario, and the game functions perfectly well with only that to lean on. We could have tried putting cutscenes in between each fight, but ultimately it would have been a lot of trouble for virtually no reward. The joke of the game is clear from the scenario, and in that sort of game, which encourages repeat plays, frequent cutscenes could be a severe annoyance for the player. Better to set the scenario and just let the player play.

However, in *Zening*, a game I directed for Kongregate, we took almost the exact opposite tack. It is, at base, a strategy game in which players control pieces on a grid against an opposing attack force. However, in this case we decided to emphasize the cutscenes, adding full voiceover in addition to the developer's already beautiful still 3D images and writing four full episodes of material. But why take such a different direction? By nature, *Zening* is a slower-paced game, more epic and persistent. The game is built on acquiring different characters (as pieces), and it felt important to give those characters weight and dimension. The episodic nature of the story also gave players a reason to keep playing outside of the gameplay.

There's no real formula for deciding if a game should have a story or not. It has to be a judgment call on the part of the writer, and largely on the rest of the development team. Can your game do with just a scenario? What will you be losing if you cut story out? Figure out those answers and then decide if story is needed.

But always, always have a "skip" button on cutscenes. A person playing the game at work (which is where a lot of casual games are played) is trying to wring every last second of procrastination time from his gameplay, and he doesn't want to have to sit through a long story scene if he's already seen it a dozen times. Above all, casual games are fortunate in that they're easily repeatable experiences. Don't make it hard on players who decide to come back for more.

16.3   Write as Little as You Can—Then Halve It

Seriously, a writer can always write less. As writers, even as game designers or artists or programmers being writers, we're often enamored with our own storytelling. We want that knight's speech to be as eloquent as possible, that space marine to be tough as nails. We want dozens of characters speaking the way you'd expect them to speak—and at the length you'd expect them to speak. But you don't have much time. For many casual game players, the story is simply a way of advancing a scenario. Make it too long and the game player will just skip it, which they should be able to do, but the point is to not make them want to. You're writing the short form of gaming. These are short stories to bigger games' novels, and you've got to trim the fat.

Below is an original script excerpt from the first episode of *Zening*. The original writer was told simply to flush out the ideas, and she did so with no limitation to length.

> Katrina: It's been a month since the operation. The cancer has stopped spreading and I want to get back to my work—you know, I'm covering the war back east. My editor says he's got me another unit he can get me embedded in—once the doctors give me the go ahead. But the dreams are getting worse. [pause—fearful] Horrible creatures—screaming my

Figure 16.1. *Zening.* Michael King, Kongregate.com.

name, chasing me and I can't get away. Until a couple nights ago when
I met Ben. He told me not to run anymore.

It seems pretty tight. The ideas come across, and it's important expositional dialogue.
But remember, this is all about speed. Like Olympic runners, tenths of a second
count. How can we shave some length off this?

Katrina: Now that I'm in remission, my editor's going to embed me in
another unit once the doctors give the green light. But the dreams are
getting worse. [pause—fearful] Horrible creatures screaming my name,
chasing me. [calmer] But a couple nights ago I met Ben. He told me
not to run anymore.

There. This was my revision. Mainly, I distilled what was important. The character
had cancer, was now getting better, was a war journalist eager to get back into the
action, but was having strange nightmares. A lot to fit in a short amount of time.
A good exercise—I would even say a fundamental one—is to boil things down to a
common denominator and look at the lines like an equation. All the cancer information you needed from the original paragraph is easily summed up by "Now that I'm
in remission..." The fact that she's a war journalist eager to get back to the action
boils down to "...my editor's going to embed me in another unit..." Subtlety and
connotation are great friends when trying to shorten things. She's in remission, so
she had a disease, probably cancer, for which that word is most often used. She has
an editor and is going to be embedded in another unit, which most will instantly
recognize as signs that she's a war reporter.

Think about every single word you use; they cost you and your player precious
seconds and should be as streamlined as possible—without losing the meaning you're
trying to convey.

16.4 Concise Copy and Instructions

Instructions are the most important words a casual game writer is going to write. Instructions are the player's first hint into understanding the game. If they're hard to understand, you've made the game a less enjoyable experience—at worst, a frustrating, impossible one.

Writing the instructions themselves is much like writing the story. Analyze and distill all the possible player actions and figure out what the common denominators are. Arrange them in a list that makes sense. Follow the list yourself and see if you've missed anything. It seems easy, but there's often confusion added by developers who don't take an analytical eye to their own game controls. Mistakes are usually made to the extremes: either too little information is given or far, far too much.

Minimalism is a good route to take when writing instructions. A picture of the up arrow key, accompanied by the word "Jump" is as clear as it can get. But have you told the player everything he needs to know to navigate the game world? Here is where you really need to pay attention to the game itself. It's a sad fact of the casual gaming world that often game design oversights get fixed in the instructions. There's an item that will give the character the super power he needs to get over that really tall wall, but he doesn't know that the huge springs floating over there are good things. To him they look like hazards. The player will inevitably discover this through trial and error, but it could be a good idea to include this little tidbit of information on the instructions screen. Be careful here of including too much; take a hard look at your game, watch new people play it, and see what needs to be explained. Also remember that if they're stuck, players will often turn to the instructions to see what they're doing wrong, even if they skipped them entirely the first time. Your words could be the deciding factor in whether the player decides to keep playing or leave in disgust.

Writing too much is even worse. Let's say your game is a complex online simulation that will revolutionize the casual game space forever. So you need tons and tons of text outlining every operational control, right? No. Trust me, there is nothing that will lose a casual player faster than multiple screens filled with text before they've even started playing the game. Try to outline the basic controls up front, the bare minimum, and prompt hints throughout the early levels. This is where bad game design can be costly; if the player has to use every single control of a complex control scheme right away, you're going to lose a lot of players simply because it's difficult to learn anything that fast, especially if it was only presented to them in the abstract before they even started playing.

Good design should ramp the complexity, and a good writer should ramp up control hints with it. It can be a good idea as well to include a more complete legend of buttons and moves that will be accessible from the game as an aid, but that should be mainly for players who saw the hints but have forgotten, or didn't get it in the first place. That legend would be quickly forgotten if shown up front.

Figure 16.2. "Floor It!" AdultSwim.com. © 2009 Cartoon Network.

16.5   Licensed Games

One of the most profitable and prevalent species of casual game is the licensed tie-in. Casual games based on shows, movies, or even retail products are a mainstay of Web gaming. The hardest part—and the part that will in most cases get the most attention from your client—is how you handle the brand. Most times that burden, especially from tie-ins with characters, will land squarely upon the writer. Are you presenting the character in a way that's consistent with the brand? Or will fans wrinkle up their noses and think, "He'd never say *that!*"

There's really no help for it but to simply immerse yourself in the brand. When I was working on the game *Floor It!*, a tie-in for the Adult Swim show *Squidbillies*, I spent hours watching and re-watching the same six 15-minute episodes of a show about redneck squids. I tried to figure out why each character was funny and what made that character unique. It's often not enough to simply ape the words of a character; they'll come out phony. Try to figure out what the creators of that character were thinking when they wrote each line and apply the same thought process to your writing. I doubt I hit on what the creators were really thinking, but I think the end result was pretty close (see Table 16.1). Early's a lost-cause uber-redneck, and Rusty often has flashes of uncommon insight, followed by a desperate need to be like his father. Hilarity ensues.

One important thing to remember, especially when writing for children's brands: adding an exclamation mark does not make your sentence exciting. It's condescending, and most kids can spot it a mile away.

Rusty and Early Exchange 01			
Voiceover for *Squidbillies: Floor It!* Rusty and Early discuss various points of interest as Rusty flies through town. These are back-and-forth bits of dialogue that will sound during normal gameplay.			
Filename	**Event**	**Character**	**Line**
RE_01_01	Normal Play	Rusty	I feel like Icarus, soarin' aloft on wings of wax and hubris.
RE_01_02	Normal Play	Early	What the Hell you sayin', boy?
RE_01_03	Normal Play	Rusty	Nothin', Daddy.

Filename	**Action**	**Character**	**Line**
RC_16	Hits Mail Box	Rusty	That there mail's gonna be late, I reckon.
RC_17	Hits Granny	Rusty	Granny? Granny! You all right?
RC_18	Hits Early	Rusty	Don't kill me Daddy! I'm sorry! I'm sorry!
EC_15	Rusty Hits Sheriff	Early	Aw, crap. Russell! Apologinate yourself to the Sheriff and, uh… hit him again.
EC_16	R. hits Anyone	Early	Well, hell. I guess you're gonna need to get his wallet, too.
EC_17	R. hits Anyone	Early	That's what you get what you's a damn sinner, ain't it?

Table 16.1. Voiceover script for *Squidbillies: Floor It!*

16.6   Voiceover

One area of casual games that has largely been avoided because of costs and other practical considerations is voiceover (VO). Should you use voiceover in casual games at all?

Well, there are a few considerations to take into account. Is the game a licensed tie-in? If so, the client may want voiceover as part of the game, to strengthen the brand. Of course, the client may also insist that you simply use existing VO from the brand, but this is rarely a good way to do it. If you're going to include voiceover at all, it's best to try to get that VO integrated with the game as best you can, which means that canned VO will rarely work.

Another thing to remember when attempting VO in a casual game is time. A good measuring standard is to assume that in every second of VO, an actor can say three words. If you have a paragraph of lines for that character, the game may suddenly become less casual as these lines take what seems like forever to finish. You should be very sure that voiceover is worth the time price you'll have to pay on top of actor fees, studio time, mixing, and sound design.

Whenever possible, hire professional actors. They have trained a long time to learn their craft, just as you have yours, so trying to do it yourself, or with your friends or co-workers, is often an embarrassing exercise in futility. Remember: the only thing worse than no voiceover is bad voiceover.

Finally, if you've gotten great VO from professionals and it all works out great, make sure you've expressed your intentions for the VO with your programmers. Integrating VO attached to game events isn't simple; the programmer must make sure the lines don't overlap or that including them won't mess up another area of his code. It will also affect the total file weight of the game, which can be a vital consideration. The average file weight of a downloadable game can be around 50 MB, but a Web-based game has to be much smaller as the load time must be as fast as possible. Your programmer may have to stream that audio in from external files—again, something he should definitely be notified about up front.

16.7   Conclusion

Casual games are a fairly new market, and as such the landscape is constantly in flux. Keep your eye on what some of the better casual games are doing and see how people are including writing in innovative ways. Don't be afraid to push the boundaries of casual game writing, but always try to remember that in the end it needs to be an enjoyable experience for the player. If in beta testing you realize that flipping through dozens of story screens is exasperating to the player, don't be afraid to rip it all out and go back to the basics. The main idea is to make the game more fun and easier to understand. If you haven't accomplished either, you haven't done your job as a casual game writer.

17

Writing for Handheld Games

Evan Skolnick

17.1   Introduction

When writing narrative content for a game on a handheld system such as the Nintendo DS or Sony PSP, there are a number of considerations that are important to understand and take into account. They largely pertain to the technical limitations of the hardware, the budgetary constraints common to this type of title, and the player's unique interactions with a handheld game system. In this chapter, we'll examine many of these considerations and explore best practices for approaching narrative development on these diminutive but important game platforms.

Let's Get Small

A writer of big-budget Hollywood action blockbusters who suddenly found himself working on a weekly TV crime drama would soon find that the expensive, special-effects-laden action scenes he previously relied on to punch up his scripts were not within the scope of his new assignment. He'd also encounter and have to adapt to some important structural conventions of writing for TV; for example, the need to design your story to work effectively around the commercial breaks, always teasing the audience enough so that they'll return after the ads have played.

Our displaced movie writer would need to very quickly learn to work within the limitations and requirements of this format, and work effectively... or he'd soon need to learn how to apply for unemployment compensation.

This reorientation process would not be dissimilar to that of a game writer whose previous project was Lead Writer on a next-generation title for a platform like the Xbox 360 who then found herself hired to produce narrative content for a Nintendo DS title. The specifics of this adaptation process would of course be completely different than in our movie-to-TV writer example, but the core aspect of putting aside old, possibly luxurious writing habits in favor of those that are more constrained (and by necessity more efficient) would probably feel very much the same.

Fortunately, nearly all professional writers are used to dealing with limitations, and game writers are no exception. The key, as always, is to understand the target medium or platform—with its strengths, weaknesses, conventions, and potential pitfalls—as thoroughly as possible before getting started.

17.2   Player Interaction with a Handheld Game

The way players interact with a handheld[1] game is often very different from the way they interact with a console[2] game. This is partly due to the size, shape, and power of the hardware itself and partly due to the times and places players generally choose to play a handheld game as opposed to a console game. As you might expect, these differences have a number of bearings on game writing.

Let's start by looking at some general differences between player interaction with a console game versus with a handheld game. We'll categorize these two player experiences via the following differentiating factors: *where* users tend to play each type of game system, *why* they choose to play on that system at any given time, and *how* their interactions and experiences tend to differ from console to handheld.

Where

At the simplest and most obvious level, the *where* of console gaming versus handheld gaming can be summarized as "at home" versus "on the go."

Console games tend to be played in the home environment, on the family television or possibly on a secondary set in the basement or in a bedroom. They're stationary and more or less permanently connected to a TV somewhere in the player's home.

It goes without saying that handheld games are anything but permanently connected; they are specifically designed to be portable and played "on the go." It does not seem unreasonable to assume that this is how they're played for the majority of the time.

There are, of course, exceptions to these rules. For example, with the right third-party accessories, a slimline PlayStation 2 can be made portable enough to play on one's lap in the back seat of a car. And there is currently no law on the books against sitting at home and settling in for a Nintendo DS play session.

However, the main distinction between console and handheld games is that one type of system you can take with you on the road and play almost anywhere, and

---

[1] For the purposes of this chapter, "handheld" will refer to small, standalone portable game systems that have no other functionality (such as PDA or phone capability). The main examples in the marketplace at the time of this writing are the Nintendo DS and the Sony PlayStation Portable (PSP).

[2] For the purposes of this chapter, "console" will refer to any modern game system one would connect to a television, such as the Xbox 360, PlayStation 3, Nintendo Wii, etc.

the other you can't. It is a major differential with multiple implications, all of which must be taken into account when designing and writing for these platforms.

Sound versus silence. The console game player is in her personal space, set up as much as possible to her preference. It's almost assured that the TV volume is on, so that game audio intended for the player to hear will actually be heard (sometimes in glorious surround sound!).

Not so with the handheld game player. She is quite possibly playing your game someplace where openly audible cutscenes, sound effects, voiceover quips, and music will not be appreciated or, in some cases, even allowed. Examples might include airplanes, buses, study hall, and even the back seat when Dad's driving and Mom's got a headache.

Maybe the player brought a pair of headphones, but maybe she didn't. Based on observational experience, it doesn't seem unreasonable to venture that a good number of people playing a handheld game in public do it with the volume turned down and without the benefit of headphones.

Shared versus solitary. The console game player, relaxing on his couch with a good game, is not necessarily the only person in the room, watching that TV.

Modern game consoles ship with four controller ports for a reason: the console experience is made for same-room, local multiplayer game sessions. You've got a couch, a big-screen TV that everyone can see, and room for drinks and snacks. What could be a better set-up for in-person, shared gaming goodness?

Even for a console game that lacks multiplayer modes, it's quite possible that other people are simultaneously taking in your content. The size of the TV screen and its natural position in the home as a center of family attention means that if anyone else is nearby, they're probably absorbing the game experience as well.

For the console game writer, this means being conscious of those extra pairs of eyes and ears. For example, parents or older siblings watching a young child playing a kid-targeted game might appreciate something thrown their way once in a while, such as the occasional Warner Brothers–style, over-the-kids'-heads adult-targeted joke.

However, the thought and effort that goes into developing that multi-tiered type of content would probably be wasted when applied to the development of most handheld games, due to the intimate nature of the handheld gameplay experience. On a portable game system, no one else can see the screen very well while you're playing. So any "over the kid's head" jokes or references will simply disappear into the ether, as opposed to entertaining a more savvy observer.

Of course, the same-room, local multiplayer experience is possible on some handheld games, via wireless ad hoc gameplay. Get some friends who own the same handheld system together in a room these days and you can have some shared fun that's reminiscent of the communal console game experience. However, due to the higher barriers to entry—you need multiple game systems and, in some cases, multiple copies of the same game—this is the exception to the handheld gameplay experience, not the rule. Additionally, the ad hoc multiplayer experience on handheld systems is often relegated to the arena of simple minigames, which don't generally require or lend themselves to narrative elements.

When it comes to handheld gaming, the majority of the time it's an intimate, private experience between the handheld game player and the game itself, one on one.

Why

They reasons *why* someone chooses to play a console game as opposed to a handheld game—or vice versa—are worthy of examination, because they affect what the player wants (and is reasonably able) to get out of the experience.

Settling down versus squeezing in. When a gamer fires up his console system, it's unusual for his intent to be to play for just a few minutes. He is generally settling down in his own home with the intention of playing for what is likely a significant period of time. Once locked in, he may play uninterrupted for hours at a stretch.

The handheld gamer, conversely, often knows he will be playing for only a short time. Many times, the handheld game system is pulled out when the player has some time to kill: waiting for an oil change, or in a doctor's waiting room, or at a bus stop. And the gameplay experience could be interrupted at any point, to be continued at some unknown time in the future.

Experienced handheld game designers know that this means they must deliver gameplay in small, bite-sized chunks and design the gameplay experience to survive interruption. A 25-minute mission in a console game would be a poor choice for a handheld SKU; it's likely the designers would try to break it into five- to ten-minute chunks. Wise handheld game writers know to follow this example and keep away from extended, noninteractive presentations of story content.

Hardcore versus casual. Because of the previously listed differences, handheld gaming tends to be more casual in nature, since casual games are easy to get in and out of, whereas hardcore games have steeper learning curves, demand a player's full attention for longer periods, and don't withstand interruption as well.

The relatively casual nature of handheld gaming is a design consideration that can affect how much writing is appropriate for the title. A gamer playing a hardcore title expects and will generally tolerate much more narrative content than he will when playing what he expects to be a casual game.

How

The *where* and *why* of a player's game system choice at any time has direct bearing on *how* he interacts with that system.

Engrossed versus interrupted. Being at home in his own, controlled environment, the console game player is generally able to devote his full attention to the game he's playing. He is not waiting for a train, sitting on a plane, riding in a car, sitting in study hall, or listening for his name while waiting in a jury duty pool.

With a handheld game, all of these possibilities are, no pun intended, in play. The handheld game player may be fully engrossed sitting at home on her couch, or she may be just killing a little time while waiting for something to start or end. Her attention may be purposely split. She is well aware that her game experience may be interrupted at any time—perhaps quite unpredictably—and expects the game (and game story) to withstand this sort of thing. She may not expect or appreciate very complex game or story elements that, if interrupted, are difficult to re-engage with at a later time.

Roundabout versus direct. The leisurely approach a console gamer may take to her game playing—stopping in a 3D level to admire the artwork, going back to get that extra collectible item, replaying the level with a different character—may be less likely to be taken by the handheld game player.

Someone who's squeezing in a little gaming time while waiting for something else to happen might be more likely to be looking for something simple, direct, and achievable in just a few minutes, with a tangible reward for doing so. Narrative clutter that gets in the way of this kind of simple goal may not be appreciated and may in fact interfere with what the player is trying to get out of the game.

17.3 Additional Considerations: Cartridge-Based Games

Until recently, all handheld gaming systems lagged very far behind their console cousins in terms of raw computing power, memory, and storage capacity for game assets.

Even console games in the mid 1990s could process thousands of 3D polygons per frame, while storing on their optical discs hundreds of megabytes of assets—including graphics capable of rendering expansive-feeling worlds, and hours of full-motion video and game audio.

Handheld systems of the time, with their relatively low-powered CPUs, limited graphics rendering capabilities, and cramped, cartridge-based storage media, were forced to rely on the use of early PC and console game development tricks such as pre-rendered sprites, severe color palette restrictions, and 2D tiling. Most significant from a narrative perspective, handheld games were unable to present full-motion video (FMV) or more than a few seconds of voiceover (VO) audio. This required handheld game writers of the time to be supremely inventive and scope-conscious when planning the delivery of story content to the player.

The technology for providing a console-like game experience in the palm of one's hand was realized in 2004 when Sony first released the PlayStation Portable (PSP), considered to be the first optical disc–based handheld gaming system. Its powerful CPU, combined with Sony's proprietary UMD disc format, promised gamers the potential to enjoy the experience of a console game virtually anywhere.

However, it may be that for handheld gaming, it's not all about high-power CPUs, eye-popping graphics, or home theater–type audio. For at the time of this writing, the dominant handheld platform continues to be Nintendo's cartridge-based DS.

Because of the DS's relatively low-powered CPU and modest storage capability, there are additional considerations a writer must take into account when developing content for it.

Hardware

Compared to a console game or the PSP, the DS as a platform is limited in terms of CPU and graphics rendering power. More importantly for narrative considerations, the ROM budget is only a small fraction of the gigabytes you see on consoles or even the PSP. By small fraction we mean around 20%, and in many cases less than 10% of consoles and the PSP. (The exact figure depends on the ROM size for that particular DS game... they do vary).

After all the game art, animation, and audio assets are on the cartridge's ROM, there is generally little to no room left over for extensive VO or FMV. These storytelling components are the bread and butter of most game writers, and without these important tools you'll find yourself falling back on GameBoy-era storytelling tools like the still picture and the caption. In other words, you might be asking your players to (gasp!) *read* if they want to experience the story content. More on that later.

Schedule and Budget

Even more potentially constricting than the hardware limitations of the DS when compared to a console game are the development schedule and budget. The budget in particular will tend to conspire with ROM storage limits to rule out the inclusion of extensive VO or FMV.

The inclusion of any FMV in third-party DS titles is less than common. Any FMV you do get will probably be re-purposed from the console version of the game—assuming there is one—or from other pre-existing footage, since the development of original FMV is enormously expensive (and therefore extremely rare).

Additionally, the development team will probably have little to no available time to compensate for this FMV shortfall by developing in-game, engine-driven cutscene content, because it requires time-consuming custom scripting and animation, which the schedule and budget will generally not support.

The news generally isn't much better on the VO front. If your DS title is a companion SKU to a console version of the same game, you might be lucky enough to get "piggybacked" onto their VO recording session, allowing you to record unique lines for the DS game. However, if there is no console SKU, you are probably out of luck with regard to voiceover, because VO casting, directing, and recording are, again, inordinately expensive.

The shorter schedule for a DS game (usually about six months versus 18+ months for a console game) also tends to put a rush on the narrative content development, usually in concurrence with the very short pre-production phase and probably spilling into the production phase. You will be under the gun and on a short cycle, with little time for major rewrites.

17.4   What to Do?

So, pretty grim, eh? Well, buck up. Soldiers need to learn to survive with or without their primary weapons; just think of this as unarmed narrative combat training. The following practices should help you succeed when writing narrative content for a cartridge-based handheld game.

Control the Overall Scope

Obviously, with this many limitations working against you, you'll need to work within them, and that means keeping the scope of your narrative content under strict control. Fortunately, the previously stated limitations for cart-based systems tend to work with you here. Handheld games cost less than console games to produce, and they cost less at retail. The audience expectations for overall gameplay length are lower, too.

That means you can expect to be delivering a shorter overall game experience. And because there is less story content that actually needs to be created, it becomes easier to manage and keep focused.

Part of keeping the story content under control and on track is to avoid overburdening the handheld narrative at any point in the game with more than it can carry, given the extreme limitations that will be on it. A big part of this task falls to the designers who are laying out the main structure of the game flow. They must not leave huge conceptual gaps in between gameplay levels that are left to the writer to fill.

For example, imagine a game in which Level 1 finds the player under the ocean fighting against robotic sharks, and on Level 2 the player is on Mars mining for rare minerals. As the writer, you're asked to link these two disparate locations and gameplay situations using only three still images (sorry, budget and ROM restrictions!) along with some caption text. What are the odds that this is going to be a narrative experience that anyone will enjoy, or even want to endure?

As a writer in this situation, you've been set up to fail by a poorly conceived overall game design. There is simply too big a gap to be filled here, and yet you must try to do so. Your cutscene will probably be either short and ridiculous, or long-winded and tedious to read. Whether the player reads the short version or skips the long one, he will suddenly find himself on the moon, probably feeling disoriented and bewildered, lacking any kind of story context for the next gameplay experience.

Keep It Simple

Story simplicity is important, because the player is going to pick up the game and put it down many times more often than a console game, due to the likelihood of shorter play sessions. Complex, subtle and multi-layered story elements can more easily be forgotten, and the player may feel lost throughout much of the game. Like general handheld gameplay itself, the story components must survive interruption. A simpler story—featuring straightforward plot points and characters with simple, easy-to-remember motivations—will keep things at all times focused and clear for the player.

In addition to keeping the story elements tight, lean, and easy to follow, you may want to reinforce the main story points again and again throughout the game, to further support the player who's returning after being interrupted.

A good analogy for approaching this is to think of a televised sporting event. When you are flipping through TV channels and happen upon an in-progress sports contest, notice the efforts made to get you up to speed. There are, obviously, the ever-present onscreen graphics that tell you the current score and what part of the game you're in (quarter, period, inning, set, etc.). But if you listen to the announcers for a while, you'll notice that every few minutes they will do a general recap of the current situation and what led up to it. They generally don't make a big deal of this—you rarely here them call out that they're recapping ("If you're just joining us, or stepped away for a while, here's what's been happening..."). Imagine your consternation if you were watching the game and the announcers said that every ten minutes! No, they weave these short summaries into their regular conversation, in a way that someone who's been watching the game from the beginning will not find annoying or obtrusive.

You'll need to find ways to accomplish the same thing in your handheld game narrative, in ways that won't feel condescending or be annoying to players who are playing straight through. Player questions you should repeatedly answer include: What is the overall conflict again? Why is/are the player character(s) on the current quest/level? What is the overarching game goal, and why? And so on.

Narrative simplicity is also aligned with the observation earlier in this chapter that the handheld gamer is generally experiencing the narrative content alone, with no observers. This allows you to aim directly at that gamer and not worry about adding multiple tiers of intricacy or humor.

Make It Snappy

Brevity is the soul of wit, as Shakespeare put it. More to the point of this chapter, it's vital to keep things tight and lean when writing for handheld games, no matter what delivery method will be used to convey it to the player. And if you are lucky enough to have VO and/or FMV as part of your toolset, it's important to know how and where to use them.

Onscreen text. As stated previously in this chapter, much of the time when you're writing for cart-based handheld games, your cutscene storytelling tools will mainly consist of static images and text. If you spend years observing play testers on hand-held games, you'll soon note that there are two basic types of players: those precious, patient few who stop and read all the wonderful narrative text you develop, and others, who tend to press the "skip" button for all it's worth in order to return to gameplay. The sad truth is that the latter group tends to outnumber the former.

However, there are many "middle of the road" players who will take the time to read your narrative text, as long as you don't push your luck by writing too much of it. The less there is, the more likely players will take the time to read it. Conversely, the more you write—especially when it's presented in a big chunk—the more likely it will be skipped.

This is an important fact of life to keep in mind if you're angsting over having to cut down your lovingly crafted but encyclopedic dialogue. It's never easy or enjoyable to slice your precious writing down to the bone. But ask yourself this: would you rather have a shorter version of your dialogue actually read by the player, or would you rather have the longer version be skipped entirely?

Also, keep in mind that the small screen size means that only a few words can probably fit on the screen at a time. If you can only fit 5 or so words per line, and only 2 or 3 lines per page, it's important to keep your writing as lean and mean as possible.

Voiceover. If you do have the opportunity to include original VO in a cartridge-based game, it will probably be pretty limited, only a few minutes total. So make every word count. Keep your dialogue snappy and direct.

You probably won't be able to carry VO all the way through the game, because there will be more that you need to say than can be covered by just a few minutes of recorded material. So consider front-loading your VO so that all your main characters get a chance to have their voices heard at least once. Assuming you'll have to resort to text for the rest of the game, granting each major character some VO early on allows the player to get a sense for each one's personality and what they sound like. This way, the text that follows will be "heard" properly in the player's head.

Full-motion video. If you are blessed enough to have budgeted, original FMV for your handheld game, it will be extremely limited, so make every second count.

When writing for handheld-targeted FMV, you'll likely have other limitations to deal with besides simple length. A 30-second animation of two characters talking with each other in a small room is a lot less expensive and time-consuming to produce than a 30-second animation featuring 500 characters storming the beaches of Normandy.

Make sure you understand what the team, schedule, and budget can actually support. How many locations can the animation(s) include? How many characters total, and how many onscreen at once? How much (if any) lip-synching is budgeted? These are all scope considerations you'll want to know before you start writing, not after. Insist on being allowed to put a synopsis, detailed story outline, or a beat script in front of the artists and animators who will be tasked with either doing or outsourcing the cutscene work, to get their buy-in on scope, before you waste time developing a full script that cannot be animated.

Because of its limited nature, placement of handheld FMV is almost as important to decide as its content. Where are the most important places to put FMV in a handheld game? Your initial instinct might be to focus on an opening cutscene, perhaps one or two in the middle parts of the game, and a closing cutscene, to be seen upon successful game completion.

But what if your FMV budget is so limited that you have to prioritize even among these choices? Well, think of it this way. 100% of the people who play your game will experience the first couple of minutes, and then as you move through the game you will start to see some drop-off—especially as you approach the end of the game.

What percentage of players will take the time to make it all the way through your game, not get stuck somewhere in progression, and see the ending? It varies from game to game, of course, but it's always less than 100%, sometimes a lot less. So where is the best place to make a good impression with FMV, for players and reviewers, and to ensure that everyone actually sees the video? The beginning.

Working with the Impatient Player

No matter what you do to simplify, streamline, and make attractive your still images with captions—as stated before, still the mainstay of handheld game cutscenes— there will nevertheless be a large number of impatient players who have no intention of sitting through these sequences. These stubborn, "I don't care about the story" types will do anything they can do to avoid noninteractive content, so they can return as quickly as possible to gameplay.

You could, of course, throw up your hands in defeat and give up on these players, but to do so would be a capitulation you should not make lightly. The narrative content in many games, when properly executed, plays an important role in filling out the game experience by providing motivation and context, improving the experience even when players don't realize it's happening. Allowing players to short-circuit this component of the game design so easily is extremely undesirable. Therefore a baseline goal of the game writer should be to get *some* narrative content into the players' heads even if they're aggressively trying to skip past it.

How do you do this? Well, you could obtain some compromising pictures of the Producer or Lead Engineer and use them to "negotiate" the removal of the "skip cutscene" button. However, a less treacherous approach might be to try what I call the "silent comic book panels" test. Think about a comic book you may have read— or at least a several-page sequence within a comic—that has no word balloons or captions whatsoever. It's 100% reliant on the visuals to tell the story. This technique can be just as powerful a storytelling vehicle as a comic book that does have dialogue and captions.

Now imagine a handheld cutscene that consists of six static visuals shown in sequence, combined with background music and captions. The player is provided a button to move to the next image, allowing them to read the captions at their own pace.

Next, picture our typical impatient game player, mashing the "next" button to get through each image in the cutscene as fast as humanly possible. Text appears at the bottom, attempting to give the onscreen characters voice, but before any of it can be read, another rapid press of the button shifts to the next image. Skip, skip, skip, skip. Oh, the humanity!

But here's the thing. Even though this player doesn't have any intention of taking in the narrative content you and your supporting artist(s) worked so hard to create, he will nevertheless be exposed to the images as they flash across the screen.

If your images can do the same thing as our silent comic book pages—tell a story purely with visuals, when viewed in order—then they will convey the core narrative information you need to get across. *This is true even if the player attempts to skip all your story content and doesn't read any of your text.*

Of course, this will only work if the images do actually fit together in a way that visually conveys cohesive narrative, and if they are simple and clear enough to be comprehended at a glance. While success or failure here rests heavily on your supporting artist(s), you as the writer might be able to have some influence on it—especially if you're describing in your script what should be seen in each still image and/or if you're having any direct interactions with the artist(s) who will be developing the visuals.

Keep Narrative Off the Critical Path

The sad truth is that with handheld games, perhaps more than any other type of game, you need to assume that a significant portion of your audience does not have the time, interest, or inclination to read through your narrative content, especially if it's not being delivered with FMV or VO (which, as covered previously, is very likely the case).

So, as painful as it may be to hear, you should avoid requiring the players to *listen* (because even if you have VO, they might have the volume turned down for privacy) or to *read* (because many of them won't want to). Notice that the word chosen was *requiring*. In other words, you can still include a modicum of narrative content, but don't make experiencing it a requirement to succeed at the game.

Now, some clever writers and designers might conspire to "force" the player to read the narrative content by embedding crucial gameplay information within it. *Want to know how to jump over this wall? Okay, read this cutscene and somewhere in there you'll find a clue!*

This approach of embedding need-to-know information within the narrative content is a perilous one indeed. While on the surface it may seem like a smart way to circumvent the player's desire to skip the story content, it stands a good chance of annoying the player, especially if the implication is the careful reading of voluminous text passages for vital information. Require this too often and too much, and you may be facing angry reviewers and players.

So avoid burying critical gameplay instructions or objectives in the middle of narrative content. For important, need-to-know gameplay info, stick with in-game iconographic or very brief text instructions that are impossible for the player to avoid.

17.5   Conclusion

Where does all this leave you as the handheld game writer? Perhaps a little ego-bruised? Jealous of your console game writing contemporaries, with their fancy FMVs and hours-long VO budget? Well, don't be.

Like all other game writers, you are not the main attraction. When was the last time you heard someone say they can't wait to hear that hot RPG sequel, or watch that new FPS title that's coming out next week? No... gamers come to play.

As a game writer, you're in a support role, bolstering and enhancing that play experience. The best you can hope to achieve—and all you should be trying to achieve–is to make a good thing better, by providing context for gameplay goals, creating the illusion of a larger world, and making the player empathize with and care about the characters. If you've managed to accomplish all that in a handheld game, you've done very well indeed.

Hold your head high, soldier. You're a handheld game writer. You do more with less. Be proud of it!

18

Writing for Mobile Phone Games

Graeme Davis

18.1   Introduction

As a gaming platform, mobile phones have a number of similarities with handheld gaming devices: screens are usually small, controls are limited, and memory and processor power can impose severe constraints. Therefore, the reader will find it useful to review Chapter 17 on writing for handheld games, which contains a great deal of information that is also applicable to phone games.

Because gaming is very much a secondary function of mobile phones, they are not optimal platforms for high-end, "core" games—and, of course, the market for mobile phones is much broader than the market for any dedicated gaming device. As a result, the overwhelming majority of mobile phone games are casual games, aimed at the notional "average" mobile phone user—in other words, just about anyone. So Chapter 16 on writing for casual games is also very useful.

This chapter addresses the unique aspects of mobile phones as a gaming platform and the specific challenges of writing for mobile phone games.

18.2   The Platform

Mobile phones have several features that are unique and others that they may share with other devices but that have a more significant impact on the game writer.

Screen Size

With a few exceptions, mobile phones offer a smaller screen size than any other gaming platform—a screen can be little more than one inch square. More expensive and function-rich phones can have larger screens, but they also have a much smaller user base. A quick visit to Nokia's website (http://www.nokia.com/) reveals that they offer phones for the North American market with screen sizes ranging from 800×480 pixels—comparable to an early-90s PC—to a mere 96×68 pixels.

Diversity

There are literally hundreds of makes and models of mobile phones on the market, all with different specifications. In order to achieve any kind of market penetration, game developers have to cater to multiple platforms. Porting a game for twenty or more different phones is not uncommon.

As you will see in the following paragraphs, there is a huge difference between a game targeted exclusively at high-end devices like the iPhone and one aimed at the more limited phones that (at the time of writing, at least) make up the bulk of the market. A writer should always make sure of line and character limits and any other constraints before starting a project.

Hardware

The vast majority of mobile phones are optimized for their primary function—to send and receive voice and text messages—rather than as game platforms. This is changing with the iPhone and its competitors, but the heart of the market remains with basic and mid-range phones. Processing power and memory are both limited, as they are with many handheld devices, and phone games suffer additional restrictions because they are not the primary function of the device.

Unlike most other game platforms, too, games are downloaded to a phone in their entirety. Every one of the game's assets, be it code, art, text, or audio, has to fit in the phone's memory. That means that every asset has to earn its place in the download. For example, a narrative sequence will almost certainly be cut if doing so allows another level, weapon, enemy class, or other gameplay-extending feature to be included in the game.

Download Size

Memory restrictions mean that mobile phone games have to be incredibly small compared to games for other platforms. At the time of writing, the new releases on the Sprint Nextel website had download sizes ranging from just over 100 kB to almost 500 kB—including all the code and art as well as the writing.

Controls

The controls on a mobile phone are unique, and again they are optimized for the device's primary function. This is as relevant to writing as it is to game design. Although it is theoretically possible to allow text input in a game using the same system as text messaging, the restricted processing power and memory—not to mention the small-team, fast-turnaround nature of almost all phone game development—mean that it is impractical to develop sophisticated text parsers. At the same time, the restricted screen size makes it difficult to display multiple-response options in a conversation tree (like those used in *Monkey Island*–style adventure games, for example). Controls for handling conversations may well be restricted to "Yes" and "No" inputs once the rest of the game's controls are assigned.

Touch screens are increasingly common among newer and higher-end models, and some have Javascript-enabled browsers such as the iPhone's Mobile Safari browser. At this point, the phone takes on more of the characteristics of a handheld device such as the PSP or Nintendo DS.

Color

These days, mobile phones with monochrome displays are rare, at least in North America, but elsewhere in the world they are still available at the bottom end of the market. However, all but the most high-end phones offer much narrower color palettes than current-generation handhelds, home consoles, and computers. Camera-equipped phones have displays capable of handling more colors, but there may sometimes be hardware issues restricting games and other non-camera applications to a smaller palette.

Fonts

The game developer cannot count on having anything but the most basic fonts and character sets—even bold and italic may not be available. On lower-end phones, a line of text can be as little as 16 characters—including spaces and punctuation. A full screen can be as little as four lines, and a line can be as little as 10 pixels high, with characters 6–8 pixels wide. Fancier text may have to be created as artwork, which is prohibitively expensive for anything except game titles and maybe—just maybe—credits.

User Behavior

Most mobile phone users do not put as much into playing games on their phone as they would on a home console, a computer, or even a handheld gaming device. Instead, mobile phone games are most commonly regarded as something to kill time: on the bus or subway, while waiting in line, or at similar times. It is a displacement activity, which can and will be interrupted at any time when something else requires the player's attention. Therefore, a game's narrative cannot unfold over an extended period of play—unless the game allows saves, which (a) cannot be counted on, and (b) may restrict the number of platforms on which the game can run.

Audio

Despite the fact that a mobile phone is primarily an audio device, game developers can't count on having large amounts of game audio—voiceovers, conversations, and the like—or even sophisticated sound effects. Again, memory restrictions are the problem—usually, there simply isn't enough memory to accommodate the necessary audio files. Things may be easier with a phone that is also an MP3 player, provided it is possible to access the MP3 memory for a game that is being played on the phone—and that cannot be taken for granted. And again, by restricting the game to such high-end units, developers are shrinking the potential market drastically.

Animation

Animation in games on current-generation phones is simple, consisting largely of 2D sprites—although some 3D games are beginning to appear for higher-end phones. Cutscenes are often too expensive, and every piece of art has to compete for its place in the download package. Sometimes, in-engine cutscenes are possible, though as on other platforms, they run the risk of confusing and frustrating the player, who might not understand why the controls have suddenly stopped working while the screen looks much the same.

Automatically scrolling text (as sometimes used in epic movies) is out for the most part, as this is also animation. However, the player can be allowed to scroll text line by line or screen by screen, using the same up and down controls as for text messages.

Don't Despair!

Given the tight restrictions imposed by the nature of mobile phones as a game platform, writers may despair of achieving anything at all in the way of storytelling. Some may even doubt their ability to write within such rigid limits.

It's vital to approach a writing assignment for a phone game with the right frame of mind. Treat the restrictions as a challenge rather than an obstacle. Imagine you're writing haiku, or imagine yourself as a skilled miniaturist. Refine and refine your text until you have conveyed your meaning with a maximum of clarity and elegance. This is actually a good writing exercise in any case.

Mobile phone games are a market that is overlooked by many writers, and although this kind of work may not lead a writer to the same kind of fame and glory as writing an award-winning story for a high-profile PC or console game, it can lead to reasonably steady work. The skills required to write well for phone games are far from commonplace, and a writer who develops these skills will also win the respect of fellow writers, who know just how challenging this process is.

18.3   Types of Writing

On mobile phones, just as on other platforms, all games require more or less the same kinds of writing. Different genres of games may require more or less of a particular type.

Instructions

The instructions for playing the game are often provided by the development team. In cases where the game has been developed overseas, though, the writer may be required to edit or rewrite the text. And don't assume the programmers know how to explain things really well in plain English. Take some time to consider ways to improve the instruction text.

Credits

Again, credits are normally provided by the development team and will seldom require anything more than a quick proofreading by the writer.

Background/Intro Text

This text sets the scene for the game and establishes the beginning of the story, if the game has one. It should not normally take up more than one screen, and if possible it should be distilled down to one or two sentences. For example:

"Defend the Earth from the attacking Zigmoid battle fleet!"

"Falthar sets out to discover who murdered his parents."

"Unlock the Maze of Myxtan to win the Treasure of the Gods!"

It is fine (indeed, it's often necessary) to address the player directly in these opening sentences. The writer can also supply an art brief for a graphic screen to run behind the text—such as Falthar's village in flames as the youth sets out, sword in hand. It is important not to forget the restrictions of screen size and resolution when writing art specifications, though—the simpler the better. The writer should also be sure to get the producer's approval for any art screens in advance, or risk the possibility that they will not appear in the final game.

Delivering Narrative

There are many ways to deliver story information (also called narrative content) within a video game. For a solid overview of writing and storytelling within a game, the reader can turn to a previous book by the IGDA Writers' Special Interest Group, *Game Writing: Narrative Skills for Videogames* (Charles River Media/Thomson Learning, 2006. Chris Bateman, editor).

For the most part, the writer will not be able to rely on cutscenes in a phone game. The occasional art screen with a couple of lines of text may or may not be available between levels. Cutscenes using the game engine and game assets may be possible, but as mentioned above, they risk confusing the player, who will often not be familiar with such gaming conventions.

A common criticism leveled by gamers and reviewers is that some games stop the gameplay too often, and for too long, to deliver chunks of narrative when all the player wants is to get on with playing the game. The result can be that the player "clicks through," ignoring the story, or simply gets bored and gives up on the game. Because phone games are smaller and cheaper than games on other platforms, they have to work harder to catch and keep the player's attention. The lower the price and the more casual the purchase, the less players feel impelled to finish the game in order to get their money's worth.

So, as much as possible, the narrative content of the game must be delivered alongside the gameplay content—within the game itself. This is actually a good principle to apply to game writing in general, as well.

To achieve this, the player should ideally work closely with the development team, weaving the story through the gameplay and level design so that the game is a single, harmonious whole. However, in many cases, the writer may come on board after the game has been substantially finished and find that there is no time, budget, or inclination to make changes in the interest of a story idea.

In these circumstances, the writer has to work within the existing limits and create the best story possible by taking advantage of what the existing levels and gameplay have to offer. As with every aspect of writing for phone games, the right frame of mind is key. Many writers actually find it easier to look at an existing game and weave a story through it, rather than starting with a blank screen and a blank mind. And like the mechanical task of writing within tight line and character counts, this is actually a good exercise for the writer, which promotes creativity and resourcefulness.

The writer should also remember the adage that a picture is worth a thousand words. Given the screen size on most mobile phones, a thousand words may be an overestimate, but it is always better to show than to tell—and best of all is to show story information within the game itself, without stopping the gameplay or requiring the creation of additional art or other assets. If a large chunk of text simply cannot be avoided—and this is the case far less often than most writers would care to admit—it should be limited to an absolute maximum of two screens of continuous text at any time, requiring one button-press to get from one to the other and a second button-press to get back to the game. Like it or not, it is the game that the player has purchased, not the writer's deathless prose.

In-Game Messages and Dialogue

Depending on the style of the game, it may be possible to include a certain amount of character speech to further the story. For example, a detective game may see the player locating and interviewing witnesses and informants to solve a mystery. These characters can be presented by means of simple head-shots, with a text space at the bottom of the screen for their dialogue. Once again, concise writing is key, as text space will be severely limited unless the conversation is one of two or three key turning points in the story. And, as with all dialogue, the text has to convey personality as well as information.

18.4   Other Issues

Game Saves

Like coin-ops and early console games, mobile phone games very rarely have the capacity for the player to save the game before quitting. Some can offer a pseudo-save function, where the player is given a code upon completing a level or chapter, which can be entered when restarting the game to go directly to the start of the next level or chapter.

This means that complex interactive narratives are out of the question. The player's game state is never recorded by the game, except perhaps as the number of the highest level completed. Interactivity may be possible within chapters, in so far as there may be more than one way for the player to reach the end point, but it cannot carry over between chapters. If the player starts Chapter Three with the BFG, then the player must not be allowed to complete Chapter Two without it—or there must be some explanation at the start of Chapter Three as to how the BFG came into the player's possession.

Choice of Words

Always favor short words over long ones. This isn't because phone game players are simple—they're not—but because breaking words across two lines is unsightly and adds another character in the dash used to indicate that the word continues on the next line. In the same spirit, keep character and place names short and keep resounding titles, like Zog the Unspeakable, Invincible Overlord of the Universe, to a minimum—otherwise there won't be room on the screen for anything other than the name.

18.5   Must-Dos

Line and Character Counts

For each piece of text (or at least each type of screen), get a firm line and character count from the producer or the lead programmer and stick to it rigorously. There is simply no room for going over length, and going under can be unsightly—not that having too much space is likely to be a problem.

Payment Terms

No writer should accept a contract that pays by the word—most of the writer's time will be spent paring down the text, therefore reducing the fee. The writer must insist on payment by the hour, or by the project (most phone games are single-milestone affairs, because of their short development cycle).

Market Research

As always, the writer needs to look at competing games—especially those in a similar genre of gameplay. This lets the writer see what restrictions and difficulties the writers of these games have faced, how they have dealt with them, and how well their solutions have worked. Often, looking at other people's solutions to problems can inspire different and better solutions.

As well as playing games on their own phones, writers can go to the websites of prominent developers and look for demos. Sometimes these are playable on a PC (which is still the main development platform), and sometimes they can even be played right in a Web browser. It is useful to look at the range of phones for which each game is available; this reflects both the installed base of each model and the ease of developing games for it. If multiple versions of a game demo are available, they can give an indication of the different capabilities of different handsets.

When a project is in the offing, it makes sense to focus this research on the target platforms for the game under development, and the writer should ask the producer for a list of them. By being aware of the differences and restrictions, the writer can discuss them intelligently with the developers and find out what the options and technical limits are.

It is a mistake to assume that writing must be based on the minimum spec for the simplest, cheapest phone on the list; the writer should be ready to discuss options for adding value to the game on higher-spec phones. Ideas won't always be accepted, but the word will get around that here is a writer who knows something about mobile phones, and that can lead to more work.

18.6   Web Resources

This list is not meant to be exhaustive but should provide enough information for basic research.

Manufacturers

Manufacturers' sites include specifications for their mobile phones.

- Motorola: http://www.motorola.com/

- Nokia: http://www.nokia.com/

- Samsung: http://www.samsungtelecom.com/

- Sanyo: http://www.sanyo.com/

- Sony Ericsson: http://www.sonyericsson.com/

Service Providers

Typing "games" in the search box at most provider sites will give a link to a list of available games.

- AT&T: http://www.wireless.att.com/

- Qwest: http://www.qwest.com/

- Sprint Nextel: http://www.sprint.com/

- T-Mobile: http://www.t-mobile.com/

- Verizon: http://www.verizon.com/

Game Developers

- Capcom Mobile: http://www.capcommobile.com/

- EA Mobile: http://www.eamobile.com/

- Glu Mobile Inc.: http://www.glu.com/

- Hands-on Mobile: http://www.mforma.com/

- Humagade: http://www.humagade.com/

- Reaxion Corp.: http://www.reaxion.com/

- Sega Mobile: http://www.segamobile.com/

- Sony Pictures Digital: http://www.sonypictures.com/mobile/index.html

- Superscape: http://www.superscape.com/

- Vivendi Games Mobile: http://www.vgmobile.com/

Others

- Games on Deck: http://www.gamesondeck.com/

- Steve Palley's "Going Mobile" column: http://www.gamasutra.com/php-bin/column_index.php?toplevel=8

19

Writing for Interactive Fiction

J. Robinson Wheeler

19.1   What is IF?

Originally known as text adventures, interactive fiction (IF) holds a unique place in game writing history, being one of the oldest genres of computer games, predated only by the original Spacewar, and the undisputed progenitor of all modern interactive storytelling. For more than three decades, IF has continued to make advances in technology and technique, guided and shaped by very bright and talented writers and programmers. Some of its early writings still educe a tingling feeling of nostalgia in gamers across the world:

- You are in a maze of twisty little passages, all alike.
- You are standing in an open field west of a white house, with a boarded front door.
- It is pitch black. You are likely to be eaten by a grue.
- ''Floyd here now!''
- What do you, the detective, want to do next?
  >

Only very recently has IF re-emerged in gaming consciousness and popularity. Its commercial heyday was a full quarter century ago, when Infocom was producing big-selling hits like the *Zork* series and its adaptation of Douglas Adams's *The Hitchhiker's Guide to the Galaxy*. Activision bought the ailing company a few rocky years later (a business software venture nearly bankrupted Infocom), and the rise of better graphics cards consigned the text-only adventure game genre to obscurity. To most people, interactive fiction was "dead."

What really happened, though, was that the medium was nurtured in obscurity by an international community of hobbyists, who created a comprehensive FTP (file transfer protocol) archive of IF games, languages, and compilers and gathered their collective thoughts on a Usenet discussion group. Electronic magazines promoting

IF (*XYZZYnews, SPAG*) were born, as were an annual competition to create new games and a regular award ceremony for the best works of the year. New IF development languages that were free, powerful, and relatively easy for new authors to learn drew new talent into the community. This infusion of talent, the potency of discussions within the group, the emphasis on dramatic new ideas and innovation, the exploration of the untapped strengths of the medium, very quickly propelled IF storytelling in the 1990s and 2000s to surpass the fondly remembered games of the 1970s and 1980s in depth and quality.

Nostalgia is still a huge factor in terms of drawing players and authors to IF. Mention them on a blog or in a game review and you'll get dozens of comments saying, "I remember text adventures! Those were great!" IF games are now rising in popularity and gaming consciousness once more, and with that there is playing out a shift in tone from, "They're still writing those?" to, "Modern IF games are awesome. If you're not playing them, you're missing out."

Moreover, one of the unique aspects of IF is the high conversion rate of people who like to play IF into people who want to write IF. Part of the appeal of this—there are a number of reasons why this might be the case—is how easy it is to make the switch. The act of writing IF is in many ways similar to the act of playing it. The act of playing IF excites your mind about the possibilities for writing and crafting stories in that medium; the availability of tools—and a community of support to answer questions you have as a new author—makes the jump possible. If you want to write IF, you can get started right now.

19.2   A Writer's Medium

The best thing about IF is that it is a writer's medium. One can toil alone, like the writer of a short story or a novel, and produce a finished work in a relatively manageable amount of time. You don't need a team of dozens. You'll need a few volunteer beta testers when the time comes, but basically, you can do it on your own.

Being an IF author requires both writing and programming. This combination means that top IF authors tend to be great at both, but very good IF authors usually have a strength in one and a decent ability in the other. Some of the best of the modern authors are professional programmers who were hobbyist writers, and so they were able to deploy their writerly ideas with great technical skill and polish. Others are professional writers who learned enough programming to do the job, sometimes excellently—in large part because, as writers, they had a firm enough idea of the story they wanted to tell and how they wanted players to interact with it that they could figure out how to write the IF language code that was required.

If you're reading this book, you're a writer and may not think of yourself as a programmer. Let me try to remove the intimidation factor from this, because writing IF is great fun, and I want to encourage everybody who isn't writing IF to start doing so. I'm going to assume you know the basics of good writing, and even that you understand what it means to write an interactive story, one with branching dialogue and player choices that matter and make a difference to the outcome. Let's say you have a story idea you're keen on, and you're thinking about writing it as an IF game, because then you can do it yourself and not worry about pitching it to a studio. But you've never written programming code in your life, and so you're freaked out. Well, please don't be.

First of all, you're not starting from nothing. There are several programming languages and tools specifically designed for writing IF. I'll talk about choosing a language later, but for now we'll talk about them in general. The task boils down to: when the player types X, the game should print Y. It is all about printing the right bit of text at the right time, and these languages are designed to make it as intuitive and clean as possible for an IF author to do just this.

19.3 The World Model and the Library

Any modern IF language comes with two pieces of underlying technology already set up for you: the world model and the library.

The world model is the game space that the player character (PC) of an IF game wanders around in. It defines a set of spatial relationships between rooms, objects, and characters, which you don't have to worry about programming. A room connects to another room, allowing travel in between. An object that has a flat surface can have things put on top of it, and the PC can possibly climb up on top of it, stand on it, or sit on it. A container can have things put into it or taken out of it. Things that can hide other objects are searchable.

This now overlaps with the library, which defines the interactive tissue that holds the world together and allows things to happen. It defines archetypal classes of items: chairs, doors, keys, non-player characters (NPCs). All of the basic command verbs are defined, allowing objects to be examined, pushed, pulled, turned, switched on or off, climbed, dropped, taken, boarded, worn, thrown, or eaten. The library allows for NPCs to be spoken to, attacked, kissed, given items, and ordered around. The PC can jump, sing, pray, lie down, stand up, swim, and sleep.

Now, what I mean by the world model and the library allowing for these things— that objects can have these properties and attributes and that these actions can be taken—is that generic versions of them exist that produce default, generic responses. It is trivial to create, compile, and run an IF game that has a couple of rooms, each with an object or an NPC in it, and a generic PC who will be able to enter all of the above commands to interact with the world. Without your having to write anything special, the game will automatically provide responses to all of that input. Of course, you can already see where I'm going: none of the responses are going to be special. You need to write them.

So, to put a chair in your game, you write some definition code that says you want an instance of a chair-type object. You specify where you want it, then you add the vocabulary that a player will use to refer to it. Not just "chair," but a "plush" and "comfy" chair. You give it a unique description, so that instead of, "You see nothing special about the chair," examining it prints, "It's a plush chair with a comfy-looking seat. The mere sight of it makes you want to settle into it and take a load off." Sitting in the chair is handled by the fact that it's a chair-type item in the first place, but all it says is: "Okay, you're now sitting in the chair." So the last thing you do is customize the library's default message so that it says, "You ease yourself into the comfy chair. If you're not careful, you might doze off before you know it."

That's one way of looking at the entirety of writing and programming IF: customizing responses. Tailoring each item in the game so that the player sees a line you've written instead of something the library and world model would generically produce if left alone. A good deal of what trained IF beta testers do is figure out holes in your game where you haven't written a custom response to something, giving you an opportunity to do so.

IF players are delighted when they enter a command and read a special bit of text in response. It fires the reward centers of their brain. When they reach a major milestone in the game, getting a big bunch of new text all at once is an even bigger pleasure. It means they did something right. Part of the dance between IF authors and IF players is that the IF author needs to always gently lead the IF player to enter the commands they've already anticipated, the ones that produce the next bit of story, or character detail, or humor. IF players can't read your mind, and they will tend to go along with you if you're encouraging them to become more immersed in the story they're playing and the world they're interacting with.

There is a place for leaving the library to do some of the work for you and produce generic messages. Generic messages are boring but are also informative, and they can also help players who are feeling a little lost, stuck, or overwhelmed to feel like they're being steered back on track. For example, if the player tries to walk in a certain direction and there's no location to move to, "You can't go that way" is a perfectly valid thing to say. If you had customized that message to something like, "As you walk to the east, a sudden crowd of people surges into your way, blocking you for the moment," a player might think this is a puzzle to be solved and waste 15 minutes trying to outsmart or disrupt this allegedly surging crowd. Then again, suppose you didn't bother to implement (create an object describing) the crowd. The player will try to interact with it and be told by the game, "You can't see any such thing" or, "I don't know the word 'crowd'." These generic messages will get them back on track.

Implementation detail is a quality of modern IF where the bar has been raised significantly over the classic games that people remember playing years ago. Load an Infocom game (Activision currently owns them but has allowed the *Zork* series to be freely played) and you'll find wonderful scene descriptions that allow almost no interaction with any of the scenery depicted. It just isn't there for players to play with. Modern IF sets a standard where practically every noun mentioned in the description of a room or a scene is expected to at least be independently examinable. This was partly due to a trend to enhance and sustain the sense of player immersion (or "mimesis" in the lingo of the community) and also from the scaling back of the average size of IF games as a result of the annual IF competition. The IF Comp, which happens every September (see http://www.ifcomp.org/), limits the games to two hours of play time. People remember playing the Infocom games for days or weeks. Some authors and players wish for a revival of long-form IF games, but from personal experience I can say that trying to create a large IF game with the same density of detail that is expected in a short game will really burn out your synapses after a while.

19.4   Using the Medium

Although the roots of IF are in adventure games (see Chapter 3 for an overview of that genre)—what is now considered "old-school" IF, heavily based in solving thorny puzzles, often to retrieve treasure items—there is no reason to limit your imagination in this regard when contemplating writing an IF game. That is not to say that there isn't a little bit of hunger out there for an old-school puzzle romp, so if you want to do that, just make sure to do a good one. Furthermore, I would argue that puzzles, in the broadest sense—of obstacles to overcome, doors to be unlocked, NPCs with demands that must be satisfied—must be part of IF storytelling, because this is how the medium delivers conflict and resolution, flow and pacing, entertainment and engagement. It is where the interactivity comes from.

The analogy I would use is to songs in a musical. In mediocre musicals, a bunch of songs are slapped together just for the sake of having them, even though they have little or nothing to do with the story, or a paper-thin story is constructed as an excuse to tie a set of songs together. The best musicals, everyone agrees, are ones where the songs naturally flow from the story, spring organically from the characters who sing them, enliven the drama (or add zest to the comedy), and drive the character development and the story forward. The best puzzles in IF these days are ones that have those same organic roots in the story you're trying to tell, that aren't just slapped together or grafted onto a thin excuse for a plot. Think about character, think about setting, the environment and its challenges to the PC, and let the challenges and obstacles grow out of them.

One of the early milestones in modern IF—in a way, the dramatic flare announcing the arrival of a new generation of authors and innovators—was a game by Andrew "Zarf" Plotkin called, appropriately, *A Change in the Weather*. The winner[1] of the 1995 IF Comp, it had a simple scenario: wandering away from a picnic gathering one summer evening, you're caught in a violent rainstorm that dramatically changes the landscape, cutting flash flood channels through formerly dry beds and turning dirt to mud, threatening your survival as well as others'. There were a small number of locations in the game, just enough to establish a clear sense of place, and what Plotkin did was write a mutable description for each location. Each turn of the game,

---

[1]There were two winners that year, one for Inform games and one for TADS games.

as the weather changed from fair to stormy, each location had a custom tailored description written for how things looked that particular turn. You could stand in one place and watch the sun set and the clouds roll in, or you could wander around and feel the change happening while you were busy exploring. No one had ever done anything like that before, and it was revolutionary.

The programming for an effect like this is relatively simple: use a variable to keep track of what turn it is (there is always a counter running that totals the number of turns the player has taken; usually this isn't used for anything). Then, each room's description property runs a check that says, on turn 1, print description 1; on turn 2, print description 2, etc. There are various programmatic shorthands for this sort of thing (`if` and `else` statements, `case` or `switch` statements), but the principle is simple. (One of the more popular languages these days has tried to replace programming code with English sentences that describe the effects the author intends, as a way of being more accessible to non-programmers. I'll explore that and other IF language options in more detail in Appendix G.)

My own version of this effect was in a time-travel game called *First Things First* (XYZZY Award winner, Best Puzzles 2001), which also kept the story confined to a fairly restricted geography but allowed the player to see each discrete location within it at various different points in time. There was also one certain location, set in the future from the PC's point of view, where the variable effects of what the PC had been doing mucking about in the past were continually updated and visible. A house might have weather damage due to inadequate protection. If the player planted a tree in the past, it might have grown overlarge and fallen over into the house instead of protecting it. The whole story was about discovering that the future was going to be a sad state of affairs unless actions were undertaken to change it back in the past, and so even though it was a classic text adventure game in one sense, containing a lot of puzzles, they all grew out of the central premise and were highly tied to the environment of the game. Solving puzzles in one place had reverberating effects and consequences throughout the story. This overall theme was also repeated in the NPCs that you met along the way. You could see what happened to them in the future and see that some of them were heading along tragic paths, and the player had an option to try to influence lives for the better.

19.5   Player Characters as Storytelling Springboards

Another rich area of creative exploration in IF has to do with player characters. It took a long time for IF to change from using a generic PC, through the cliché of amnesia-suffering PCs, to the modern conception where the PC is a particular person, with a particular point of view on the world he inhabits, through which the story's events are seen or possibly filtered.

A great deal of interest has been generated by games that explore the friction between the PC and the player. The tradition in IF of using second-person narration ("You are in a large cavern of limestone and travertine. Your lamp is starting to grow dim.") tends to make players wonder whether they are supposed to feel that they themselves are the actor in the story, or if they are somehow intended to role-play whomever it is that the author has specified. What if the player wants to take an action that is out of character for the PC? What does the PC do? What does the author allow? Would a PC with a particularly active sense of self start to notice that they feel something like a puppet?

There was an IF game by Stephen Bond a few years ago called *Rameses* (XYZZY Award winner, Best Individual PC 2000) that told the story of a particularly moody and recalcitrant young man. In effect, he was so emotionally ungrounded that he often rebelled against commands the player tried to issue, making the meta-point of the game the difference between the PC's internal motivations and sense of moral inertia and the player's interests in what he'd like to make the PC do in the story. It generated a lot of earnest newsgroup discussion and is still pointed to as an example of thought-provoking use of the medium itself.

One of my own experiments into the realm of player characters was *Being Andrew Plotkin* (XYZZY Award winner, Best Game, Best NPCs 2000), which riffed on the title and the premise of the Charlie Kaufman and Spike Jonze movie *Being John Malkovich*. I noticed that the premise of the film—traveling into the head of someone else and witnessing and directing their movements from behind their eyes—was a rather close parallel to the schism between PCs and players in IF. It was also a chance to explore something that IF allows you to do but that hasn't been used by many authors yet, and that is multiple player characters, with the player switching viewpoints between different characters as the story progresses. It also folded back into the other territory of mutable scene descriptions. As one particular location in the game was traversed a series of times, each time with the player directing a different PC, the room description changed to be from that PC's point of view. Same furniture, but each character had a different attitude, a different set of things that they would notice about the environment.

I also had fun in a couple of games that followed that one, of breaking the tradition of starting the game with a character who is empty-handed (and who is expected to eventually acquire a large range of objects in the course of the game) to one who comes fully-stocked, on the first turn, with a full inventory of clothes and gear, all of which was there to help describe who the character was as well as the world he was inhabiting. Furthermore, examining all of the items gave you the PC's personal take on them, how he saw his own possessions. This was very different from the standard way of describing things in IF, which traditionally uses an omniscient narrator's perspective. I was also catching the modern wave of making self-examination, the command "Examine myself" (abbreviated to "x me" in all standard IF games), print an introduction to the PC for the benefit of the player. Here's an example from the first turns of my game *Centipede*:

```
>x me
You're in good health for a guy who's been awake and on active
duty for 76 straight hours.  The stimulants they rationed you
```

```
seem to be working fine with no side effects.  You're pumped
and ready to kill some bugs for God, planet and country.
>i
You are carrying:
a combat suit (being worn)
a waterproof boots (being worn)
a helmet (being worn)
a set of night vision goggles (being worn)
a belt of ammo clips (being worn)
a backpack (being worn and closed)
Charlene
```

You get up to speed pretty quickly by examining yourself and then looking at what you're carrying (and wearing). The order of the inventory isn't accidental, either. Controlling when items are mentioned in lists and descriptions is one of the ways an IF author can draw attention to the more interactive items. Here, all of the combat gear tends to group into a collective, since it all kind of looks the same, and rightfully so. Then comes a surprise, "Charlene"—what?

```
>x charlene
This is Charlene, your plasma rifle.  You know every dent and
scratch on her curved metal body.
>polish charlene
You prefer to polish Charlene in the privacy of your
quarters.
```

There was a recent argument on the newsgroup as to whether players should now feel obligated to type "x me" and "i" ("inventory"—the command for listing one's possessions) at the start of the game even if they'd rather do other things because they might "miss out" on information the author intends them to know—and, conversely, whether authors are now obligated to make sure those commands print something useful because many players now are trained to try them automatically.

I usually come down on the side of letting authors do what they like and tell their stories however they want to, but, as a player, I think I lose a tiny amount of faith in the author when I type "x me" and see the generic result, which is, "You look about the same as always."

As for how you write the code to do this, the player character in IF games is always, at a basic level, just another game object like everything else and has a description property just like everything else. It can also be conditional and change based on variables. The PC might go through a bunch of different looks as the story wears on. And I note, one more time, that "x me" is by nature a reflexive action: it's the character giving his own self-assessment, describing himself, which is a deeply subjective act. There have been a few experiments in having unreliable narrators in IF (I'd tell you what they are, but that would constitute spoilers, wouldn't it?)—stories where seeing the world from that particular PC's perspective leads the player to make some wrong conclusions about the situation—but there is a lot more that can be done.

19.6   Conversation Styles

There are two approaches to character conversation in IF games, usually described as "ASK/TELL" versus "menu-based" dialogue. ASK/TELL is called that because those are the verbs you use to carry out interaction with NPCs—you either ask them about topics you're interested it, or more rarely, you tell them about topics in order to get their reactions. Sometimes this is augmented with the ability to show items to NPCs, as a gestural form of asking them to comment on whatever object is at hand. The vast majority of the time, ASK is all you need to do:

```
Fred is here, whistling as he cleans the countertops with a
gray rag.
>Fred, hi
You greet Fred.

''Hey there,'' says Fred.
>ask fred about fred
''Tell me about yourself, Fred.''

''Well, shoot, what's there to say?'' Fred says,
scratching the back of his neck. ''I'm mainly here to make
sandwiches.''
>ask fred about sandwiches
''What kind of sandwiches are there?'' you ask.

''Glad you asked!  Today's special is a hot meatball sub, for
$4.99. Or if you're really on a budget you can get the cold
cut combo on rye. That's only 99 cents.''
>ask fred about me
''Do you know who I am?'' you ask.

Fred looks at you, a little puzzled. ''I'm not sure what to
say,'' says Fred. ''You're a good customer and all, but I don't
know a lot about you.''
>tell fred about me
''Fred, this is going to sound strange,'' you say. ''But I'm
actually a time traveler from the amazing future year 9 hundred
billion. I've come to deliver a warning to all humanity that
it must change its course.''

Fred fidgets with his cloth rag. ''Are you sure you
don't just want a sandwich?'' he says.
>ask fred about me
''What do you think about me?'' you ask.

''Um,'' says Fred. ''To be honest you seem a little more loopy
than I first figured.''
```

There are several things encoded into the above example that are worth noting. One is the convention—actually somewhat new, though I approve of it—of making sure to include the PC's dialogue before printing the NPC's answer. That used to not be the convention. You'd only get Fred's response, and the PC would be effectively mute, sort of like hearing only one half of a phone conversation. The PC's dialogue wasn't considered that important, but of course it is.

The other things to note are:

- Allowing some words of greeting before launching into pelting a character with questions.

- "Ask [npc] about [npc]" meaning the same thing as "[npc], tell me about yourself."

- "Ask [npc] about me" being a way of getting the NPC to comment on the player character. Sometimes, this is more useful than other times, but generally you need to remember to cover this response no matter who the NPC is.

- Repeated asking of the same question getting a different response after some intervening conversation changes the relationship between the characters. Now that Fred knows more about you, maybe too much, he answers the question differently.

ASK/TELL requires a lot of patient, detailed work on the part of an author, because you've got to anticipate every conversation topic that a player might pull out of thin air, especially if they relate to what the NPC is purportedly interested in. In the above example, Fred will have to know a lot about making sandwiches and the ingredients used. Or, if not, he should have a generic response to an unknown topic that is an improvement over the library default, which is either, "Fred says, I don't know anything about that," which is often terribly wrong (a sandwich maker who knows nothing about cold cuts or bread), or a message that the character "doesn't appear interested," which reduces most characters to wooden robots who are apathetic about the most remarkable topics of conversation, like time travel.

Still, with a little diligence and a lot of testing, ASK/TELL can yield marvelous results. One of the most famous games of modern IF is one called *Galatea* (XYZZY Award winner, Best Individual NPC 2000), which Emily Short wrote for the IF Art Show, a semi-annual boutique for works that are more like conceptual experiments than games. In the piece, the player engages in conversation with a living statue. That is the entirety of the work, but because of the incredible detail that went into the responses, as well as the underlying code that charted the flow of the conversation, such that topics could be delved into more deeply and change the emotional state of the character as it went, it proved to be a rich, immersive experience, and one that put Ms. Short on the map as someone to be reckoned with.

Menu-based conversation is generally more familiar to game writers because it appears in other types of video games, such as RPGs. In IF, you generally start a conversation either through a greeting or a "TALK TO [npc]" command. Once conversation is started, a menu of possible dialogue responses pops up, and players choose which line they want to say. When the NPC responds, the menu updates, following the flow of the conversation until it gets to an end point, or by looping back to offer choices that the player didn't take the first time. There is also usually a way to exit the conversation early if the player has better things to do.

This type of dialogue also requires a lot of preparation and work on the part of the author, because you have to prepare for all of the different ways that a conversation could possibly go, and they all have to sound good. It is also increasingly popular to offer players a choice in terms of how belligerent or conciliatory the PC's dialogue will be at any given moment, a choice that can influence the development of the story in both the short term (how well the NPCs like talking to you) and the larger arc of the overall storyline.

```
>talk to fred
1:  ''Tell me about yourself, Fred.''
2:  ''What kind of sandwiches are there?''
3:  ''I'm actually a time traveler from the amazing
future year 9 hundred billion.''
4:  ''Gotta go.''

>>2
''What kind of sandwiches are there?'' you ask.

''Glad you asked! Today's special is a hot meatball sub, for
$4.99.''
1:  ''I'd love a meatball sub.''
2:  ''Is that all you have? What kind of lame deli is this?''
3:  ''I'm actually a time traveler from the amazing
future year 9 hundred billion.''
4:  ''Gotta go.''

>>4
''Gotta go,'' you say.

''Come again!'' says Fred.
```

Note that if you want to get across a major plot point in the conversation, you can clue players into this by keeping it alive in the menu no matter what other train they may be following, as with the time travel line in the above example. They could keep asking about sandwiches all they want, but you're keeping it in their heads that asking Fred about time travel is ultimately more important. The next time you engage Fred in conversation, it's possible you could skip mentioning anything about sandwiches and only offer the time travel option. Or you might change how a seemingly persistent menu item is answered.

```
1:  ''I'd love a meatball sub.''
2:  ''Is that all you have? What kind of lame deli is this?''
3:  ''I'm actually a time traveler from the amazing
```

```
future year 9 hundred billion.''
4:  ''Gotta go.''
>>2
''Is that all you have? What kind of lame deli is this?''  you
sneer.
''Hmph!''  says Fred.  ''If you don't like it, you can stuff
the meatballs up your shirt for all I care.''
1:  ''I'm actually a time traveler from the amazing
future year 9 hundred billion.''
2:  ''Gotta go.''
>>1
''I'm actually a time traveler from the amazing future year
9 hundred billion.''
''You're a lunatic, and a rude one at that!''  says Fred.
''Okay, that does it, outta my shop!''


With that, Fred tosses you out on your ear and slams the door.
When you look up again, the sign in the window says ''Closed.''
```

If it's actually important to enlist Fred's help to reach the best outcome of the game, the player has made a serious blunder here. Or possibly not—there might be another way to approach Fred later on. It might even open up a subplot that wasn't available without insulting him and having him close the shop on you.

One controversial aspect of menu-based dialogue is that many players have a tendency to want to see everything on the menu. They feel a little disturbed, as if they're missing out on something important, if dialogue choices they didn't select the first time through are closed off and never offered again. It doesn't matter that you, the author, know that they weren't actually very important—the players don't know that and are likely to get antsy if they do not get to satisfy their completionist streak.

This is one of the reasons that there is a philosophical disagreement about whether ASK/TELL is better than menu-based conversation. Because ASK/TELL in effect hides from the players the full extent of possible conversation, they do not know what they're missing and thus don't feel that same sense of itchiness about not getting to select every last possible dialogue option every time. It is also true that players who thoroughly exhaust dialogue menus admit that even as they do this, they feel themselves lose immersion in the game momentarily, as it becomes a mechanical exercise of going through menus instead of sustaining the illusion of a simulated conversation between characters. On the other hand, it is arguable that this is inherently a fault of dialogue menus, which are otherwise a perfectly good way of handling conversation in games.

One way to go about writing interactive dialogue like this is to pick one through-line of the conversation and write all of the back and forth, then start at the top and look at each step of it on a second pass to see what else the characters might say, or say differently, then follow that line. The other is to write one menu at a time, pausing at each to consider all of the options, and keep track of which ones you've written and which you haven't. All of this branching can get rather dense and bushy if you keep at it in such a manner, and generally each conversation in and of itself doesn't need to have more than a few beats back and forth. You might want to use a large sheet of paper and draw arrows around, or use some system of note cards. It seems like a software tool that aids game writers in keeping track of branching dialogue as they write it would be useful, but as of the time of publication, such a tool does not yet exist, even for IF games. (In the larger game world, the game editor that comes with the *Neverwinter Nights* CRPG has an internal tool for writing conversation trees.) In terms of programming conversations, whether ASK/TELL or menu-based, each IF language has its own methods for handling it. In general, though, there will be a way of designating topics and a way of assigning variables to lines of dialogue that (1) keep track of whether the line has been spoken yet or not, and (2) whether speaking that line activates (or deactivates) other dialogue options, so that the next conversation menu that is printed is up-to-date. (See Appendix G for examples.)

19.7   Notable IF Games

While there is a lot of difference of opinion out there, what with the IF community being conspicuously composed of prickly, opinionated, and voluble personalities, there has shaken out, in the scheme of things, a modern canon. These are the games that, for one reason or another, have risen to the top and are continually cited when newbies pop up looking for a list of games to try, or on blog threads about IF where people make random recommendations of games that struck them the most. Some of these games have buoyed up in general estimation since their initial release, where they were regarded as interesting but flawed or controversial, and are now seen as modern classics.

1. *Shade* (Andrew Plotkin)

2. *9:05* (Adam Cadre)

3. *Galatea* (Emily Short)

4. *Photopia* (Adam Cadre)

5. *Spider and Web* (Andrew Plotkin)

6. *Shrapnel* (Adam Cadre)

7. *Slouching Towards Bedlam* (Daniel Ravipinto and Star Foster)

8. *1893: A World's Fair Mystery*[2] (Peter Nepstad)

---

[2]This game is for sale on CD by its author, Peter Nepstad, rather than being freeware. Demo available.

9. *Worlds Apart* (Suzanne Britton)

10. *Anchorhead* (Michael Gentry)

Here's my own B-list of games that come to mind.

1. *Muse: An Autumn Romance* (Christopher Huang)

2. *The Moonlit Tower* (Yoon Ha Lee)

3. *Ad Verbum* (Nick Montfort)

4. *The Edifice* (Lucian P. Smith)

5. *Savoir Faire* (Emily Short)

6. *Bad Machine* (Dan Shiovitz)

7. *Whom the Telling Changed* (Aaron Reed)

8. *Lost Pig* (Admiral Jota)

9. *Fallacy of Dawn* (Robb Sherwin)

10. *Babel* (Ian Finley)

11. *Rematch* (Andrew Pontious)

12. *Aisle* (Sam Barlow)

Playing these games will give you a taste of the modern era of IF and the kinds of writing and storytelling (and yes, puzzle design) that have excited the most dedicated IF players and authors for the past decade. IF is starting to grow beyond serving just its own community, though, and now is a perfect time for an infusion of new ideas and new authors who will continue the growth and experimentation.

19.8   Go for It

Of course, the field is wide open in terms of storytelling possibilities for IF. You are, of course, encouraged to write whatever you want and make it work as IF. All genres are up for grabs, not just fantasy, science fiction, or horror. I've been thinking for a while that nobody's done a cracking good IF courtroom drama, even though the tropes of that—investigation, assembling evidence, and interrogating witnesses on the stand—seem like they'd translate well. A friend and I have been talking for a while now about making an IF game resembling the farcical adventures of the P. G. Wodehouse characters Jeeves and Wooster. My first game was in essence an historical fiction whose setting was the MGM film studio where the Marx Brothers were making their first movie in 1935. People have written psychological dramas and

Lovecraftian horror, madcap slapstick and Machiavellian intrigue. There have been IF games where you play as animals, or as aliens, or even as babies. One of the great things about IF is that you have the freedom to experiment.

As for how to dive in and start going about it, I'm a strong advocate for starting with a mock transcript of what I imagine playing the game would look like when it's finished. I imagine the actions that players will take, and I craft the responses to them. This gives me a blueprint to follow when I start writing the code that will print the right bits of text in the right places. I can then cut and paste the writing from the mock transcript into the code, then play through it and see if the game's output looks like the draft model. I usually find that I want a different flow than I planned for and start breaking up the text in different ways, and of course there quickly come all sorts of extra ideas for commands to enter, and fun responses to give to them, that I didn't think of when I wrote the transcript.

And then there is the fun of finding all of the horrible ways your code is wonky and doing something completely strange. During the process of coding and de-bugging, you often feel like you're playing a meta IF game, trying to solve puzzles of your own design. Rather than wondering, "How do I get that locked door to open?" you lie awake wondering, "How do I write the code to make that locked door tricky to open?" Long walks and deep ruminations in the shower become the places where the "Aha!" solutions to programming problems come to you, just like the way people remember solving the more devious puzzles of *Zork II*, *Planetfall*, and *Trinity*.

19.9   The IF Community and Its Resources

The best part about writing IF is the tremendous resource that the IF community represents. It is an active network of authors with years of collective experience trying to work out how to do probably the very things you're attempting to figure out. If you've made a good-faith effort to work it out on your own, presenting the case to the newsgroup and asking for help will always get prompt and thoughtful responses.

Before you start writing, though, you might want to start playing. Just like people who want to become screenwriters are always told to watch a lot of movies and read a lot of scripts, you should start by playing a lot of IF games and reading a lot of IF source code. The IF Archive (http://www.ifarchive.org/) has piles and piles of freely available source code to look through, which will often show you how someone else went about getting a similar effect.

Most important of all, though, are the freely available games. There are so many of them, in fact, that there are now a number of resources devoted to helping you sort through them and find the best ones. The IF Archive itself is just that—a rather dense library whose stacks you can get lost in without some sort of guide. That's where Baf's Guide to the IF Archive (http://wurb.com/if/) comes in. Eventually, people built more tools that interfaced with the guide, creating the IF Ratings site, the IF Wiki, and the IFDB. (See Appendix G for these and other links.)

19.10   Finishing Up

Suppose you sort all this out, and you manage to write a game. What do you do with it? There are two things to do. One is to simply upload it to the IF Archive and then post an announcement to rec.games.int-fiction (available via http://groups. google.com) inviting people to play it. The other is to enter it into the IF Comp, because that is the best way to get the most feedback about your game, because it attracts the largest number of players, many of whom write reviews of every game they play.

Everyone is encouraged to write games for the IF Comp, because it's where great new authors and games are discovered each year. It provides a deadline to shoot for, which is something any writer should appreciate having as motivation. Competition is stiff, though, so you should familiarize yourself with the quality of the top games each year. Also worth noting are the games that get the worst reception every year, and the sorts of games, or game tropes, that are deeply unpopular.

Many of these used to be staples of the genre. Mazes used to be popular, but now they are loathed. Puzzles where you can't carry very many items, or necessitating the need to eat or sleep on a regular basis, or games where you can make the game unwinnable without realizing it, or that kill you and end the game unexpectedly and frequently—all of these are out (that is, unless you find a very creative and original way of using them, which some authors have dared to do and succeeded). In general, players like the experience to be much friendlier than they used to. Cruelty is out. The other thing you want to avoid, as a new author, is releasing a game that is very obviously set in a recreation of your own apartment or house, because this is a newbie thing to do and is very obvious to experienced players when they come across it. There was a run of games set in office cubicle hell for a while there, and after the fifth or sixth one, they all started to blur together.

Finally, and this is a silly point, but I'll make it anyway: just because it's "realistic" to have them there doesn't mean you need to implement bathrooms. They are a real problem, because if you're going to do them at all, they require a tedious amount of work implementing faucets (sink and bath, hot and cold) and flushable (and usable?) toilets, drain stoppers, bath mats, bars of soap, and mirrors that players will try to break or breathe on. Troublesome (or bored) players will turn the taps on and leave them running just to see what happens. None of that work on your end ultimately adds up to much value to the player, or to the story you're supposedly trying to tell. Sure, if you have a crucial scene requiring pills in a bathroom medicine cabinet, or you're adapting *Psycho* or some such, then go for it. But otherwise, be aware that no one is going to think it's weird that your game's setting fails to have a bathroom in it.

19.11   Step 3: Profit?

Some of you out there, being professional writers, may be wondering where the paycheck is in writing IF. Well, it is possible to win some money by placing first in the IF Competition, and there is at least one company, Textfyre, that is aiming, at the time of this writing, to bring commercial IF to the market once more. (Full disclosure: I've been doing some work for them.) It does seem to be the trend that IF is being rediscovered right now. Companies are finding excuses to publish IF games as fun promotional extras, and there might be more of that in the next few years. Casual game sites are becoming interested in promoting new and interesting IF games to a growing audience.

On the whole, though, IF is still largely in the hands of amateurs in the original meaning of people who do it out of the love of it. You might look at it as an opportunity, a creative outlet for ideas that you weren't able to successfully pitch to a company but that you were sure would make a great game. People can play IF on iPhones now, so there's no shortage of potential players.

Why write interactive fiction? Because you can! You can, right now, write IF.

What do you, the writer, want to do next?

>

A

Appendix for Chapter 1

Steve Danuser and Tracy A. Seamster

Here's a blurb from the style guide for *Echoes of Faydwer*, the third expansion for *EverQuest II*.

Writing Style Guide for *Echoes of Faydwer*

Please keep the following guidelines in mind when writing any text that the players will be exposed to in this expansion, especially when it comes to NPC dialogue. Adhering to the same writing and spelling guidelines helps ensure a more consistent world for our players.

Proper Names

- **The Greater Faydark, The Lesser Faydark**—The residents of Faydwer would always use "the" when referring to their great forests. They see these forests as living entities, and always refer to them with respect.

- **The Faydark**—A more general term that refers to the sum of the forests on Faydwer. Still used with respect.

- **The Fae**—The racial name of the Fae. Please do not use "Fay" to refer to this race. "Fay" can be used as a generic term to refer to magical races, but all references to the new Exp03 race should use "Fae."

- **Ak'Anon, Klak'Anon**—Note the capitalization of the second "a."

The following is a spreadsheet showing some of the racial voiceover barks/call outs for *EverQuest II*. These are what gnomes say when they run into other characters, so the Token field denotes to what other race a gnome would make the Script comment.

Token	Emote	General Reaction	Voice Direction	Script
gnome	curtsy	Friend	**Warm**	May all your gears and whistles work as well as you imagined them.
gnome		Friend	**Offering to share a rare, important gift**	If I had only one goggleblender, I'd definitely share it with you.
status	bow	Gnome level 40+	**Awestruck, seeing a celebrity**	Didn't you calculate the circumference of a fragitory dolamidden to within three fippins? Amazing!
status		Gnome level 40+	**Eager to learn**	Let's sit down and compare blueprints sometime. I'm sure I could learn a thing or two from you!
halfling		Friend	**Curious and cheerful**	Have you got a foozlebit in your pocket? I sure wish I did!
halfling		Friend	**Inviting**	Next time I'm working on a fwinger, I'd love to have you over to help!
barbarian		Cold	**Irritated**	Watch your step, you rusty-pated, slow-witted, half-turned knob on a cognizoid! Can't you see I'm busy?
hail		Neutral generic hail	**Lighthearted anxiety**	Have you any spare foozlebits? Don't you just hate being one foozlebit short of a fwinger?
hail		Neutral generic hail	**Cheerful**	Cheers and boggle chippers to you!
dwarf		Neutral generic hail	**Lightly envious**	I sure wish I had some of the metals I heard you dwarves discovered.
erudite	wave	Neutral generic hail	**Calling out to someone who's not interested**	Hey! Sometime I'd like to show you my latest invention! All right, well, maybe next time!
froglok	duck	Neutral generic hail	**Embarrassed but cheerful**	Ooh, about that little incident with the hair-growth stimulator... who knew? Oh, guess that wasn't you – never mind!
halfelf	ponder	Neutral generic hail	**Curious**	Say, is that a minor absinthesizer you're wearing? I've never seen one used quite that way before.
highelf		Neutral generic hail	**Trying to be helpful**	I have something that might bring back your eyebrows... or, no, maybe not.
human		Neutral generic hail	**Giving advice**	You'd be so much better off if you humans just picked one thing and followed through to the end.
kerra		Neutral generic hail	**Embarrassed but cheerful**	Ooh, about that little incident with the hair-growth stimulator... who knew? Oh, guess that wasn't you after all – never mind!

woodelf		Neutral generic hail	**Reluctant to criticize someone else's homeland**	The woods are fine, but give me a bucket of foozlebits and sprockets and I'm much happier, thanks.
darkelf		Betrayer Citizen	**Shoo! Shoo!**	What!? There's no underground city for you here to cause trouble here.
iksar		Betrayer Citizen	**Surprise in first two sentences hastening away last two**	Greasy Sprockets!!! What is an Iksar doing here... Oh! I must be going now.
ogre		Betrayer Citizen	**Speaking to herself first sentence, sentence then extremely irritated at the interruption**	Flapsockets, flizgigs and more... Ack! Watch where you're going ya brute, I lost track of something important I was working on!
ratonga	ponder	Betrayer Citizen	**Curious, peering at a specimen in a jar**	Yes yes, you are the most curious creature I've come across. I never thought I see a Ratonga this side of Norrath.
troll	grumble	Betrayer Citizen	**Furrowing brow, nose-pinched irritation**	Rusty Cogs!!! I can't get any work done with this bad stench lingering about.

B

Appendix for Chapter 7

Stephen Dinehart

```
Company of Heroes: Opposing Fronts
      The Battle for Caen

              by
      Stephen E. Dinehart
      and the COH Team
```

```
        Current Revisions:
    Version 0.1, Nov 30, 2006
    Version 0.5, Dec 14, 2006
    Version 1.0, Dec 18, 2006
     Version 1.1, Jan 3, 2007
     Version 1.5, Jan 8, 2007
     Version 1.7, Jan 9, 2007
    Version 2.0, Jan 12, 2007
    Version 2.1, Jan 18, 2007
    Version 2.2, Feb 2, 2007
    Version 2.3, Feb 14, 2007
    Version 2.4, April 3, 2007
   Version 2.5, April 20, 2007
    Version 2.6, May 10, 2007
```

<u>MISSION 1: AUTHIE</u>

N01_01 ARRIVAL ON THE FRONT

SUPER TITLE: "GOLD BEACH, NORMANDY"

FADE IN:

EXT. OUT OF GOLD - THE ROAD TO CAEN - DAY

SUPERIMPOSITION:

"Buron - Authie Road: British Second Army Sector"

"1342hrs, June 7th, D-Day +1"

"3rd Battalion Mobile HQ"

The Armored Commonwealth Command barrels forward at a steady
pace, down a dirt road, escorted by two Cromwell tanks. A
caravan of the 3rd Battalion extends well up Authie road. The
French countryside lies half eaten by the ravages of War.

Muddied boots travel at a steady pace alongside the Allied
Armor. The earth shakes under the weight of the heavy steel
beasts, as they rattle down the road.

Fires burn in the distance.

THE CAMERA PANS UP THE LINE OF ARMOR.

Men lounge atop a Cromwell candidly engaged. A stencil on the
tank shows the 3rd Battalion symbol and the words "Boudica's
Boys".

                DILLINGHAM
...a wall of 'em.

                HAZARD
Seven, Dillingham, seven.

                WALLIS
So Major Blackmore empties his clip
on 'em, and realizes, shite,
there's one left. He dives, on our
poor friend Jerry, grabs his
bayonet...

                SEVILLE
Two cuts?

2.

                         DEGNAN
                Two cuts.

                         TENNANT
                Baldy didn't even loose his pipe.

CAMERA PULLS AWAY TO:

Another conversation, three soldiers sit atop an adjoining
Cromwell. A stencil on the tank shows the Royal Dragoon
Guards symbol and the word "BOSS" (the tank's nickname).
While watching the landscape roll by, they speak:

                         BRITISH SOLDIER1
                Poor Frenchies, Jerry really did a
                number on 'em.

                         SCOTTISH SOLDIER1
                We'll thin them out back to Paris
                without so much as a zap. Wankers.
                Should only take us a day.

                         CANADIAN SOLDIER1
                The General says Caen isn't too
                far.

A LOW RUMBLE SUDDENLY ENTERS HARD RIGHT AND SLOWLY PANS LEFT

A look of caution comes over the mens faces. Within moments
they are rocked by blasts from off-screen Panthers. . .

FIZZZZ....KER-PLOWWWW!

The soldiers are blown into fiery bits. Their tank folds as
if imploding. Men fall in all directions as continued fire
comes in.

As the Battalion is rocked by the days first enemy fire, Axis
infantry appear from hidden slit-trenches; firing upon the
Commonwealth Infantry.

                                                   CUT TO:

OUR FIRST LOOK AT MAJOR BLACKMORE!

CLOSE-UP - CONTINUOUS

A hundred yards off from the enemy barrage, one foot raised,
on the roots of a tree stands a war-aged man in his late
thirties, smoking a pipe.

                                                                    3.

                           MAJOR BLACKMORE
                      (under his breath)
                      Bloody Jerries . . . here we go.

A wisp of smoke waves past his brow as Major Blackmore puffs
his pipe and quickly calculates.

                           MAJOR BLACKMORE (CONT'D)
                      Captain Cutting, remind me to
                      gather my own intelligence in the
                      future! Tell 3rd Battalion to pull
                      back, and dig in. We need to
                      protect HQ.

He gently puffs the pipe once more. The Intelligence officer
crouching next to him picks up a radio handset and begins to
shout.

                           CUTTING
                      (into his radio)
                      Boudica, silence that Panther, pull
                      back, dig in, and protect HQ;
                      again. . .

Major Blackmore looks at the combat ahead.

                           MAJOR BLACKMORE
                      (with subtle power)
                      Doubt not ye, the Gods have
                      answered. . .

SEAMLESS TRANSITION INTO DEFAULT GAMEPLAY CAMERA

                           CUTTING
                      (with increasing intensity)
                      3rd Battalion, pull and defend the
                      HQ; Major Blackmore's orders.

P01_01 DESTROY PANTHER AND INFANTRY SQUADS

Length: 5 Minutes

The 3rd Battalion pulls back his infantry and light Armor to
protect the Allied HQ from the Panthers spawning off-map just
beyond Authie (the other side of the mission map).

                                                      CUT TO:

```
       Company of Heroes: Opposing Fronts
            The Witches Cauldron

                    by
             Stephen E. Dinehart
             and the COH Team
```

```
             Current Revisions:
          Version 0.1, March 3, 2007
          Version 0.5, March 10, 2007
          Version 0.9, March 16, 2007
          Version 1.0, March 18, 2007
          Version 1.5, March 23, 2007
          Version 1.7, March 26, 2007
          Version 1.8, March 27, 2007
          Version 2.0, March 28, 2007
          Version 2.2, April 3, 2007
          Version 2.3, May 10, 2007
          Version 2.4, May 25, 2007
          Version 2.5, May 29, 2007
```

MISSION 1: WOLFHEZE A

N01_01 A SUNDAY SURPRISE

                                                    FADE FROM BLACK:

Germany's 3rd Empire consumes most of Europe. As Voss speaks
a propaganda film plays.

                         VOSS
                    (in German)
                    During the past five years our
                    quest for German living space has
                    placed most of Europe under the
                    rule of the 3rd Empire. All that is
                    changing.

                                                    CUT TO:

SUPER-TITLE:

"Wolfheze, Holland: German 2nd Fallschirmjaeger Army"

"1258hrs. September 17th 1944"

                                                    DISSOLVE TO:

EXT. OUTSIDE WOLFHEZE - TRAIN STATION - MONOCHROMATIC

A train pulls into the station at Wolfheze.

New recruits move about to their assignments, a voice echoes
from the stations loudspeakers.

                         STAUDEGGER
                    Willkommen in Holland!

                    Sie alle sind ausgewählt worden, um
                    unserem Vaterland in der
                    Kampfgruppe Lehr zu dienen.

                    Im Namen von Majorgeneral Voss
                    heiße ich sie Willkommen. Melden
                    Sie sich unverzüglich bei ihrem
                    zuständigen Offizier, um ihre
                    Befehle entgegen zu nehmen. Sollten
                    sie dieser Aufforderung nicht
                    nachkommen, müssen sie mit
                    Disziplinarmaßnahmen rechnen.
                    ~~WELCOME TO HOLLAND! YOU HAVE BEEN SELECTED TO~~
                    ~~SERVE YOUR COUNTRY WITH THE KAMPFGRUPPE LEHR!~~
                    ~~MAJORGENERAL VOSS WELCOMES YOU.~~
                         (MORE)

2.

                         STAUDEGGER (CONT'D)
          ~~PLEASE REPORT TO YOUR COMMANDING OFFICERS~~
          ~~IMMEDIATELY, ASSIGNMENTS HAVE BEEN PROVIDED.~~
          ~~THOSE THAT FAIL TO DO SO WILL BE ASSIGNED~~
          ~~ADDITIONAL DUTIES.~~

The soldiers, young and old, move about in an organized
fashion, few seem to even acknowledge Stuadegger's thundering
voice. A few voices stick out over the crowd.

                         DEINHARD
               (in German)
          You heard the man!

                         HENZE
               (in German)
          Yes, commander! On my way sir.

                         GENERIC SOLDIER1
               (in German)
          Move it already you sorry bastard.
          I can't help if you mama over fed
          you out of my way!

                         DEINHARD
               (in German, commanding)
          Get that look off your face and
          keep moving!

CAMERA CRANES DOWN AND PANS TO A FIELD NEARBY

                         WOLFGANG (O.S.)
               (in German)
          Just look at them, what are we
          going to do?

                         ALDRICH (O.S.)
               (in German)
          Train them, what else?

                         WOLFGANG (O.S.)
               (in German)
          Father always said you where a
          positive thinker!

                              FADE TO COLOR:

Fallschirmjaeger Luetnant Aldrich Berger looks into the sky,
admiring the beautiful day. Next to him stands his brother,
Wehrmacht Oberst Wolfgang. Reinforcements report to their
assignment in the field nearby.

>   WOLFGANG (CONT'D)
>   These boys and old men are so green
>   they haven't even fired rifles
>   before and yet these are the best
>   the Führer can provide us!

>   DEINHARD (O.S.)
>   Move it soldiers! Into position!

Aldrich looks into the sun.

>   ALDRICH
>   Enjoy the War while you can,
>   Wolfgang, the peace will be hell.

Aldrich looks to Wolfgang.

>   ALDRICH (CONT'D)
>   Remember what mother used to say,
>   "Make Earth your heaven."

Wolfgang looks down to his brother and smiles.

>   WOLFGANG
>   If this heaven little brother, then
>   we best stay away from hell.

The brothers both laugh uncomfortably a bit.

THE RUMBLE OF ALLIED AIRCRAFT INTERRUPTS THEM

Aldrich seems to pay no attention. Wolfgang looks to the sky
nervously.

>   ALDRICH
>   Relax! Just watch your head.

The preliminary allied bombardment begins.

BOOM!

An unmanned Flak position, near the Berger Brothers is hit,
Clouds of black smoke race towards the sky.

Through the smoke is seen a formation of Allied P-47
Fighters. The sky grows dark with their numbers.

The Berger brothers look at each other, and quickly snap into
action.

>   WOLFGANG
>   At action stations!

4.

SEAMLESS TRANSITION INTO DEFAULT GAMEPLAY CAMERA

P01_01 SHOOT DOWN THE ALLIED P47S

Under the direction of the Berger brothers the German forces
mount a defensive against the oncoming Allied invasion. Axis
Flak positions pummel the sky, filling it with hot munitions.

SR01_01 THEY CAME WITH FRIENDS

The Allies seem to have brought light vehicles with them in
the drop. The Kampfgruppe Lehr must take them out.

P01_02 GLIDER ATTACK AND JEEP ASSAULT

Three waves of Jeeps assault Kampfgruppe Lehr, with aims of
taking the Wolfheze train station. Aldrich's Commando Squads
blitzes each wave of Jeeps and cuts them off before they get
too close.

MISSION 2: WOLFHEZE B

N02_01 SEPTEMBER SNOW

                                        FADE FROM BLACK:

SUPERIMPOSITION:

"Wolfheze, Holland. 1330hrs. September 17th 1944"

EXT. OUTSIDE WOLFHEZE - HOLLAND - EARLY AFTERNOON

They sky, now blackened, is obscured by the Allied airborne
parachutists over Wolfheze.

The Brothers Berger look skyward. Oberfeldwebel Henze and
Oberst Deinhard stand next to them. Little white specks, as
if snow flakes, Allied airborne troops fall from the sky.

                         DEINHARD
                    (Sarcastic)
                    A September snow is upon us!

Deinhard smiles at his friends the Berger Brothers.

                        HENZE
                (nervous, clueless)
                I don't recall ever seeing autumn
                snow before, and on such a warm day
                no less!

Deinhard laughs a bit. Wolfgang puts on his spectacles,
focuses on the distance, and cocks his machine gun.

                        WOLFGANG
                (a bit condescending)
                I've seen things you wouldn't
                believe. Swarms of troopers
                storming Paris, the power of the
                Blitzkrieg, a beach made fortress.
                The beauty of the war machine has
                subtle power.

He smiles into the distance.

                        ALDRICH
                (comforting)
                Our enemy falls from the heavens,
                Henze.

Aldrich looks to the young NCO. Then back to the speckled
sky.

SEAMLESS TRANSITION INTO DEFAULT GAMEPLAY CAMERA

SR02_01 DROP 1

The Kampfgruppe Lehr must defend against the drop on Zone 1.

P02_01 GLIDER ATTACK 1

The Kampfgruppe Lehr eliminates the Allied forces at drop
zone 1.

SR02_02 DROP 2

The Kampfgruppe Lehr must defend against the drop on Zone 2.

P02_02 GLIDER ATTACK 2

The Kampfgruppe Lehr eliminates the Allied forces at drop
zone 2.

6.

SR02_03 DROP 3

The Kampfgruppe Lehr must defend against the drop on Zone 3.

P02_03 GLIDER ATTACK 3

The Kampfgruppe Lehr eliminates the Allied forces at drop zone 3.

N02_02 THE LAST GOODBYE

> FADE FROM BLACK:

SUPERIMPOSITION:

"Wolfheze, Holland. 1550hrs. September 17th 1944"

> DISSOLVE TO:

EXT. OUTSIDE WOLFHEZE - AFTERNOON

An Allied glider lies burning, next to another which seems fully intact. Oberfeldwebel Uschka Henze approaches the wreck.

Peering inside he notices a leather-bound portfolio. Reaching to it, his eyes light up with excitement, as he realizes they are Allied plans.

> FADE TO BLACK.

THE PORTFOLIO

The Allied treasure is handed off, not once but twice.

ACROSS THE TABLE

The portfolio slides across a tabletop towards Oberst Deinhard, the Berger Brothers, and Majorgeneral Maximilian Voss.

> VOSS
> (With a firm hand)
> Why didn't you radio sooner?

> ALDRICH
> It's another one of Tommy's tricks!

                         DEINHARD
              They want Majorgeneral Voss.

                         WOLFGANG
              No Germany is their aim.

He examines the plans with calm intensity.

                                          CUT TO:

DEINHARD'S GAZE

Deinhard admires Voss's Iron Cross.

                                          CUT TO:

P.O.V. THE IRON CROSS

The medal of the Majorgeneral twinkles in the sunlight.

                                          BACK TO:

THE GROUP

Wolfgang looks on with his brother and Deinhard at his side,
waiting for Voss to speak.

                         WOLFGANG
                    (excitedly)
              What does it mean, Majorgeneral?

Voss looks up after a moment, and turns toward the men.

                         VOSS
              Are you familiar with the tale of
              Hansel and Gretel?

The Berger Brothers exchange a skeptical glance, speaking
without words.

Voss looks at the puzzled Wolfgang for a moment.

                         VOSS (CONT'D)
              We have found the children's
              crumbs,there will be no way home!

Voss smiles sinisterly.

                                          CUT TO:

8.

P.O.V. VOSS

The Map shows Allied arrows moving up Highway 69 and several
drop zones.

>   VOSS
>   (confidently)
>   The plans only confirm my
>   suspicions...

>   MATCH CUT TO:

SM02_03 THE PLANS

MAP OF HOLLAND — THE ALLIED PLANS

>   VOSS
>   We are losing more than 70 miles a
>   day on the front to British and
>   American forces. They now seek
>   passage into Germany. Holland would
>   be their gateway.

As Voss speaks the drop zones light up.

>   VOSS (CONT'D)
>   The British 1st and 3rd Parachute
>   Battalions are moving towards
>   Arnhem, and the 4th to the rail
>   bridge near Oosterbeek. The
>   American 82nd and 101st Airborne
>   are pushing for Best and Nijmegen.

Allied arrows with a XXXth Corps symbol moves slowly up
Highway 69 as Voss continues.

>   VOSS (CONT'D)
>   Using their beloved XXXth Corps
>   they intend to push up Highway 69
>   towards Arnhem, uniting paratrooper
>   drop zones along their path.

Before the XXXth Corps Arrow is able to connect with any drop
zones, it encounters a firm swift stall from and arrow ridden
by a Kampfgruppe Lehr symbol.

```
                              VOSS (CONT'D)
                     Kampfgruppe Lehr is to stall XXXth
                     Corps advancement and destroy the
                     enemies precious drop zones. We
                     must stop this Operation Market
                     Garden!
```

From the Kampfgruppe Lehr symbol splits two arrows with the
9th Panzer Regiment and 2nd Fallschirmjaeger Corps symbols
atop them, they pierce the enemy drop zones on either side of
the highway.

```
                                      FADE TO BLACK.
```


<u>MISSION 3: OOSTERBEEK A</u>

N03_01 OOSTERBEEK BRIDGE

```
                                      FADE FROM BLACK:
```

SUPERIMPOSITION:

"Oosterbeek, Holland. 1149hrs. September 18th 1944"

```
                                      DISSOLVE TO:
```


EXT. OUTSIDE OOSTERBEEK - AXIS HQ - LATE MORNING

Half-tracks approach the Axis HQ. Oberst Wolfgang Berger
awaits them quietly with his hands drawn behind his back. The
vehicles pull up alongside him, Aldrich rides atop one of
them.

```
                          WOLFGANG
                     We must destroy the bridge!

                          ALDRICH
                     Fear not brother, Oosterbeek will
                     not be lost.
```

Wolfgang nods to Aldrich. Luetnant Berger signals his men
forward.

```
                          ALDRICH (CONT'D)
                     (yelling over the rain)
                     To the bridge!
```

SEAMLESS TRANSITION INTO DEFAULT GAMEPLAY CAMERA

C

Appendix for Chapter 9

David Wessman

C.1 *Blood Wake* Samples

Fish in a Barrel Mission Design

Filename: Mission_01.mis

Title of mission & Act #: *Fish in a Barrel* (Act 1, Mission 1, Always)

Type: Raid

Summary: Attacking a small port that houses a variety of armed and unarmed sampans.

Context: Introduces player to the forces of the Jade Kingdom, the main enemy of the first part of the story, and puts the player in a pirate position story wise.

Objective(s): Sink all Jade Kingdom sampans in the bay of Suei Pu island.

Captain Difficulty Sequence of Play:

You drive a Barracuda-class speedboat and are accompanied by Gamal. You enter the bay of a Jade Kingdom island from the northwest, led by Gamal the Knife. Gamal leads you in then runs away, leaving the player to fend for themselves. Along the shore are three sets of docked / anchored sampans (some are unmanned.) Buildings on shore and fuel dumps may also be targeted and used to cause extra damage to the unmanned sampans.

Three swordfish class sampans are mixed in with the docked boats and come out of hiding to attack the player when the player gets within a set range of them. After three of the unmanned sampans are sunk, a piranha (med and hard only) and a swordfish class sampan set come in to attack the player. Once six of the unmanned sampans are sunk, five more piranha class sampans come in.

Ensign Difficulty Changes: Less one piranha in the incoming boats.

Admiral Difficulty Changes: Plus one piranha in the incoming boats.

Duration: 5 minutes

BRIEFING:

KAI (A BIT ADMIRINGLY)

A local named Achmed's been showing me around, telling me about old man Zeng and the Shadow Clan.

ACHMED (PROUDLY)

"We hunt the coastal shipping, especially boats from the Jade Kingdom. We live well enough, and our ships are the envy of the Dragon Sea!"

KAI (COCKY)

"I could get to like it here. Who's that?"

ACHMED (WARY)

"Watch out: that's Gamal the Knife, one of Ped's senior men."

GAMAL (CONTEMPTUOUS)

"So you think you're a pirate, *boy*? Bah! You got to earn the right to run with us. Time for a little test."

"All you gotta do is sink a bunch of Jade Kingdom sampans roped up at Suei Pu. That idiot merchant, Anam Pok, has hired 'em as 'protection' against us. We gotta show him that this is a *bad* idea. They'll be easy targets – just make sure you find 'em all."

"Even a *navy man* shouldn't be able to screw this up."

KAI (DEFIANT)

"All right, but I'll need one of your speedboats with chainguns, and I take Achmed here as my first mate."

KAI (DETERMINED)

"Then I'll show you wartholes just what a *navy man* can do."

Voice Script:
M01A01_TARGETS_AHEAD
Achmed (EAGER): Targets dead ahead. Let's get started!

Deleted M01A02_ARENT_ACCURATE
Achmed (INSTRUCTING): Chain guns aren't very accurate at long range.

M01A03_CLOSE_RANGE
Achmed (INSTRUCTING): Chain guns are deadly accurate at close range!

M01A04_NEVER_A_WORRY
Achmed (INSTRUCTING): Best of all, you never run out of ammo!

Deleted   M01A05_PLENTY_OF_AMMO
Achmed (A WARM HAPPY THOUGHT): We always have plenty of chain gun ammo!

Deleted   M01A06_GOOD_START
Achmed (REASSURING): A good start; keep it up!

Deleted   M01A07_OVERHEAT_GUNS
Achmed (GENTLE WARNING): Be careful not to overheat the guns..

Deleted   M01A08_GUNS_TOO_HOT
Achmed (GENTLE WARNING): The guns are too hot, that's what makes them jam up!

M01A09_SHORT_BURSTS
Achmed (INSTRUCTING): Just fire short bursts!

M01A10_USE_RADAR
Achmed (INSTRUCTING): Use your radar to locate targets.

M01A11_LINE_OF_SIGHT
Achmed (INSTRUCTING): Remember, it works by line of sight.

M01A12_HIDDEN_BEHIND
Achmed (INSTRUCTING): Targets can be hidden behind things.

Deleted   M01A13_YOURE_DOING_WELL
Achmed (REASSURING): You're doing well!

M01A14_CROSSED_PED
Achmed (PUN INTENDED): Anam Pok will be sorry he crossed Ped Zeng!

Deleted   M01A16_TEACH_BRANA
Achmed (GLOATING): That'll teach Brana some respect!

M01A17_SHOOTING_FISH
Achmed (BOASTFUL): It's like shooting fish in a barrel!

M01A18_SINK_EVERY_SAMPAN
Achmed (EXCITED): We've got to sink every last sampan!

Deleted   M01A19_WAKING_UP
Achmed (SARCASTIC): Looks like they're finally waking up!

Deleted   M01A20_DONT_LET_ESCAPE
Achmed (EAGER/RUTHLESS): Don't let any of them escape

M01A21_COMPANY
Achmed (WARNING): We've got company! Enemy reinforcements!

M01A22_CLOSE_TO_FUEL
Achmed (WARNING): Don't be too close to fuel tanks when they blow!

Deleted   M01A23_FOG_CLEARING
Achmed (OFFHANDEDLY): Look, the fog is clearing.

M01A24_FOLLOW_GAMAL
Achmed (EAGER): Follow Gamal! He'll lead us to the target!

M01A25_REPAIR_CRATE
Achmed (WORRIED): We're taking damage! Try to pick up a repair crate!

M01A27_FIRE_CONTINUOUSLY
Achmed (INSTRUCTING): Chain guns jam up with continuous fire!

M01A28_USE_TURBO
"Use turbo for a burst of speed."

M01G01_ON_YOUR_OWN
Gamal (CONTEMPTUOUSLY): You're on your own kid!

M01G02_DONT_PUSH
Gamal (ANGRY WARNING): "Don't push me boy, you will regret it!"

M01G03_NOW_DIE
Gamal (DIRE THREAT): "Ok fool, now you die!"

Camera Subtitles:
Intro:
M01G04_SINK_ALL_SAMPANS
Gamal (COMMANDING) Sink all enemy sampans in Suei Pu Bay

M01A26_SHOW_US_THE_WAY
Achmed (INSTRUCTING): Gamal will show you the way

Victory:
M01A15_GREAT_JOB
Achmed (VICTORIOUS, HAPPY): Great job! Ped Zeng will be pleased.

Player Craft & Armament:
Barracuda-class speedboat: chain guns

Friendly Craft & Armament:
Pike-class speedboat: auto cannon & rockets

Enemy Craft & Armament:
Minnow-class sampans: unarmed
Piranha-class sampans: chain guns

Special Features:

Design Notes:
This is the first mission and must include rudimentary instructions for the radar, turbo and primary weapons. Issues:

- Need messages for turbo.
- Messaging steps on it self and needs to be lessened.

Setting
World: Archipelago_C.WLD
Where: Jade Kingdom territory
Terrain: Suci Pu Bay

Environment
Atmosphere: Gray
Sky Body: Sun
Weather: Clear

Base Atmospheric Conditions
Wind Velocity / Direction: 10 knots, 10 degrees
Wave Height / Suppression: 5 / 0.5
Rain / Lightning Density: 0 / 0
Fog: White, 50-500m

Timed Atmospheric Conditions
Delay: 3 minutes
Wind Velocity / Direction: 20 knots, 20 degrees
Wave Height / Suppression: 6 /1
Rain / Lightning Density: 0 / 0
Fog: White, 100-1000m

Assets: (buildings, objects, sound)
Building: Wooden buildings, docks, tropical trees, and watch towers.
Objects: Fuel tanks, and shore batteries.
Sound:

Story Document

Prologue (Red-lit text fading in against black background)

The sea boils with war. Death charges forth in sleek hulls. Chaos rules the waves.

Act 1, Act Intro 1

Baptism of Fire

ZHAN (TIRED AND RESIGNED)

Floating on a piece of wreckage, waiting to die, gives you time to think. I thought I knew Shao Lung. He had often told me he would rule the Northern League, that he was willing to kill anyone who stood in his way.

I thought he was joking.

ZHAN (SUDDENLY ANGRY)

I was wrong.

—ART: Zhan floating on wreckage

—SCREEN BREAK—

ZHAN (CONTINUING ANGRY)

The attack came out of nowhere.

I was an officer with the Fleet of the Northern League, patrolling the Gulf of the Moon, when the explosions first ripped through our ships. We were set up like sheep for the slaughter. Within minutes our squadron was nothing but flaming hulks.

I watched two of our own ships steaming away after the attack, lead by the battleship Dragon. The traitorous bastards were machine-gunning our drowning men as they left ...

That's when I knew who'd betrayed us: Shao Lung himself, admiral of our fleet, commander of the Dragon ...

ZHAN (REALLY BITTERLY)

... and my brother.

—ART: Explosions, Shao Lung

—SCREEN BREAK—

ZHAN (SLIGHTLY SURPRISED)

I was rescued by Ped Xingh, Warlord of the Shadow Clan.

The sea raiders had arrived to scavenge the battle site. They hauled me from the water and had just put a knife to my throat when Xingh made his entrance. He stopped their knives with just a gesture.

ZHAN (MILDY SARCASTIC)

I appreciated his timing.

A mysterious – but lovely – woman appeared at his side, murmuring in his ear. Xingh turned, examined me for a long moment, and then offered me his hand.

ZHAN (RESIGNED AND CYNICAL)

Did I really have a choice? I took it.

ZHAN (CONTINUING)

And so began my career as a sea raider of the Shadow Clan.

I owe these people my life, and I am grateful, but I've also got a score to settle. And I swear on our dead mother's talisman that I will find out what my brother is doing ... and why he wanted me so very dead.

ZHAN (SOUNDING COCKY)

But for now, I'll play pirate. After all, how hard can it be?

—ART: Zhan pulled from ocean, Ped holding out

—SCREEN BREAK—

Act 1, Mission 1 Briefing
Running The Gauntlet

ZHAN (A BIT ADMIRINGLY)

A local named Achmed's been showing me around, telling me about old man Xingh and the Shadow Clan raiders. These people make their living by pirating local shipping, especially that of Iriyan, the Jade Kingdom, to the west.

They live hard but well, and their boats are armed to the teeth, designed for pure speed and maneuverability

ZHAN (COCKY AGAIN)

I could get to like it here.

—ART: Achmed standing portrait and little portrait of Achmed's head..

—SCREEN BREAK—

ZHAN (A BIT LESS ARROGANTLY)

Still, my naval uniform just seems to make me a target. Only my skills with a
boat matter to these guys. In fact, I've been challenged to a race by Gamal the
Knife; a raider with a seriously ruthless rep. I've been loaned a speedboat and
Achmed's even signed on as my co-pilot. All right.

The challenge seems simple enough. All I have to do is keep up with Gamal as
we circle the island back to the starting dock ... while running a gauntlet of sea
raider boats who'll be trying to drive me into every available reef or rock ... if
I'm lucky.

ZHAN (CYNICALLY)

Gamal's even been so kind as to give me a head start, claiming he won't move
until I pass the first buoy. And a guy with the nickname, "the Knife," has just
got to be trustworthy, right?

ZHAN (DETERMINED)

So now it's time to show these wartholes just what an officer can do.

—ART: Gamal Art, Dock photo

—SCREEN BREAK—

Spotter Scripts
Achmed: "Once past the 1st buoy the race is on."
Achmed: "Stay close to the shore, but avoid the rocks!"
Achmed: "Just a little further!"
Achmed: "Do not sink him, Zhan. They will have our heads for sure"
Achmed: "We made it. You did a great job!"
Gamal: "Hurry it up fool, I do not have all day!"
Gamal: "You will never catch me, boy!"
Gamal: "A soldier can never have a pirate's ruthlessness!"
Gamal: "Your career ends today child!"

Act 1, Mission 2 Briefing

Fish In A Barrel

ZHAN (EXCITED)

Having survived that last little party game, I've been given the chance at a mission. Ped Xingh himself called me in, but he didn't seem very impressed. He
spent most of the time puffing on a huge cigar and looking at me like something
that should be dragged behind a boat rather than piloting one.

PED XINGH (RESERVED/ASSESSING)

"You've bought yourself some time, crab bait, but now you've got to earn your
keep. Let's see if your gunnery is a match for your piloting."

PED XINGH (DOWN TO BUSINESS)

"I am sending you to sink a number of freight barges at anchor at Suei Pu. They'll be easy targets, since their crews'll be ashore. The tricky part will be finding all of them – the coast there is riddled with coves and hiding places."

"I've no interest in capturing the cargoes; I want them destroyed. Anam Pok, their pig of an owner, hasn't paid his tribute to me in over a month."

PED XINGH (THREATENINGLY)

"He's going to bleed for that ... until he squeals. Now, go."

—ART: Ped Xingh with cigar, Photo of

—SCREEN BREAK—

Spotter Scripts
Achmed: "A good start; keep it up."
Achmed: "You're doing well."
Achmed: "Anam Pok will be sorry he crossed Ped Xingh."
Achmed: "Great job! Ped Xingh will be pleased."

Act 1, Mission 3 Briefing

A Lesson In Violence

ZHAN (CONFIDENCE RETURNING)

My "-busting' has earned Achmed and I some credit ... and another mission.

ZHAN (ADMIRINGLY)

Xingh's advisor, the Lady Helen, delivered this latest briefing. She's a bit of a mystery, a real beauty with a heart of steel.

During the meeting, she handled that pack of cutthroats like she could gut every one of them, and they treated her words as if they fell from the lips of God.

LADY HELEN (BUSINESS-LIKE BUT SEXY)

"Our last raid was just to attract Lord Brana's attention. This attack is to punish him for withholding our tax on commerce in the archipelago."

"You're to sink any Jade Kingdom sampans you encounter. Kill only when you have to, but don't let any boats escape."

LADY HELEN (SUDDENLY HARD AND DETERMINED)

"We'll teach them who owns these islands."

ZHAN (CURIOUS)

What's the Shadow Clan got against Lord Brana and the merchants of Jade Kingdom? This is beginning to sound like a blood feud.

> ZHAN (EXCITED)

Still this Lady Helen has me intrigued. Now there's a woman worth getting to know better!

> ZHAN (DETERMINED)

But it'll have to wait; I can only fight one battle at a time....

—ART: Portrait of Helen (from original character sketch), Silhouette of her standing in front of group of pirates, Photo of Sampans

—SCREEN BREAK—

Spotter Scripts
Achmed: "These Jade Kingdom traders need a harsh lesson."
Achmed: "Don't let them get away!"
Achmed: "Ha! Some have the gall to fire back!"
Achmed: "You've done well; your ancestors would be proud!"

Act 1, Mission 4 Briefing (Act Finale)

Knife Fight

> ZHAN

I've learned that my mate's full name is Achmed Rahman bin Sul. Now there's a mouthful. Still, he's a good man, with sharp eyes and steady nerves. I trust him in a fight.

> ZHAN (TURNING SERIOUS)

And I need a friend right now.

Gamal and another of Xingh's lieutenants have proposed a dangerous but doable plan to finally earn my way into the sea raider brotherhood.

I'll act as bait to lure a flotilla of heavily armed Jade Kingdom sampans into a bay with a very narrow entrance. Then my two new "allies" will charge out of hiding to complete the ambush.

—ART: Gamal sketch (close-up of him sitting on dock), Smaller image of Gamal and other raider standing, talking to you

—SCREEN BREAK—

> ZHAN (GETTING EXCITED)

Together, we ought to be able to blow the trapped Iriyani to pieces. Achmed's even scrounged up two rapid-fire chain guns to give our boat a meaner bite.

This is my chance to finally show Lady Helen – and Lord Xingh too, of course – just how good I am.

ZHAN (DETERMINED)

Still, I'm holding on to my mother's good luck charm and praying that Gamal keeps his word ... this time.

Let's do it!

—ART: Drawing of minicannons, photo of mini cannons on boat

—SCREEN BREAK—

C.2 *Star Wars: X-Wing Alliance* Cutscene Scripts

Cutscene Master Character List

Character (cutscenes appearing in)

Aeron Azzameen (C02)
Player's sister: Older than player. Her specialty is code slicing, i.e. code cracking, and general computer hacking, player's trainer, confidante and link to the family throughout the story, but particularly after player has joined the Rebellion. Central character and heroine.

Antan Azzameen (C01)
Player's uncle: Brother to player's father, long time partner and founder of family shipping and storage business. Takes leadership of family after father killed. Central character, key figure in major plot twist of story.

Emon Azzameen (C02)
Player's brother: Older than player. Hot headed brother, modeled after Sonny Corleone of the "Godfather," a great pilot but quick tempered. Spends most of the story seeking retribution and revenge for his father's and brother's death. The target of this vendetta is the head of the rival family, K'Armyn Viraxo.

Tomaas Azzameen (C01)
Player's father: Head of family business. Sympathetic to Rebellion but outwardly neutral. Killed early in story.

Galin Azzameen (C01)
Player's brother: Oldest in family, heir to family business , killed along with father early in the story.

Olin Garn (C01, C05, C07, C12)
Sister's friend: A fighter pilot in the Alliance. Is there to train the player when the player joins the Alliance at the beginning of battle 1. Older, wiser and more experienced pilot than player

Commander Kupalo (C05)
Rebel Briefing officer: imperial mole/spy, on board the Cruiser Liberty

Commander Zaletta (C06, C07, C08)
Rebel Briefing officer: on board the Cruiser Liberty

Admiral Nammo (C02)
Rebel commander of Cruiser Defiance, calamari

Admiral Ackbar (C08)
Top military commander of Alliance, commander of Cruiser Independence, calamari

Rebel Officer #1 (C05)

Rebel Officer #2 (C06)

Rebel Pilot #1 (C10)

Rebel Pilot #2 (C10)

Admiral Holtz (C02, C03)
Imperial commander: commands task force searching for rebel fleet after Battle of Hoth

Admiral Zaarin (C04)
Imperial commander (battle 2) from TIE Fighter, in charge of many different research projects

Lord Darth Vader (C06, C08, C09)

Emperor Palpatine (C06, C08, C09)

Imperial Officer #1 (C03, C09)

Imperial Officer #2 (C03, C10)

Imperial Officer #3 (C04, C10)

Imperial Officer #4 (C11)

Imperial Zero-G Stormtrooper (C01)

Imperial TIE Interceptor Pilot (C11)

Cutscene 1—Opening
Main Elements:
- Rebel escape from Hoth
- Credits
- Rendezvous at a Family Platform

Ships:

- Corellian YT-1800 Transport *Otana* (Family Transport)
- Corellian YT-1300 Transport *Sabra* (Player's Craft)
- MandalMotors *Pursuer*-class Enforcement Ship *Andrasta* (Emon's Craft)
- Medium Transport
- Corellian Action VI Transport
- Tugs
- X-wings
- Imperial-class Star Destroyer(s)
- TIE Fighters
- Super Star Destroyer?
- Assault Shuttles?

Voices:

- Tomaas Azzameen (Father and captain of the Family Transport)
- Galin Azzameen (eldest brother and co-pilot of the Family Transport)
- Antan Azzameen (Uncle and Platform Director)
- Olin Garn (X-wing Pilot #1)

Shot 1: The *Otana* leaving Hoth escorted by a pair of X-wings flies directly toward the camera. The camera tracks the transport and as it flies past and away from the camera, a Star Destroyer is revealed moving to block its path.

TOMAAS AZZAMEEN mordantly

"What a great day to pay a visit to the Rebels! I can see why you're going to need so much bacta!"

The Star Destroyer is hit by ion cannon blasts coming from behind the camera.

OLIN GARN reassuringly

"Don't worry, we've got you covered."

As the ion blasts hit and the Star Destroyer begins to list, two pair of TIE Fighters come into view flying toward the camera spitting laser fire.

Shot 2: Switch to a view that shows the TIEs are making a firing pass on the transport.

OLIN GARN determined

"Green Two, bracket high-low now!"

The X-wings have broken out high and low relative to the *Otana* and turned back to intercept the TIEs. The TIEs end up caught in the crossfire. One pair is simultaneously toasted by a single quad burst from one X-wing. The other pair is taken out in quick succession, rear craft first. The ball of one of the TIEs explodes near enough to the Family Transport to pepper it with small bits of debris and cause it to shudder.

TOMAAS AZZAMEEN earnestly, then wryly for last phrase

"Great shooting, but that was way too close for comfort. Thanks for your help, we are outta here!"

The *Otana* jumps to hyperspace sporting a few ragged and glowing little holes. The X-wings have turned back to cover the next ship off of Hoth. (Note it would be cool if the background could show a bunch of Imperial ships, especially Assault Shuttles and other planetary attack craft. Isn't the Executor part of this fleet?)

Shot 3: Tracking the *Otana* through hyperspace while the TG credits run. Panning/rotating camera view or series of fly-bys showing off the details of this new-to-the-Star Wars-universe ship. At least one medium shot sufficient to show two bobbing heads in the cockpit to place the two voices for this shot.

TOMAAS AZZAMEEN concerned

"It doesn't look like we got away so clean after all, Galin. We're losing coolant pressure in the primary reserve tank."

The camera zooms in on the damage done by the exploding TIE. It affects only a few spots on the hull, but the damage isn't insignificant. There is some residual glowing, random sparking and what appears to atmosphere venting through a tiny hole in the hull.

GALIN AZZAMEEN slightly worried

"You want me to see what I can do?"

TOMAAS AZZAMEEN relaxing

"No, we're close enough to stop at our service platform in the Roccus system for repairs."

GALIN AZZAMEEN slightly taken aback, then somewhat mocking

"Isn't Uncle Antan going to be there? When he sees this damage he's going to say, 'I told you not to get involved with the Rebels.'"

TOMAAS AZZAMEEN resigned

"I'd rather put up with that than risk trying to get all the way home without that primary reserve."

GALIN AZZAMEEN resigned

"Fine by me. It's your call."

Shot 4 [B-list]: The *Otana* comes out of hyperspace near a space platform where a variety of transports can be seen docked. They include any number of the following: Medium Transport, Corellian YT-1300, Kuat Systems Engineering Firespray-class Patrol and Attack Ship (Slave One), MandalMotors Pursuer Enforcement Ship (Slave Two), Corellian Action VI Transport, Lambda-class Shuttle, Tugs etc. Ships are moving about the platform and various docking operations are being carried out while the following argument goes on as long as necessary for the LEC credits.

TOMAAS AZZAMEEN business-like

"Hailing Twin Sun Service Platform, this is Captain Tomaas Azzameen of the Corellian Transport *Otana* requesting emergency repairs!"

ANTAN AZZAMEEN surprised

"Tomaas! What happened? It looks like you've been in a fight. You didn't actually contact the Rebels did you?"

The camera moves around the platform taking it all in as the *Otana* moves in. LEC credits run while Tomaas and Antan argue.

TOMAAS AZZAMEEN still business-like (trying to minimize the gravity of the situation)

"Everything was just fine until an Imperial fleet showed up. I accomplished what I set out to do and we got away with only minor damage. How quickly do you think you could patch up my primary reserve tank?"

ANTAN AZZAMEEN sympathetic, then suspicious

"I'd have to bump a bunch of ships that have been waiting ... it's going to cost us if I do that. You're not in any particular hurry are you?"

TOMAAS AZZAMEEN disingenuously

"Well, yes..."

ANTAN AZZAMEEN deeply suspicious, then accusatory, then angry, then bemoaningly

"What are you telling me? You're under pursuit aren't you? Blast your idealism! I told you this would happen! As if the Imperial authorities aren't already difficult ... "

TOMAAS AZZAMEEN weakly apologetic, then conniving

"Now, Antan, I took precautions and I know we weren't IDed. Look, the sooner I get out of here, the better for all of us, right?"

ANTAN AZZAMEEN furious

"No way! This is bantha spew and you know it. You can make it home just fine as you are. I suggest you leave immediately before I report you myself!"

TOMAAS AZZAMEEN astonished, then angry

"Why you ... are you refusing to help me out?"

ANTAN AZZAMEEN furious

"You're damned straight! I told you we can't afford to get mixed up in this Rebellion. Maybe this will make you realize I'm serious. We'll talk about this after you get home and cool off. Twin Sun Platform out!"

Cutscene 2—End of Prologue

Main Elements:

- Escaping Imperial Seizure of Family Platform
- Rendezvous with a Rebel fleet

Ships:

- Family Base
- Corellian YT-1800 Transport *Otana*
- Corellian YT-1300 Transport *Sabra*
- MandalMotors *Pursuer*-class Enforcement Ship *Andrasta*
- Imperial-class Star Destroyer
- TIE Fighters
- Assault Shuttles
- Zero G Stormtroopers
- A-wings
- Y-wings
- Calamari Cruiser *Defiance*
- Nebulon-B Frigate
- Corellian Corvette
- Rebel Medium Transport

Voices:

- Aeron Azzameen (Sister)
- Emon Azzameen (Hothead Brother)
- Admiral Nammo (Captain of the *Defiance*)
- Garreth Holtz (Imperial Commander)
- Imperial Zero-G Stormtrooper

Shot 1: The three family transports are flying toward the camera with TIE Fighters in hot pursuit. In the background an Imperial Star Destroyer looms upon the family base.

GARRETH HOLTZ imperious

> "In the name of Emperor Palpatine, the personnel on this station and all ships in the area are under arrest. Cease your flight and return to the platform at once or be destroyed!"

The *Andrasta* suddenly executes an impossibly tight loop and unleashes a sustained burst of rippled single-fire cannon blasts that catch the nearest of the pursuing TIEs completely by surprise.

EMON AZZAMEEN surly

> "Not today, bootlicker!"

The *Andrasta* rejoins the other two transports for the jump into hyperspace, and the remaining TIEs break off and turn back toward the base.

Shot 2: Switch to a view that shows the Assault Shuttles making a firing pass on the base using their ion cannons. Zero-G Stormtroopers are deployed in their wake.

IMPERIAL ZERO-G STORMTROOPER overconfident

"Securing the station now, sir!"

The Stormtroopers use their maneuver packs to reach the hangar opening where they are caught in a large explosion.

Shot 3: Family transports come out of hyperspace near a large pale gas giant. Panning reveals that the planet is orbiting a double star. Further panning reveals a Rebel fleet orbiting the planet.

EMON AZZAMEEN mordantly, then serious

"Wish I could've seen the look on that Imperial Commander's face when they found your little present, Aeron. Anyway, looks like the co-ordinates your boyfriend gave us were right on the money. Why don't you give them a hail and see what kind of reception we get?"

AERON AZZAMEEN serious

"Hailing Rebel Commander, this is Aeron Azzameen. The Empire has just driven my family and me from our home. We seek sanctuary, may we approach?"

ADMIRAL NAMMO surprised, then sympathetic, then inquisitive

"You're Tomaas Azzameen's kids? He was a good man, I was sorry to hear of your loss. You're certainly welcome to join us, but how did you know where to find us?"

Two flights of A-wings have moved into escort positions.

AERON AZZAMEEN slightly flustered

"Uh, I'm a friend of Olin Garn, one of your starfighter pilots. Is he there?"

ADMIRAL NAMMO businesslike

"Well, we can discuss that in person. Follow your escorts to the Cruiser Defiance."

The trio of family transports and their escorts fly toward the Calamari Cruiser.

Cutscene 3—Battle One: Clearing the Way
Main Elements:

- Rebel fleet escaping into hyperspace
- Admiral Holtz's ISD repair problems

Ships:

- Mon Cal Cruiser
- X-Wing
- A-Wing
- B-Wing
- Nebulon-B Frigate
- Corellian Corvette
- Imperial Star Destroyer

Voices:

- Imperial Admiral Holtz
- Imperial Officer #1
- Imperial Officer #2 (Communications)

Shot 1: A large collection of Rebel capital ships moving in formation. Various Rebel starfighters are moving with the fleet, like small insects darting around the ships in formation (Like the scenes at the Battle of Endor in ROTJ). The fleet jumps into hyperspace together. Hopefully the shot can show the fleet in the familiar blue hyperspace tunnel).

Shot 2: The shot would show the ISD slightly adrift in space.

> IMPERIAL OFFICER #1 carefully choosing his words, the emphasis should
> be on "top efficiency"

Admiral Holtz, Engineering reports that they have completed their repairs. They wish to inform that without adequate parts or tools, they cannot be certain the hyperdrives will function at top efficiency

> ADMIRAL HOLTZ

Very well. Was the Sensor station able to repel the Rebel attack?

> IMPERIAL OFFICER #2 nervous, aware that they are all in a bad situation

Negative Sir, we lost communication with them an hour ago. Gunboats from Tau squadron have reported that they are lost. Incoming report sir, Command has given us new orders. We are to return to Coruscant for an inquiry into the Rebel attack.

> ADMIRAL HOLTZ fatally resigned, he knows that his inability to prevent the
> Rebels from escaping has ended his career, and possibly his life

Of course. Signal command, inform them that we shall arrive in two weeks. Navigation set course for Coruscant, engage hyperdrive.

Shot 3: The shot would then show the Hyperdrive engines flicker to life, the ISD would move for a short distance, then come crashing out of hyperdrive with small fires in the engine section. Various warning sirens are going off.

> ADMIRAL HOLTZ emphasis should be placed on the phrase "three weeks."
> This is something of a funny remark, since how could things get any worse?

sigh Less than top efficiency indeed, Lieutenant. Tell command to expect us at Coruscant in three weeks.

Cutscene 4—Battle Two: Secret Weapons of the Empire

Main Elements:

- Tugs operating in debris field
- Admiral Zaarin speaking with Imperial officer

Ships:

- Tug
- Debris (various bits and pieces)
- ISD

Voices:

- Admiral Zaarin
- Imperial Officer #3

Shot 1: The debris from the battle is spread out, parts of craft still burning in space (yeah I know, internal fires?). Suddenly several tugs are shown collecting debris. An ISD comes into view with TIE Fighters on patrol.

IMPERIAL OFFICER #3 businesslike

We have recovered the damaged remains of the facility's computer core, Admiral Zaarin. Our techs are looking at it now. It appears that we will be able to recover a significant amount of data.

ADMIRAL ZAARIN brisk

Excellent, and what of Director Lenzer?

IMPERIAL OFFICER #3 businesslike

The log shows he fled the scene in a shuttle. That is all the information we have sir. There is a high probability that his shuttle was destroyed in the battle.

ADMIRAL ZAARIN unmoved

A shame, but the project will continue. The data recovered from the prototypes will prove valuable to us as we move in the second stage. As soon as the tugs are all onboard, set course for research station Obsidian.

IMPERIAL OFFICER #3

Yes sir.

Shot 2: Many tugs (more than the previous scene) collecting the debris from the battle.

Cutscene 5—Battle Three:

Main Elements:

- Commander Kupalo steals a shuttle and escapes, wreaking havoc along the way.

Ships:

- Calamari Cruiser
- Nebulon-B Frigate
- Shuttle
- X-Wings

Voices:

- Rebel Officer #1
- Olin Garn
- Commander Kupalo

Shot 1: The landing ramp of the Shuttle closes, and as the shadow of it recedes, a security guard is revealed, face down and motionless.

Shot 2: The shuttle lifts off from the hangar bay of the Cruiser, as a Rebel officer's voice is heard.

REBEL OFFICER #1 businesslike

Shuttle AA-23, you are not authorized for launch. Power down your engines, and submit your flight plan. [No response].

Shot 3: The shuttle continues and nears the open hangar door.

REBEL OFFICER #1 starting to yell

Shuttle AA-23, you are ordered to comply. Power down your engines and...

Shot 4: Just as the shuttle leaves the hangar bay, a large explosion rocks the hangar.

Shot 5: X-Wings are scrambled and launch from the secondary hangar bay. They approach the shuttle, opening their s-foils into attack position.

OLIN GARN angry

AA-23, we have you in our sights. Power down at once or we will open fire.

COMMANDER KUPALO sarcastic

I'll take that into consideration.

Shot 6: The Shuttle drops a few homing mines, which immediately lock onto the X-Wings and start tracking them. The X-Wings try to avoid them, but end up getting blown to smithereens. The Shuttle escapes to hyperspace.

Cutscene 6—Battle Four:

Main Elements:

- The Imperial computer is decoded by the Rebels, revealing the Death Star construction.
- Vader and Emperor discuss their plans to trap the rebels.

Ships:

- Rebel Base (interior)
- Super Star Destroyer
- Star Destroyers
- TIE Fighters

Voices:

- Rebel Officer #2
- Commander Zaletta
- Darth Vader
- Emperor

Shot 1: Inside a rebel base, the Imperial computer captured by Bothans is decoded.

REBEL OFFICER #2 hesitant

Okay, I think I've got it. I'm routing it to the display now.

Shot 2: A few officers stand in front of a large display as the Death Star II is revealed. A few gasps and sounds of amazement and dread can be heard.

COMMANDER ZALETTA shaken

Get this information to High Command at once. We have a new priority, people. I only hope it's not too late.

Shot 3: Cut to Endor to show actual Death Star under construction.

Shot 4: Cut to Imperial Fleet, and the Executor. Various TIE Fighters patrol the area.

Shot 5 (B-list): Inside the Executor, Vader kneels before a holo-image of the Emperor.

EMPEROR

Your report, Lord Vader.

VADER

The plans are now in Rebel hands, my master. Our forces gave chase, but allowed them to escape as you commanded.

EMPEROR

You disapprove?

VADER (slight pause)

It is not my place to disapprove, my master.

EMPEROR

Quite so. On Prince Xizor's advice, I allowed the plans for the new Death Star to fall into Rebel hands. When their trust in him is complete, he will deliver the Rebels to us, and we will crush them at our leisure.

VADER

Yes, my master.

Cutscene 7—Battle Five: Mustering the Fleet

Main Elements:

- X-Wing moving through large cargo ship convoy (smuggler)

Ships:

- X-Wings
- Cargo Craft (2-5)

Voices:

- Olin Garn
- Commander Zaletta

Shot 1: Various cool looking smuggler cargo ships transferring cargo to Rebel cap ships. Fighters will be flying around looking over the operation. The shot could follow an X-W as it flies near several of these exotic cargo craft.

COMMANDER ZALETTA businesslike

Red 4, what's your status (a pause). Red 4 I say again, what is your status?

OLIN GARN snapping to attention, then sheepishly

Everything checks out Commander. Sorry about that, it's just with the Imps out of our hair for a while things seem almost relaxing.

COMMANDER ZALETTA businesslike

We haven't won this war yet. Keep those status reports coming in on schedule

OLIN GARN businesslike

I roger that.

Shot 2: The X-W kicks in its engines and continues its patrol.

Cutscene 8—Battle Six:

Main Elements:

- Ackbar narrowly escapes
- Rebel fleet gathers at Sullust
- Vader and the Emperor plan the ambush (B-List)

Ships:

- Calamari Cruisers
- Nebulon-B Frigate
- Corvettes
- Rebel Transports
- Variety of Rebel Fighters
- Star Destroyer
- Imperial Fighters
- Death Star observation tower (exterior)
- Emperor's Throne Room (interior)

Voices:

- Admiral Ackbar
- Commander Zaletta
- Darth Vader
- Emperor

Shot 1: A Star Destroyer (or two?) pursues Rebel forces as they head for their rendezvous at Sullust, firing madly. A variety of Rebel and Imperial fighters twist and turn embroiled in combat.

Shot 2: Inside the Independence, a blast rocks the Cruiser violently.

ACKBAR concerned

How long until we can make the jump to hyperspace?

COMMANDER ZALETTA excited

We're almost there, Admiral! But at the rate they're gaining, it's going to be close!

Shot 3: More cool battle stuff, some pilot chatter, lotsa things going boom. The Cruiser escapes to hyperspace, and there is much rejoicing.

Shot 4 (B-List as in ROTJ): Inside the Emperor's Throne Room, Darth Vader stands before the Emperor, and awaits his orders.

VADER

What is thy bidding, my master?

EMPEROR

Send the fleet to the far side of Endor. There it will stay... (Deviously)...until called for.

VADER

What of the reports of the Rebel Fleet massing near Sullust?

EMPEROR (dismissively)

It is of no concern. (More sinister) Soon the Rebellion will be crushed [and young Skywalker will be one of us]. [All is as I have foreseen]. Your work here is finished, my friend. Go out to the command ship and await my orders.

VADER

Yes, my master.

Cutscene 9—Battle Seven: Endor Part 1

Main Elements:

- Order to fire Death Star
- Fire initiation procedure

Interiors:

- Emperor's Chamber
- Death Star Gunnery Station

Characters:

- Emperor Palpatine
- Darth Vader
- Luke Skywalker
- Imperial Officer #1
- Death Star Gunnery Crewman

Voices:

- Emperor
- Imperial Officer #1 (reassigned from Adm. Holtz)

Shot 1: (In the movie the Emperor is seated with Vader behind him and Luke looking out the window.)

EMPEROR PALPATINE gloating

"Your friends have failed. Now witness the firepower of this fully armed and operational battle station! Fire at will, commander!"

Shot 2: Gunnery crew responding to order.

IMPERIAL OFFICER #1 decisive

"Fire!"

Cutscene 10—Battle Seven: Endor Part 2

Main Element(s):

- Super Star Destroyer Executor collides into Death Star

Interior(s):

- Gun Tower

Ships:

- Death Star
- Super Star Destroyer
- B-wing
- A-wing
- TIE Interceptors
- Any variety of other Rebel and Imperial starfighters and capital ships

Characters:

- Gun Tower Officer
- Gun Tower Crewman

Voices:

- Rebel Pilot #1 (Green 5)
- Rebel Pilot #2 (Blue 7)
- Imperial Officer #3 (reassigned from Adm. Zaarin)
- Imperial Officer #2 (reassigned from Adm. Holtz)

Shot 1: Near the surface of the Death Star, B-wing Green 5 shooting past a pair of TIE Interceptors which quickly loop around to chase the Rebel fighter.

> REBEL PILOT #1 grim and determined, random stress from violent
> maneuvers

"Blue 7, I'm starting my run on the surface...please get these squints off my back."

An A-wing swoops in behind the TIEs.

> REBEL PILOT #2 excited

"No problem, 7!"

The A-wing launches a missile at the rear Interceptor. The target immediately jinks away in a futile attempt to evade the missile. The lead craft loops around to deal with the threat of the A-wing.

Shot 2: From behind the B-wing as it heads toward a gun tower.

> REBEL PILOT #1 determined

"Torpedoes away!"

A pair of proton torpedoes shoots forward as the B-wing pulls up out of frame.

Shot 3: From inside the gun tower, looking out the viewport at the oncoming torpedoes.

IMPERIAL OFFICER #3 panicky

"Ignore the fighter, target those warheads!"

IMPERIAL OFFICER #2 nervous

"Yes, sir!"

Both warheads are destroyed by fire from the gun tower just moments before impact.

IMPERIAL OFFICER #3 relieved

"That was close!"

IMPERIAL OFFICER #2 in shock

"Oh, no!"

Looking upward to see the SSD's bow barreling directly toward them. Screen whites out with the explosion.

Shot 4: B-wing hurtling toward the camera out of the expanding fireball of the exploding SSD, with the Death Star taking up the background.

Cutscene 11—Battle Seven: Endor Part 3

Main Element(s):

- Red and Gold Group enter Death Star Interior

Ships:

- Death Star
- Millennium Falcon
- X-wing
- Y-wing
- A-wing
- TIE Interceptors

Interior(s):

- Cockpit of TIE Interceptor

Voices:

- Imperial Officer #4
- Imperial TIE Interceptor Pilot

Shot 1: Cockpit of TIE Interceptor, over the shoulder pilot's POV, chasing Rebel craft over surface of Death Star.

IMPERIAL OFFICER #4 commanding

"Stop those Rebel fighters, they're headed toward an access tunnel that will allow them inside the station."

> IMPERIAL TIE INTERCEPTOR PILOT calm

"Yes, sir!"

Shot 2: Chase view of TIE Interceptor as it shoots down an Y-wing. As it turns to engage the Falcon, it and assorted Rebel fighters enter tunnel opening.

Cutscene 12—Battle Seven: Endor Part 4

Main Element(s):

- Destruction of Death Star

Ships:

- Death Star
- Millennium Falcon
- X-wing
- Y-wing
- A-wing

Voices:

- Olin Garn

Shot 1: Death Star blows. Rebel ships flying toward the camera out of the explosion.

> OLIN GARN ecstatic and very loud (a proper Rebel yell that makes Lando's
> seem rather pitiful)

"YEEEE-HAAAWWWW! We did it! We really did it!"

Shot 2: Victory rolls, celebration etc.

D

Appendix for Chapter 14

Wendy Despain

D.1 Big-Picture Plan for Proposed Game *Starfall*

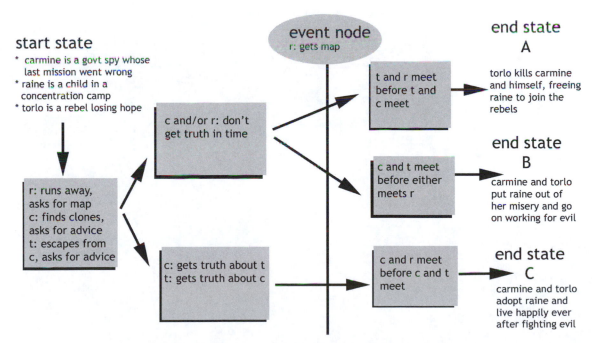

start state

* carmine is a govt spy whose last mission went wrong
* raine is a child in a concentration camp
* torlo is a rebel losing hope

r: runs away, asks for map
c: finds clones, asks for advice
t: escapes from c, asks for advice

c and/or r: don't get truth in time

c: gets truth about t
t: gets truth about c

event node
r: gets map

t and r meet before t and c meet

c and t meet before either meets r

c and r meet before c and t meet

end state A

torlo kills carmine and himself, freeing raine to join the rebels

end state B

carmine and torlo put raine out of her misery and go on working for evil

end state C

carmine and torlo adopt raine and live happily ever after fighting evil

Sample Big Picture Plan for proposed game: *Starfall*
by Wendy Despain   created fall 2008

E

Appendix for Chapter 16

Chris Pasley

E.1 Casual Game Wireframe

On the following page is a very simple example of a wireframe of a fictional shooter game with a story. You can be as simple or as elaborate as you like with the construction of the wireframe; use it to map out every screen and every word of copy, or just the general flow, as I've done here.

The main idea with this is to document how much copy is needed, in what order, and how it affects the user's experience within the game. A valuable exercise is to print each frame out on a separate piece of paper and flip through them as if they were screens already made. Ask yourself: could I remove this page and the game still work?

WORLD WAR TWELVE

Single Player   Multiplayer   Options   How to Play

[Scenario]

They said it couldn't happen. Not a twelfth time...

[Story, First Level Objective]

Still Image:
Space Marines suiting up as the sergeant lays out their
objectives. One looks up, haunted.

JOE: (V.O) War always looked so glamorous in
the video games.

SGT. INORITE: Today, we're gonna be hitting a
munitions factory on Europa...

Level One Gameplay

[Story, Level Two Objective]

Back in the briefing room.

SGT. INORITE: Good work, men. You may not be
the lazy screwups I thought you were. Now, our next
job is to take out anti-spacecraft guns hidden on Io...

Level Two Gameplay

F

Appendix for Chapter 18

Graeme Davis

The following screenshots illustrate different presentations of text at a typical screen size for mobile phone games.

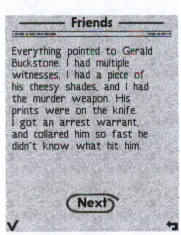

Figure F.1. A full screen of text, allowing space for interface elements. Even with a small point size, the maximum amount of text that can be displayed on a single screen is around 50 words. *Detective Puzzles* © 2006 Reaxion Corp.

Figure F.2. A partial screen of text, with image. Notice the scroll bar at the right of the screen, which allows for larger blocks of text. As with games on other platforms, though, scrollable text is seldom an ideal solution. *Detective Puzzles* © 2006 Reaxion Corp.

Figure F.3. Dialogue may be restricted to a small area at the bottom of the screen, as here, and accompanied by a character graphic. Only one character's speech may be presented per screen, since displaying two character graphics would leave next to no space for the actual text. Long conversations become tedious to click through, so conversations should be kept down to two to three speeches per character. *Houdini's Infinite Escapes* © 2008 PressOK Entertainment.

Figure F.4. Dialogue may also be presented in speech bubbles in the main screen area. This permits longer speeches, but conversations should still be kept short. *Parisian Puzzle Adventures* © 2008 Reaxion Corp.

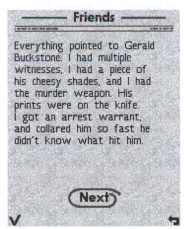

Figure F.5. Text-based minigames, such as quizzes, can also offer work to the writer. Question and answers must be kept short. *Parisian Puzzle Adventures* © 2008 Reaxion Corp.

G

Appendix for Chapter 19

J. Robinson Wheeler

G.1 >Help

In order to play IF games, you'll need to download what's called an interpreter, the software that runs IF games. There's an interpreter for each IF language for each operating system, which makes it complicated. Recently, all-in-one interpreters (Gargoyle for Windows and Spatterlight for MacOS) have been created that try to run all games for you without much fuss. Similarly, for each language you want to use to write IF, you need to download the library and the compiler that go with your operating system. The best resource for navigating through these issues and getting yourself all set is the Brass Lantern website (http://brasslantern.org/), which has a Beginners section that teaches you how to play IF and a Writers section that instructs you in how to find the materials you need to get started.

Choosing a language to use is a separate issue, and of course everyone has their own preference. The most popular languages are Inform and TADS, with a system called ADRIFT enjoying a special popularity of its own because it has a graphical interface and does not require much if any programming to create IF games.

Inform was created by Graham Nelson, who specifically designed it so that he could write Infocom-style games that compiled to the same game file format that Infocom invented, called a Z-machine file. This means that Inform games can be played on all platforms that Infocom games are playable on, and that is extensive—it comprises everything from Commodore 64s and Apple II+'s to modern laptops and even mobile phones. Inform 6, which was used to create many of the best IF games of the past decade, is a programming language that somewhat resembles C or Java. (C and Java programmers would disagree, but it is more or less true, especially to a non-programmer.) In 2006, Graham Nelson, in collaboration with eminent IF author Emily Short, released a next-generation update, Inform 7. Eschewing programming language syntax for English sentences, and bundling it (on MacOS and Windows) with a development application that includes a suite of special features and language documentation, Inform 7 is unique and growing in popularity. For more about Inform, take a look at http://www.inform-fiction.org/.

TADS (Text Adventure Development System) was originally a shareware software product written by Michael J. Roberts. TADS version 2 became freeware around the time that Inform

6 became popular, and for most of the 1990s and the early 2000s there was roughly equivalent popularity between the two languages, with great games being written in both. Recently, Michael J. Roberts released his next-generation update, TADS 3, comprising a workbench development application (on Windows only), the most extensive world model and library ever developed for IF authoring, a compiler, and an extensive suite of language reference manuals and documentation. TADS games will run on many different platforms but compile to their own "virtual machine" rather than the Infocom Z-machine format. This makes them playable on all modern computers and on Java applets running on websites but unavailable on platforms such as mobile phones. The TADS language is indisputably a C-like programming language, and programmers find themselves more comfortable with it than writers might, but the richness of the world model is a strong selling point. For more about TADS, see http://www.tads.org/.

G.2   Coding Examples

Speaking personally, I am still a fan of Inform 6 and TADS 2, since I know them fluently and have written XYZZY Award–winning IF games with each of them. I then entered a period of indecision as regards making the jump to one or another of the next-generation versions of these languages that I have not emerged from. I have been experimenting with each, but only you can decide whether you like Inform 7 or TADS 3 better. Or, like me, perhaps you'll find the older versions worth a look. Inform 6 and TADS 2 are still supported, and they have accrued extensive collections of library extensions and game source code for study—all still freely available in the IF Archive.

Here's an example of TADS 2 code containing a variable room description (the `ldesc`, or long description, in TADS 2 syntax). It makes use of a `switch` statement whose outcome depends on the value of the variable `future.state`.

```
SouthOfHouse: room
    sdesc = "South of house"
    ldesc =
    {
        if ( future.state < 4 )
            "This is not your house as you expected to find it, but
            a scene of devastation.";

        switch( future.state )
        {
            case 1:   /*  no rod, no tree, yes roof  */
                "The house has been damaged by fire. Though the roof
                remains intact, the insides have been burnt out,
                leaving a brittle, soot-stained shell that you can
                hear wind whistling through.";

                if ( tinyTree.location = self )
                {
                    "Beside the house is a scrawny, dead tree.";
                }
```

```
        break;

    case 3:   /*  no rod, yes tree, yes roof  */
        "The beautiful tree you planted has split from its scorched
        trunk and smashed into the side of your house. From what you
        can see, the roof has been torn open by the weight of it, and a
        terrifying hole gouged out to fully halfway down the wall.
        However, the fire seems not to have spread thanks to the fire-
        resistant shingles. Broken splinters of wet and rotting wood
        lie everywhere, kept moist by recent rains.";

        break;

    case 5:   /*  yes rod, no tree, yes roof  */
        "The house is older and sagging, with long ruts where splinters
        have broken off, but otherwise looks the way you remember it.
        The ground slopes down slightly here, and the wall of the house
        looms an extra story high because of it. The tiny window high
        in the wall has been crudely boarded shut.";

        if ( tinyTree.location = self )
        {
            "Beside the house is a scrawny, dead tree.";
        }

        break;

    case 7:   /*  yes rod, yes tree, yes roof  */
        "The house is older and sagging, with long ruts where splinters
        have broken off, but it otherwise looks the way you remember.
        The ground slopes down slightly here, and the wall of the house
        looms an extra story high because of it. The tiny window high
        in the wall has been crudely boarded shut.";

        "A large and sagging tree grows here, leaning its bulky canopy
        toward the house. A large branch has snapped from the middle of
        its trunk and lies in the mud.";

        break;
}

"To the southwest is the old rock and, farther, the clearing. ";

if ( future.state == 1 )
    "You can walk around the burnt ruins to the northwest.";
else
```

```
                    "You can walk around your house to the northwest.";
        }

        sw = Clearing
        nw = FrontOfHouse
;
```

Here's some sample Inform 6 code. This is some of the code that goes with the *Centipede* transcript, showing a player character with a variable self-description property and some of his items of inventory. The syntax is cosmetically different from TADS 2 but shares an underlying approach to defining objects and descriptions.

```
Object Mitchum "Mitchum"
    with name 'Ray' 'Mitchum' 'Corporal' 'cpl',
    description [;
        if ( combat_suit hasnt worn )
            "You're buck naked and freezing. We're talking major
            shrinkage, soldier. ";
        if ( game_counter.number > 66 )
            "You are quickly drowning in poisonous marshwater.";

    switch ( game.state ) {
        0,1,2,4,5:
            if ( helmet has general )
                "You're feeling a little shaky from that blow to the
                head, and there's a searing pain in your right arm.
                The stimulants are giving you the adrenaline to
                ignore all of this, and you're still alert and ready
                to kill some bugs for God, planet and country. ";
            "You're in good health for a guy who's been awake and
            on active duty for 76 straight hours. The stimulants
            they rationed you seem to be working fine with no side
            effects. You're pumped and ready to kill some bugs for
            God, planet and country. ";
        3: "You're freezing to death, and in imminent danger of
            drowning. ";
        6: "You're pumped and ready. The pain in your arm is a
            distant annoyance.";
        7: "You're almost hyperactive now, alert to every sound,
            every movement.
            You feel nothing but your own body heat, like a roaring
            furnace. ";
        }
    ],
    has male proper
;
```

```
Object -> combat_suit "combat suit"
    with name 'combat' 'suit',
    description "Your standard-issue insulated combat suit. ",
    before [;
        Disrobe:
            if ( location ~= marshlands ) {
                give self ~worn;
                "You strip off your combat suit, leaving yourself naked to
                the elements. You won't last long like this, but you don't
                need to.";
            }
            "You'll need that suit on to survive in the freezing
            marshlands. ";
        Drop: if ( location ~= marshlands ) {
                if ( self has worn ) {
                    give self ~worn;
                    print "You strip off your combat suit, leaving
                        yourself naked to the elements. ";
                }
                remove self;
                "With bare-ass bravery, you drop your combat suit into the
                murk, where it sinks and disappears. You won't last long
                like this, but you don't need to.";
            }
            "You'll need that suit on to survive in the freezing
            marshlands. ";
    ],
    has worn transparent
;
```

Here's an ASK/TELL conversation example from *First Things First*, written in TADS 2.
The system I'm using is modified from how the TADS library generally handles it, but I think
it makes it clearer how to use it.

```
future: Topic
    sdesc = "future"
    noun = 'future'
    state = 0

    verDoChange( actor ) =
    {
        "Everything you do changes the future. ";
    }

    askingAboutMe( who ) =
    {
        switch( who )  // matches with NPC class objects
```

```
        {
            case Fred:
                "Fred says, \"The future? Heck, I bet in ten years
                I'll be the manager of this place. Maybe I'll even
                own the franchise. Sure, I'll have a big house, the
                wife and kids. Yeah.\" ";
                return( true );
            case Laura:
                "Laura says, \"Well, after I go to business school --
                or maybe law school, I haven't decided yet -- I
                figure I'll be able to do whatever I want. But you
                never know what the future will bring!\" ";
                return( true );
            case Angela:
                "Angela says, \"I visited a fortune teller once. She
                told me that, if I wanted it, I could reach the top
                of the world. Then she said that I shouldn't want
                that. I got angry at her, I'm not even sure why. It
                just sounded phony, you know? Heck, I could do worse
                than reaching the top, you know? I should have such
                problems.\" ";
                return( true );
            case Homeless_Guy:
                "The homeless guy coughs and says, \"I have no
                future. Not one I can face. But let me tell this
                in my own way.\" ";
                return( true );
            case Architect:
                "He says, \"I always like to think ahead, but I'm
                always surprised by what the future brings.\" ";
                return( true );
            default:
                return( nil );
        }
    }
;
```

The verDoChange definition is the code that runs if the player happens to type "change the future" at the command prompt. This is a non-standard verb that doesn't come with the library, but since some players might think to try it, I added it myself. Here's the rest of that verb definition, including the default response (Thing is a generic object class) that will be printed most of the time.

```
changeVerb: deepverb
    verb = 'change' 'modify' 'alter' 'adjust'
    sdesc = "change"
    doAction = 'Change'
```

```
;

modify Thing
    verDoChange(actor) =
    {
        "That isn't something you can change.";
    }
```

Just for fun, here is the Inform 6 equivalent of the above definition (skipping the conversation):

```
Topic future "future"
    with article "the",
    name 'future',
    before [;
        Change: "Everything you do changes the future.";
    ]
;

Verb 'change' 'modify' 'alter' 'adjust'
    * noun -> Change
;
[ ChangeSub;
    "That isn't something you can change.";
];
```

And, just to dip one toe into the next generation, here is the Inform 7 version:

```
Changing is an action applying to one visible thing.
Understand "change [something]" or "modify [something]" or "alter [something]"
or "adjust [something]" as changing.
Instead of changing something: say "That isn't something you can change."

The future is scenery. Instead of changing the future: say "Everything you do
changes the future."
```

For more thorough language comparisons, check out Roger Firth's Cloak of Darkness page, which implements a simple IF scenario in every available modern language, so that you can see all of the differences and similarities for yourself. (See below for URL.)

G.3 IF Resources

- Cloak of Darkness (http://www.firthworks.com/roger/cloak/index.html)
- Brass Lantern's Beginner Resources page (http://www.brasslantern.org/beginners/)
- Brass Lantern's Writers page (http://www.brasslantern.org/writers/)
- Baf's Guide to IF (http://www.wurb.com/if/)
- IF Archive (mirror site, loads faster) (http://mirror.ifarchive.org)
- IF Competition (http://www.ifcomp.org/)

- IF FAQ (http://nickm.com/if/faq.html)
- IF Ratings (http://www.carouselchain.com/if/)
- IF Wiki (http://www.ifwiki.org/index.php/Main_Page)
- IFDB (http://ifdb.tads.org/)
- IF authors usenet community (rec.arts.int-fiction)
- IF players usenet community (rec.games.int-fiction)
- Past r.a.if topics archive (http://www.ifwiki.org/index.php/Past_raif_topics)
- David Welbourn's IF Walkthrough archive (http://webhome.idirect.com/~dswxyz/sol/index.html)
- *XYZZYnews* (http://www.xyzzynews.com/)
- *SPAG* (http://www.sparkynet.com/spag/)
- XYZZY Awards (http://www.ifwiki.org/index.php/XYZZY_Awards)
- Social gathering spot: ifMUD (http://ifmud.port4000.com/)

Author Bios

Sande Chen

Sande Chen, co-founder of Writers Cabal, has been working in the game industry for 10 years. Her past game credits include 1999 Independent Games Festival winner *Terminus* and 2007's PC RPG of the Year, *The Witcher*, for which she was nominated for a Writers Guild of America Award in Videogame Writing. She is the co-author of *Serious Games: Games That Educate, Train, and Inform* and contributed to *Professional Techniques for Video Game Writing* and *Secrets of the Game Business*. In 2006, she was profiled on Next Generation's list of the Game Industry's 100 Most Influential Women. She holds degrees in economics, writing, and cinema-television from the Massachusetts Institute of Technology, the London School of Economics, and the University of Southern California. She has spoken at the Game Developers Conference, Serious Games Summit D.C., and other game-related conferences around the world on such topics as narrative and social design, serious game development, and women in game development. In 1996, she was nominated for a Grammy in music video direction.

Richard Dansky

The author of the critically acclaimed horror novel *Firefly Rain*, Richard Dansky is the Manager of Design at Red Storm Entertainment and the Central Clancy Writer for Ubisoft. Richard's horror game experience includes the horror shooter *Cold Fear*, as well as contributions to over 100 books for White Wolf's *World of Darkness* tabletop RPGs. You can find him online at http://www.richarddansky.com.

Steve Danuser

Steve Danuser, known in the online world as "Moorgard," was the co-foudner of Mobhunter, on of the first websites dedicated to game design analysis and discussion. He focused his knack for informative and entertaining discourse into the job of Community Manager for *EverQuest II* at Sony Online Entertainment, founding one of the strongest and most vibrant communities in the MMO gaming space. He later became a designer on *EverQuest II* and contributed to the title's ongoing expansions, adventure packs, and live updates, including the popular *Echoes of Faydwer*. In late 2006 Danuser left SOE to join 38 Studios, founded in Maynard, Massachusetts by Boston Red Sox pitcher Curt Schilling. Steve serves as Lead Content Designer on the studio's upcoming MMOG project, codenamed Copernicus. The highly story-driven game features a world envisioned by best-selling fantasy author R. A. Salvatore. Danuser continues to discuss game design on his blog, Mobhunter.com.

Graeme Davis

Graeme Davis is an independent game writer and designer with credits on 18 shipped computer and video game titles over a 15-year career. He started out writing for tabletop role-playing games, working for Games Workshop, White Wolf, TSR (now Wizards of the Coast), and Steve Jackson Games, among others. Switching to video games in 1992, his work has been published by Microprose, Microsoft, Psygnosis, America Online, So-Net Japan, Activision, Sega, and others. He has worked as a freelance writer and editor on multiple phone games. He is also a published writer of fiction and nonfiction.

Wendy Despain

Wendy Despain writes dialogue and does narrative design for video games through International Hobo. Her credits include writing for the console game *Bratz: Forever Diamondz*, the MMOG *ArchLord*, and ARGs for two Gene Roddenberry properties. She moonlights in science and video game journalism, writing for *Gamasutra* and *The Escapist*. She is chair of the IGDA's Game Writing Special Interest Group and a contributing editor to the book *Game Writing: Narrative Skills for Videogames*. Online, she's found at http://www.quantumcontent.com.

Stephen Dinehart

Stephen Dinehart is an artist, writer, designer, and acclaimed video game storyteller. He created the role of "Narrative Designer" for THQ in 2006 and since has been forging a path in narrative-driven game development in hopes of helping the industry as a whole embrace AAA storytelling techniques. His list of credits spans genres and roles having worked in the industry as a producer, writer, designer, QA tester, and developer. He was final Nominee for "Best Writing for a Game Production" for *Company of Heroes: Opposing Fronts* at the 2nd Annual Canadian Awards for the Electronic and Animated Arts (2007), and the game won "Nokia Award for Outstanding Innovation in Gaming." Mr. Dinehart received his MFA in Interactive Media from the University of Southern California's School of Cinematic Arts in 2006 and his BFA in Digital Media from the College for Creative Studies (Detroit) in 2001.

Daniel Erickson

Daniel Erickson started his professional career in the games journalism biz, working for notables such as *PC Gamer* and the late *Next Generation* before going on to help found the online site *Daily Radar*. After a few years, he was challenged to put his money where his exceptionally critical mouth was and took a design job for Electronic Arts Canada. Four years of learning the trade and doing lead design work on the *NBA Street* and *SSX* series later, he returned to his first love and embraced the makers of his favorite games, joining BioWare as a writer on *Dragon Age*. Today Daniel is lead writer for BioWare's Austin studio where he is responsible for the training, steering, and cohesiveness of the largest group of in-house professional writers in gaming.

John Feil

John Feil is a game industry veteran whose duties have spanned from Quality Assurance, to Technical Writing, and finally to Level Designer and Designer. He's worked on such titles as *Star Wars: Jedi Starfighter*, *Star Wars: Battle for Naboo*, *Microsoft Flight Simulator*, *Forza Motorsports*, and *Justice League: Heroes*. John has written a book called *Beginning Game Level Design*, is a member of the board of directors for the International Game Developers Association, the Chairperson for the IGDA Credits Committee, and has a website at http://www.gamefeil.com.

Chris Klug

Chris Klug's first published game was *Universe*, a science-fiction role-playing game, published by Simulations Publications in 1981. That was followed by *DragonQuest* (fantasy RPG, SPI, 1981); *Damocles Mission* (sci-fi strategy, SPI, 1981); *Horror Hotel* (horror strategy, TSR, 1982). The last four games Chris designed were *Aidyn Chronicles: The First Mage* (fantasy RPG, THQ, Nintendo, 2001); *Dominion Wars* (science fiction real-time strategy, Simon & Schuster Interactive, 2001); *Earth & Beyond* (science fiction MMO, EA, 2002); and *Stargate Worlds* (science fiction MMO, Firesky, 2009). Chris is a member of the Writer's Guild of America, West.

Haris Orkin

Haris Orkin has written for television, stage, film, and video games. He wrote the script for *Dragonshard*, a 2005 PC game from Atari and Liquid Entertainment. *Call of Juarez* was released in 2007 by Ubisoft. Besides writing the script, Haris also cast and directed all the voice over actors. For EA's *Command & Conquer* series, Haris wrote the scripts for *Kane's Wrath* and *Red Alert 3*. In 2009, *Red Alert 3* was nominated for a Writer's Guild of America Award. Currently, he's working on the sequel to *Call of Juarez*.

Chris Pasley

Chris Pasley is the Director of Games for Kongregate.com, a social gaming website. Before that, he worked on the AdultSwim.com gaming initiative for Cartoon Network, where he wrote for and provided direction on dozens of Web games.

Ahmad Saad

Ahmad has been designing games for the past four years, during which he has served on an unannounced sandbox game that is close to completion. He has also been involved with the IGDA Game Writers SIG's last two publications as editor and is currently serving as a design lead and trainer at Ubisoft's Chengdu studio. Ahmad can be contacted at ahmad99@gmail.com.

Tracy Seamster

Tracy Seamster's gaming career began in 1996 as a designer/GM with Simutronics Corporation where she held a variety of positions including Senior Game Master and Product Manager for *Alliance of Heroes*. She became a game designer with Sony Online Entertainment in 2004, designing and implementing quests for *EverQuest II* and its first four expansions. Tracy also worked on *Free Realms* and currently writes background stories for *The Agency*, SOE's forthcoming spy MMO. A member of Women in Games International and IGDA, Tracy has also been a speaker at the 2007 GDC and the 2008 Vancouver International Games Symposium. She also writes the official SOE blog for SOE's Gamers In Real Life (G.I.R.L.) initiative.

Lee Sheldon

Lee Sheldon has written and designed 18 video games, including a successful recent series based on Agatha Christie novels. Other titles include the award-winning *The Riddle of Master Lu*, *Dark Side of the Moon*, and *Wild Wild West: The Steel Assassin*, and the early ARG (alternate reality game) *The Light Files*. He has worked on massively multiplayer worlds for companies such as Cyan (*Uru: Ages Beyond Myst*) and Disney (*Disney's Virtual Magic Kingdom*), as well as an experimental multiplayer Xbox project for Microsoft. His book *Character Development and Storytelling for Games*, published by Cengage/Thomson Learning in 2004, is being used as a primary textbook in game design programs at some of the world's most distinguished universities. He is a contributor to the recent books *Game Design: A Practical Approach* from Charles River Media, *Second Person* from MIT Press, and *Visual Storytelling* from Cengage/Wadsworth. Before his career in video games, Lee wrote and produced over 200 popular television shows, including *Star Trek: The Next Generation*, *Charlie's Angels*, and *Cagney & Lacey*. As head writer of the daytime serial *Edge of Night*, he received a nomination for best writing from the Writers Guild of America. Lee has been twice nominated for Edgar awards by the Mystery Writers of America. His first mystery novel, *Impossible Bliss*, was re-issued in 2004. Recently a consultant on an online multiplayer world recreating jazz clubs of the 1940s and 1950s in Oakland, California for the University of California at Berkeley, Lee is currently a professor at Indiana University where in addition to teaching he is leading the design of his own narrative-driven virtual world, *Londontown*, and designing *The Skeleton Chase*, an ARG under a grant from the Robert Wood Johnson Foundation that ran from September 24th through November 12th, 2008. He is also Creative Consultant on a new Sci-Fi Channel reality show called *Danger Game*, writing and designing his fourth Agatha Christie video game, and writing his second novel, *The Keys*.

Evan Skolnick

Evan Skolnick brings nearly 20 years of entertainment content development experience to his role as Producer and Editorial Director at prominent video game developer Vicarious Visions. A former journalist, Evan has also served as an editor and writer for Marvel Comics and as a creative director for Acclaim Entertainment. He has authored and presented multiple lectures and tutorials on the subject of game writing at the Game Developers Conferences held in San Francisco and Austin.

At Vicarious Visions Evan has participated in narrative development on over 20 handheld games, including portable titles such as *Spider-Man 2* and *3*, *Over the Hedge*, *Marvel: Ultimate Alliance*, *Kung Fu Panda*, *Batman Begins*, *Shrek 2* and *3*, *Transformers*, and many others.

Lucien Soulban

Lucien Soulban (http://www.luciensoulban.com/) is a scriptwriter and novelist living in beautiful Montreal. He was narrative designer and scriptwriter for *Rainbow Six: Vegas*, as well as having written for numerous other games including *Warhammer 40K: Dawn of War*, *The Golden Compass*, *Kung-Fu Panda*, *Monster House*, and *Kim Possible 3*. He's written five novels, including *The Alien Sea* and *Renegade Wizards* for Dragonlance and *Warhammer 40K: Desert*

Raiders, and contributed to numerous anthologies including *Horrors Beyond 2* and the Horror Writer's Association anthology, *Blood Lite*.

Maurice Suckling

In the last ten years, Maurice Suckling has worked on over 20 games, across a range of genres and platforms, most often as a writer, but sometimes as a voice director, a designer, a creative director, a mo-cap director, a consultant, and/or a producer. Since 2005 he has also worked as part of The Mustard Corporation (http://www.themustardcorporation.com), which specializes in team-based interactive writing projects, where their clients include 2K, Atari, AQ Interactive, BBC, EA, Empire, Nintendo, SEGA, and Ubisoft. Some of the most recent titles he has worked on include *Wii Fit*, *Unsolved Crimes* on the DS, and the online interactive world *Papermint*. Maurice holds a PhD in Creative Writing from Newcastle University.

Anne Toole

Anne Toole lays claim to over five years' experience in the popular media as a writer for computer games and television. After writing for *Days of Our Lives*, Anne acted as Head Writer on MMO *Stargate Worlds* and earned a Writers Guild of America Award nomination for her work on *The Witcher*. She co-founded Writers Cabal, a freelance writing partnership, with Sande Chen. Since then, she has collaborated remotely on both serious and entertainment-oriented MMOs and single-player games. In addition, she has spoken on narrative design at South by Southwest and the ION Game Conference and has contributed a chapter to *Professional Techniques for Video Game Writing* (A K Peters, 2008). A citizen of the EU as well as the US, Anne holds a degree in Archaeology from Harvard.

Andrew S. Walsh

With credits across television, film, theater, radio, and animation, Andrew has amassed more than 35 video game credits and counting. A dedicated game player as well as writer, narrative designer, voiceover director, and story consultant, Andrew has worked on titles such as *Prince of Persia*, *Harry Potter* (*Half-Blood Prince* and *Order of the Phoenix*), *Dirk Dagger*, *SOCOM*, and *Heavenly Sword* for games companies including Ubisoft, Electronic Arts, Sony, Creative Assembly, SEGA, Side, THQ Wireless, Koch, Nokia, Jadestone, Razorback, BAM, Vis Interactive, and G5. Andrew has spoken about writing for games at numerous places including Austin GDC, Animex, BAFTA, WGGB, TAPs, and E.I.E.F. and to organizations such as Channel 4 the BBC. He has written on the subject for The Writers' Guild of Great Britain and *The Writers' Handbook 2005*, *The Screenwriters' Handbook*, and IGDA's games writing series. His directing credits include *Medieval Total War 2*, *X3: Reunion*, and *Shinobido*. He is Chair of the Videogames Committee of the Writer's Guild of Great Britain and is on the Executive Committee of IGDA's Writing SIG. Currently working on several more titles, he occasionally breaks off from games to research tea, coffee, beer, scuba diving, and motorbikes (though not at the same time) and can be found lurking at http://www.andrewwalsh.com.

David Wessman

David Wessman entered the game industry as a QA tester at (then) Lucasfilm Games in 1991. He soon discovered that the man responsible for the World War II air combat games he was most interested in was actually an independent contractor named Larry Holland. Fortuitously, Mr. Wessman was given the opportunity to join the test team assigned to *Secret Weapons of the Luftwaffe*. David immediately set himself to impressing Mr. Holland with his passion, dedication, knowledge, and creativity in order to convince Larry into hiring him for his next project—which turned out to be *X-Wing*. Though hired to lead an internal test team, David soon took the initiative to demonstrate his writing skills by rewriting a "sell sheet" prepared by the marketing folks at LucasArts. This was the first small step on a path that would lead Mr. Wessman to becoming the lead writer on the entire *X-Wing* series. He soon showed the same initiative with the mission editor and became a mission designer as well. David was a co-founder of Totally Games and eventually became the studio's "gameplay and story lead." Subsequently, he worked at Stormfront Studios, Starbreeze Studios (in Sweden), Volition, Backbone Entertainment, and Destineer Studios. He is currently teaching game design at the University of Advancing Technology in Tempe, AZ.

J. Robinson Wheeler

J. Robinson Wheeler is a freelance creative writer, artist, and filmmaker from Austin, Texas. His interactive fiction stories have been nominated for a total of 11 Xyzzy Awards and have won five, including Best Game of the Year 2000 for *Being Andrew Plotkin*. Rob received his B.A. in Communication from Stanford University and subsequently dropped out of the USC film school MFA program to write and direct an indie science fictio feature, *The Krone Experiment* (2005). An erstwhile member of a once-infamous gang of Austin cartoonists, he illustrated the first six volumes of an online graphic novel, *ACX: Academy X*. Frequently found haunting Austin's 24-hour cafés, Rob occasionally blogs on issues of transparency and privacy for the non-profit League of Technical Voters, where he served on the advisory board. He has been a committee member of the IGDA Game Writers SIG since 2008.

Index

international game
developers association

The International Game Developers Association is the largest non-profit membership organization serving individuals that create video games. The IGDA is committed to advancing the careers and enhancing the lives of game developers.

The IGDA connects members with their peers, promotes professional development, and advocates on issues that affect developers.

Advance your career. Advance the game industry. Advance the art form of games.

Our community is over 14,000 strong. Become a member today!

http://www.igda.org/join

Together, we will play an active role in shaping the future of digital games.